ECONOMIC ISSUES, PROBLEMS AND PERSPECTIVES

KEYNESIAN POLICIES - A NEW DEAL IN THE EUROPEAN NARRATIVE

EMPLOYMENT, EQUALITY AND SUSTAINABILITY

ECONOMIC ISSUES, PROBLEMS AND PERSPECTIVES

Additional books and e-books in this series can be found on Nova's website under the Series tab.

ECONOMIC ISSUES, PROBLEMS AND PERSPECTIVES

KEYNESIAN POLICIES - A NEW DEAL IN THE EUROPEAN NARRATIVE

EMPLOYMENT, EQUALITY AND SUSTAINABILITY

NORALV VEGGELAND
EDITOR

nova science publishers
New York

NOTICE TO THE READER

Additional color graphics may be available in the e-book version of this book.

Library of Congress Cataloging-in-Publication Data

ISBN: 978-1-53614-026-2
Library of Congress Control Number: 2018949283

Published by Nova Science Publishers, Inc. † New York

CONTENTS

PREFACE

In this book, *Keynesian Policies - A New Deal in the European Narrative: Employment, Equality and Sustainability,* nine scholars discuss theories, developments and challenges, and comparative approaches to understand the important principles of Keynesianism and New Deal Policy.

The study of international policy in traditional political science in the years following World War II had the tendency to use theories that explain policies in relation to the development of institutions and the regulation by agreements between sovereign states. Overseen was the political Keynesianism. Political economic analyses, which emphasized a national government-centered perspective. This happened both to the techno-economic paradigm rooted in Keynesian state intervention principles of effective-demand and to the socio-institutional paradigm of central overall planning deduced from just political Keynesianism.

One of the main elements of John Maynard Keynes' (1883-1946) major macroeconomic theory, "General Theory of Employment, Interest and Money" from 1936, came in response to the inter-war depression and employment crisis. He promoted the need for governments in times of crisis to "fill the hole" in the lack of overall demand rising, in particular demand for labor. Keynes argued that the solution to the Great Depression was to stimulate the country ("inducement to invest") through some combination of two approaches: A reduction in interest rates (monetary policy), and government investment in infrastructure (fiscal policy) guided by central planning.

In the nineteen thirties Western countries suffered a massive amount of unemployment and social inequality. The national economies suffered from a downward spiral of effective demand. Keynes' theory formed the basis for Western countries Keynesian policy in the postwar years with the goal of full employment. Keynes pointed out that effective demand must be achieved by the government interventions to heal market failure. This is done by spending and investing money to create new jobs and reduce social inequality. He even recommended financing the government spending by loan taking if necessary. When the employment rate increases economic growth comes up as a positive consequence – and this generates uttermost new jobs in a positive spiral of development.

A new Keynesianism of today, based on the classic Keynesian theory, is also stressing the need for governmental, institutional and economic interventions when unemployment rises and a recession is occurring nationally and internationally. While the classic variant was designed mostly as national policy, neo-Keynesianism is additionally targeting international crisis measures. In Europe, it might be action taken under the auspices of the European Union (EU) and its Central Bank (ECB).

Keynes focused the large cyclical fluctuations of capitalism, not the microeconomic fluctuations at the institusjonell- and enterprise level. Such an approach is emphasized by the neo-Keynesianism. Inspired by neo-Keynesian thinking and adopted by the USA government as a countercyclical policy came up when the financial crisis arrived in 2007/8. With rising unemployment to more than ten percent as a consequence the federal government intervened and granted the staggering sum of $ 800-trillion dollar as a stimulus and demand measure. The goal was to create macro- and microeconomics demand to reverse the market trend back towards normal economic growth. The US government succeeded. In 2016, the unemployment rate came down to just over five percent. In 2018 the unemployment rate is even lower, about four percent.

According to the neo-Keynesian approach, it may involve both short-term and long-term government interventions that aim job creation. This approach has unintendedly influenced especially European social democratic governments and have made them tom deny budget austerity as an economic policy recommended by the EU. The argument against austerity is that such a measure will only result in further unemployment in a vicious circle. It does not help to reduce bank interest rates to near zero as a mean towards economic recovery. For the lack of effective demand in the economy prevents investments regardless of interest rates. The use of monetary means like reduction of tax to increase investment is not an effective instrument, is what is stated.

The two American Nobel Prize winners in economics, Joseph Stiglitz, and Paul Krugman are two of our time most famous exponents for the neo-Keynesian economic theory and its mechanisms. These two economists are representing academic prestige at a high level, but their approaches are so far been partially rejected by ruling governments in office in the EU and Europe. Neo-liberalism and monetary mechanisms dominate their economic thinking and policy strategies. Such policy is demonstrated by the EU and the IMF when it comes to economic support to distressed countries like Greece, Portugal, Spain and even Italy. It is austerity which counts.

Political Keynesianism were picked-up especially by European social democrats, and became the basic economic road to build after war II wealth and the European welfare states. It became the European version of Franklin D. Roosevelt's New Deal in the USA. The New Deal was a Keynesian rooted policy, consisting of a series of federal programs, public work projects, financial reforms and regulations enacted in the United States during the 1930s in response to the Great Depression. From our book, you will learn more about Keynesianism and New Deal initiatives of our time. Let us go to the nine chapters to give a short summon up of the contents of each of them.

Chapter 1: This chapter is a story about two economic paradigms representing two different views on the public policy-makers' possibility to manage the economy. Keynes theory represented at radical break with mainstream economics when it put the policy maker in the driver seat. Policy makers should control aggregate demand in order to secure full employment. When the theory was used in practice in the 1950s it seems to function so well that researchers and policy makers were convinced that the unemployment problem was permanently solved. However, in the beginning of the 1970s something unexpected happened. A radical different economic situation alien to Keynes theory emerged which opened for the rebirth of Friedrich Hayek's and the Austrian Economic School thoughts. For them the economy is the sum of the behaviour of myriads of actors in a constantly changing society. Due to the large complexity public policy makers cannot manage the economy. Their role is reduced to control the public finance and the monetary supply. This neoliberal paradigm dominated the 1980s and 1990s. In 2008 policy makers were concerned that the global financial crisis should result in a deep recession and they felt a need to take an active role and returned to the Keynesian paradigm. An expansive fiscal policy was combined with light monetary policy. This policy mix should according to the theory result in lower unemployment and higher inflation. To general surprise the inflation did not raise making room for an almost boundless fiscal stimulation. It was a Keynesian dream world only shadowed by growing public debt. What will happen when interest rates raises or next recession arrives?

Chapter 2: The chapter states the following. Given the policies pursued by Franklin Roosevelt during the New Deal, one might assume that FDR was an ardent and early follower of Keynesian economics. Many of the policies that Keynes' advocated in his direct communication with Roosevelt, such as massive expenditures on public works and the use of deficit financing, are in line with what happened during the course of the New Deal. But in fact FDR is perhaps best described as a "reluctant Keynesian." Indeed, if we look at the rhetoric and policies pursued by FDR in his first few months and years as President, we might come to the opposite conclusion about Roosevelt's willingness to embrace Keynes' ideas. For the early FDR was much more inclined to tilt towards fiscal orthodoxy than the economic policies promoted by Keynes. FDR repeatedly called for a balanced federal budget and of his first moves as President was to push through the Economy Act, a relatively obscure piece of legislation that called for a cut of a half billion dollars from a federal budget. This gave the President broad powers to cut and reorganize the federal government and to slash federal salaries by up to 15 percent. Yet by the end of the 1930s and early 1940s it was clear to all concerned that many of the economic policies his administration had adopted—including the use of massive government borrowing and spending—were essentially those advocated by Keynes.

Chapter 3: The chapter states*:* For most of the post-war period, discussions on economic growth focused on demand, productivity and employment. The Financial Crisis of 2007/2008 made banks in many countries unable to serve their clients. Economic activity seized to grow or declined.

Economic growth has in the last decade been close to zero in large parts of the developed world following the Financial Crisis of 2007/2008. We discuss the reasons for the crisis and the impacts on economic developments in various regions.

What can we learn from a longer view of the history of the causes of financial crises? It seems that housing booms have been a major cause for many of the banking crises. Financial crises recessions are more costly than normal recessions in terms of lost output. What can be done to ensure a high degree of Financial Stability and thus ensure an environment where stable economic growth can be achieved? Actions are required both to ensure solidity in individual banks, create stability in the financial system and prevent the build-up of new booms in housing and real-estate.

Chapter 4: The chapter is a narrative of political economy and response to financial crises in the largely capitalist economy of the 20th and 21st century – starting from a review of pre-20th century classical economists and culminating with operative insight regarding the necessary proactive economic policy to avoid financial crisis. It elaborates on how from Keynesianism to neo-interventionism and neo-Keynesianism, policies either fail to address the problem of debt, or manage to address it only as an intermediary solution, rather than a long-term one.

The chapter concludes by introducing the theory of "neo-Keynesian" economist Steve Keen, who turns the spotlight on debt as a key factor in the supposed inevitability of financial crises. Keen argues that apparent financial flourishing while allowing debt to grow is merely sustaining the economy on borrowed time – a crisis is bound to happen sooner or later.

Only through controlling debt – beginning with a conceptual change in the perception that debt should continue to hold its established place as a driving force of contemporary capitalism could future financial crises be avoided.

Chapter 5: The focus point of this chapter of *Keynesian Policies: A New Deal in the European Narrative; Employment, Equality and Sustainability* is based on Keynes's original contribution in *The General Theory of Employment, Interest and Money.* I demonstrate that his path-breaking new macroeconomic theory can be represented as a theory of the implications of *structural* private sector excess savings. The private sector is according to Keynes's analysis not self-adjusting. So, more often than not the private sector gets stuck in an unemployment equilibrium. To establish full employment an external stimulus of effective demand is needed. Within a closed economy analysis, which Keynes employed, the government could act as such an external force by executing expansionary fiscal policy. As long as the private sector has an excess financial saving, a public sector deficit can be finance automatically. If the private excess savings vanish, there is no longer a need for publish sector deficit spending to secure full employment. Hence, Keynes's conclusion: 'Look after unemployment, and the budget will look after itself'.

Chapter 6: According to this chapter, international markets contribute in determining a ceiling to the national room for political maneuvering, and contributes to a "race-to-the bottom" for cost-driving national policies. Due to import leaks, too strong unilateral expansionary macroeconomic policies is also difficult to do, especially for small countries. At the same time, as markets shape, or restrict, political behavior, politics also shape markets. In the EU, rules and regulations emplaces a floor on how far down international competition can push cost-driving regulations and taxes. National autonomy is reduced to act within the ceiling and floor that international competition and EU regulations create, and balanced against the benefits from international trade to achieve higher standards of living. Hence, the more a country is exposed to international competition, the more probable it is that policy will converge with other countries with the same international exposure. Domestic change must then often be done via international cooperation. Countries need joint efforts in industrial and economic policies, as well as in macroeconomic regulations, to generate income to pay for the welfare state. At the same time, national interests concerning degrees of autonomy and sovereignty, conflicting interests between and within countries, and inertia in markets and politics often contribute to a slowing down of the integration processes and the ability to make common decisions. In a neo-functionalist view, public managers, as in, for example, the EU Commission, are the driving force towards more integration. In an intergovernmental view the counter-parts are more often other nations and governments and, often, seen as an advanced form of diplomacy. When common actions are needed, not only long-term and short-term economic interests are confronted, but also domestic winners and losers from free trade, and the visions of the EU as a neo-functional or intergovernmental regime.

Chapter 7: The chapter concerns New Deal policy in its beginning. The Tennessee Valley Authority (TVA) was one of the most important organizations and symbols of the New Deal. The organization solved economic and social problems, and generated both new technological and organizational solutions. This chapter focuses on some of the organizational ideas that can be drawn from it, in other words, what is here called the institutional-organizational legacies. A special focus is devoted to the Norwegian context and narrative. Examples of findings are: the idea of grassroots democracy had in TVA two forms; citizen participation and intergovernmental collaboration (e.g., partnerships), whereas the latter is almost a lost organizational legacy. In contrast, it is elements such as planning, regional development and, to some extent, other form of grassroots democracy, had dominated the Norwegian narrative of the TVA. This study also shows that studying these partnerships may teach us about organizational mechanisms for legitimization, as well as about coping with internal and external power realities.

Chapter 8: The chapter states that the Norwegian agriculture is heavily supported, with as much as 1% of gross domestic product. Naturally, more or less support is needed if Norwegian agriculture shall survive. We discuss the *proper* size of the sector. This depends on the public goals, most imporatantly food security. In addition, Norway has to meet international obligations. Foremost concerning trade policy, but also a obligation to promote a greener society. Here we base our analysis on Norway's promise under the 2015 UN climate change agreement to reduce greenhouse gas (GHG) emissions with 40%. We show that it is possible to achieve a 1/3 reduction in agricultural support without compromising food production measured in calories and protein. The main explanation for the result is that we today have a consumption pattern with a high share of ruminant products, products where the level of subsidies are relatively high. So it is efficient to shift production away from ruminant products to vegetable products. This has consequences for the consumers' diet, involving a 30% reduction in meat consumption and a 10-20% reduction in consumption of dairy products. Our results are based on experiments using a detailed sectoral model of Norwegian agriculture. We conclude that only 2/3 of the current support is needed to fulfill proper goals for the agricultural sector. So enforcing this policy gives us as much as 1/3% of gross domestic product to use on needed public expenses.

Chapter 9: The chapter tells us that since its introduction to the wider public by the Brundtland Commission Report "Our Common Future" in 1987, "sustainable development" has established itself as a key notion in political and academic discourse over how to tackle the multi-faceted ecological crisis. Unfortunately, little progress has been made when it comes to solving the crisis, be it in terms of emission reductions, loss of biodiversity or extinction of species. In practice, the notion of "sustainable development" has proven to have none of the bite needed for the required break with business as usual to happen. This is no coincidence: the notion fails to question the twin imperatives of growth and profits that continue to prevail in the now globalized capitalist economy. Hence advocating the notion on a world-wide basis, involving so-called developing nations and emergent economies (China, India, Brazil), has amounted to thirty lost years. What is needed is a clear-cut, conflict-oriented change of policies that actively seeks for the reduction of humanity's ecological footprint, in stark contrast to its increase in today's world, an increase that is inseparable from the basic dynamics of capitalism - as we know it.

ACKNOWLEDGMENTS

As the Editor of the book. I would like to take the opportunity to thank very much my colleagues of chapter authors working on different universities and institutes in Sweden, Norway, Denmark and the USA. It has been so good to work together with you on this book project. Thousands of thanks to you all. I would also take the opportunity to thank Nova Science Publishers for enduring effective cooperation and kindly support over many years.

Noralv Veggeland
The Editor
Lillehammer, Norway
March 2018

In: Keynesian Policies
Editor: Noralv Veggeland
ISBN: 978-1-53614-026-2

Chapter 1

NEW KEYNESIAN POLICY: THE REVIVAL OF EACH POLICY MAKER'S DREAM

Jan-Evert Nilsson, PhD*
Blekinge Institute of Technology, Blekinge, Sweden

ABSTRACT

This is a story about two economic paradigms representing two different views on public policy makers' possibility to manage the economy. Keynes' theory represented at radical break with mainstream economics when it put the policy maker in the driver seat in charge of securing full employment by controlling aggregate demand. When the theory was used in practice in the 1950s it seemed to work so well that researchers and policy makers were convinced that the unemployment problem was permanently solved. However, in the beginning of the 1970s something unexpected happened. A radical different economic situation alien to Keynes' theory emerged. A window of opportunity for new ideas was opened which opened for the rebirth of Friedrich Hayek's and the Austrian Economic School thoughts. For members of this school the

* Professor of economics at Blekinge University. By education he holds a doctorate in regional economy. He owns a long list of national and international publications. janevert.nilsson@jena.se.

economy is the sum of the behavior of myriads of actors in a constantly changing context. Due to large complexity public policy makers cannot manage the economy. The role of polic makers is reduced to control the public finance and the monetary supply. This neoliberal paradigm dominated the 1980s and 1990s. The global financial crisis in 2008 opened for a revival of the Keynesian paradigm when policy makers were concerned that the global financial crisis should result in a deep recession. They felt a strong need to try to avoid this by stimulating demand. An expansive fiscal policy was combined with light monetary policy. This policy mix should according to the theory result in lower unemployment and higher inflation. To general surprise, the inflation did not raise making room for an almost boundless fiscal stimulation. It was a Keynesian dream world only shadowed by growing public debt. What will happen when interest rates raises or next recession arrives?

Keywords: Keynesian policy, fiscal policy, stagflation, Austrian School of Economics, Kondratieff waves, System of innovation, Innovation policy

INTRODUCTION

In the 1920s the conventional wisdom was that business cycles were like natural laws that people were deemed to live by, as they were obliged to live with. This view placed strict limits to endeavor. Attempts to alter the laws of economics would at best lead to unintended consequences. According to mainstream economic thought the economy normally was in equilibrium characterized by full employment or on its way to such equilibrium. Economic booms and busts were seen as temporary deviations caused by external accidents. Fiscal policy was based on an analogy between the family and the state. What is prudent in the conduct of a private family was also prudent in the conduct of a state. In practice this view was translated into a norm that public budgets should be in balance, and that deficits were tolerated only in extraordinary circumstances. The most common extraordinary circumstance was war. Deficits emerged primarily during periods of war while budget surpluses were produced during the following peacetime in order to repay the debt created during war emergences.

The balanced public budget norm gave policy makers a narrow room for action. Their main task was to control the public expenditures to avoid public deficit. The conventional wisdom was that in a free market economy, prolonged unemployment could not occur since unemployment would adjust real wages downward with increased demand for labor as a result. The price mechanism was assumed to ensure the maintenance of full employment. In situations of economic problems economists sought to calm down policy makers telling them that the economy would soon return to equilibrium and full employment. It was as a response to this promise Keynes concluded, "*in the long term we are all dead.*" (Keynes 1923 p.80). The economy could be described as a swing board that swings up and down around an equilibrium position. The policy makers were placed in the back seat with no tools to manage the economy at hand. They had to be patient and wait for better times.

TIME FOR A REVOLUTION

The great American stock market crash in October 1929 started a period of turmoil that was followed by a ten years long depression. The long depression, with high unemployment and growing poverty, demanded another answer than wait for better times. The depression opened a window of opportunity for somebody who could present a plausible proposal about how to handle the difficult situation. John Maynard Keynes took the opportunity and presented such a proposal. He had in fact articulated his new ideas already some years before the stock market crash. But at this time the economic situation gave no room for new radical ideas. The window of opportunity was not yet open and Keynes' ideas aroused no interest.

The economic depression gave Keynes a second chance to present his ideas. Keynes' central idea was the existence of a clear distinction between savings and investment. The conventional wisdom at the time preached that over time savings and investment were of equal value. The conventional wisdom was derived from Say's law postulating that *as the value we can buy is equal to the value we can produce, the more men can produce, the more they will purchase*. (Say 1834 p.3). Keynes summarized Say's law as an assumption *that the whole of the costs of production must necessarily be spent in the aggregate, directly or indirectly, on purchasing the product.* (Keynes 1936 Ch. 3). The statement *Supply creates its own Demand* summarized the classical doctrine Keynes challenged. His point of departure was that Say's law was false.

Keynes' argument was that because people who save and people who invest is not the same an imbalance tends to occur. In situations when savings run ahead of investment, a state of depression occur, accompanied by deflation and unemployment. The imbalance is caused by the banks, which create credit irrespective of the society's ability to save. The crucial importance of the gap between savings and investment opens new possibilities to manage the business cycle. Keynes argued that in situations where saving exceed investment further public investment might cure the depression. Following this deficit spending has to be accepted when savings exceed investment. Keynes put emphasis of the effects in the economy rather than on the size of the budget as such. He changed focus from budget balance to aggregate demand. This twist of focus gave budget deficits an instrumental value and opened up for an active role for policy makers.

Keynes unveiled his new idea in a speech to the Liberal party in March 1928 in front of the election the following year. His message was so clear that it could not be misunderstood. *Let us be up and doing, using our idle resources to increase our wealth. With men and plant unemployed, it is ridiculous to say that we cannot afford new developments. It is precisely with these plants and these men that we shall afford them.* (Keynes 2012 p. 765).

In the pamphlet "Can Lloyd George Do It?" he presented his idea even more simple in two short sentences: *There is work to do; there are men to do it. Why not bring them together*? (Keynes 2010 p. 93).

The Liberal party, which was Keynes' spiritual home, was the big looser in the election the following year and the party was reduced to a small group in the parliament. The Conservative Party won and formed a government. Among the conservatives Keynes was seen as antibusiness and therefore not worth listening to. The Labor Party, on the other hand, swung leftward after their defeat in the same election. Members of the party were not interested in Keynes' prescriptions for a doomed capitalist system. The new political situation indicated that Keynes had no longer access to the power. He decided to write an academic book, which he immodestly called the general theory, in which his arguments should be soberly presented in a logical tight way. The book was, as he writes in the preface, *chiefly addressed to my fellow economists* (Keynes 1936). Despite its complex obscurity Keynes' book was immediately recognized as a revolutionary work. His theory demoted the neoclassical economic theory to the status of an explanation of a special case unlikely to be encountered in the real world. Thus, in a Keynesian perspective neoclassic economic theory has no practical relevance.

The key element in Keynes' general theory was the multiplier and fiscal policy was the most important channel through which the economy could be kept in the straight path of full employment. Keynes argued that during a slump increased government expenditure did not crowd out private activity. In an economy operating below capacity the stimulus will make use of idle resources. The incomes of those companies who receive government contracts will boost. These companies will in turn employ more labor and invest to increase their production capacity. Unemployed persons get job and income and they will spend more, which in turn increases income for other actors. In a similar way the investment undertaken by companies receiving government contracts leads to orders in other companies. In this way the initial government spending causes a cumulative process that make production increase and unemployment decrease. This cumulative effect of the public spending makes the final impact of the spending much larger than the initial public spending. The income generated in this cumulative process putting jobless into work will pay for the public investment made and cover the deficit in public budget caused by the public spending.

Decreasing government spending creates a corresponding cumulative contraction process. Reduced public investment lowers the incomes of those companies who loose government contracts. The companies will in turn reduce staff and investment to lower their production capacity. Employed persons lose their jobs and income and will spend less, which in turn decreases income for other actors. The reduction in investment is manifested in reduced orders for other companies. The cumulative effect of reduced public spending makes the final impact of the reductions much larger than the initial change in public expenditure. Applied in a policy context the multiplier effect means that a modest initial increase or decrease in public spending will initiate a significant change in income and spending and thus in aggregate demand. Keynes' multiplier effect gave policy makers a powerful instrument for managing aggregate demand in the economy.

The general theory turned policy-making upside down. Policy makers should no longer passively wait for the up-turn in the business cycle. Instead they should react on a down-turn with an active demand policy that through the multiplier created a cumulative causation process recreating full employment. The government should increase investment in periods of slump and decrease investment in periods of boom. More important the theory gave policy makers an important role in managing the short-term economic development. Policy makers now moved from the back seat to the driver seat. Their new task was to tune monetary and fiscal policy in order to control that no gap between savings and investment emerged. This fine-tuning would tame the business cycle. The tool was management of aggregate demand. The Keynesian approach seemed to offer policy makers the tool to relegate economic depressions to history. The golden message to the policy-maker was that the right thing to do is what will earn the policy maker popularity if he does it. It was a tempting offer for policy makers in a period of economic depression. However it was only a theory built on weak empirical foundation and still it was an open question how the theory would function in practice.

THE KEYNESIAN ERA

The years after the Second World War were a period of uncertainty. The economic turbulence after the First World War and the depression in the 1930s casted a long shadow. The Swedish Keynesian economist and social democrat Gunnar Myrdal wrote a popular book in which he warned for peace optimism (Myrdal 1944). The Cold War made it urgent to show that capitalism could deliver full employment and wealth. Depression was considered to be the great enemy and real threat. Keynes' theory offered tools that could manage the problems. It was an attractive approach promising benefits to all groups including government and bureaucracy,

Now, it was time for a large-scale test of the theory. It started with the Marshall plan, an American initiative in which The United States gave financial assistance to help rebuild Western European economies after World War II. The years of the Marshall Plan, 1948-1952, saw a period of fast growth. The importance of the Marshall Plan in the rapid recovery has been debated. The aid accounted for less than 3% of the combined national income of the recipient countries between 1948 and 1951 (Magid 2012). The direct economic Keynesian effect of Marshall Plan seems small. The Marshall Plan's indirect economic effects on institutions were more profound.

Financial instability was pervasive in post-World War II Europe. Assistance expenditures sent budgets deep into deficit and government responded to inflation by retaining controls, supporting the growth of black markets. For the budgets to be balanced and the inflation to be halted, a political compromise, in terms of a broad agreement on a tolerable distribution of burdens, was needed. The Marshall Plan did not remove the need to sacrifice, but it added resources that reduced the sacrifices required and thus facilitated the efforts to reach such a compromise. The Marshall Plan also secured the market economy, in the European version a "mixed" economy, in the recipient countries. Through there was support in Europe for the restoration of a market economy it was far from universal. Communist and socialist ministers opposed a return to market economy. It was also unclear when the transition would take place. On this issue the conditions attached to the Marshall Plan left the recipient countries with no choice. Each recipient had to sign a bilateral agreement with the United States in which they agreed to balance government budgets, restore financial stability, and stabilize exchange rate. This institutional set-up was an important element in the reconstruction of Western Europe in the aftermath of World War II and it appears to have created economies capable of dynamic economic growth in an order of magnitude stronger than had previously ever been seen in Europe.

In the quarter of a century following World War II, growth rate in the industrial world was higher than before in history. Between 1950 and 1970 the European gross domestic product grew on the average about 5.5% per annum and 4.4% on a per capita basis. Industrial production rose even faster, at 7.1% a year. Only Japan of the major countries outperformed Europe in the 1950s and 1960s. U.S was, with an average growth rate of 4% and a per capita growth rate at 2.2%, outperformed by as well Japan as Europe. The difference in growth rates between Europe, Japan and U.S. partly reflects the scale of post-war reconstruction in the three areas. The recessions in this period were short periods characterized by deceleration in growth while boom periods, periods when growth rate was higher than the secular trend, were long. High investment ratios, which, in part, can be explained by the reconstruction after the war, were the main engine behind the stable economic growth.

The government's role in the economy did change dramatically in the post-war period. Governments accepted a wider range of responsibilities including overall management of economic activity and they used a greater variety of policy measures to achieve their objectives than their counterparts before war. The measures taken were considered more appropriate and better timed than measures taken in the inter-war period (Lundberg 1968).

In his study of wage inflation and unemployment in the U.K. from 1861 to 1957 the New Zealand economist William Phillips, professor at London School of Economics, found a consistent inverse relationship between unemployment and wage increase (Phillips 1958). When unemployment was high wages increased slowly and when unemployment was low wages increased rapidly. Phillips' study supported Keynes's theory with empirical evidence and it offered a reasonable reliable variable of capacity utilization in unemployment rate. Changes in the level of capacity utilization seemed to correspond opposite to changes in unemployment rate. According to this reasoning fluctuations in unemployment rate could be regarded as observable manifestations of changes in the underlying pressure of aggregate demand.

The Phillips curve represented the average relationship between unemployment and wage behavior over the business cycle. The curve showed the rate of wage inflation that would result if a particular level of unemployment persisted for some time. Phillips' study was followed by many similar studies for other developed countries. Most of these related general price inflation, rather than wage inflation, to unemployment. Also these studies showed in general a close fit between the estimated curve and the data. The Phillips curve supported Keynes' theory, which implied that during a recession inflationary pressures are low while inflationary pressures are high in periods of an economic boom.

The empirical studies carried out by Phillips and other confirmed the existence of a trade-off between unemployment and inflation. His study also confirmed that unemployment rate was a reliable indicator of capacity utilization. The conclusion was that an increase in capacity utilization caused by an expansive fiscal policy was mirrored in a reduction of unemployment rate. Fluctuations in unemployment rate can therefore be regarded as an observable manifestation of changes in the underlying pressure of aggregate demand.

The close fit between the estimated curve and the data encouraged many economists to treat the Phillips curve as a policy menu. Gradually economists came to look upon the Phillips curve as a trade-off relation in the sense that policy makers could choose where on the Phillips curve the economy should be placed. When policy makers were interested in reducing unemployment by a certain amount, the new conventional wisdom told them to compare the benefits of lower unemployment to the cost of a higher rate of inflation.

Fiscal and monetary policy could be used to move up and down the Phillips curve as desired. From a Keynesian perspective fiscal policy was the most important tool to control employment. The lesson learned was that policy makers could choose which combination of inflation and unemployment they would achieve and thus control fluctuations in the economy. The problem with deep recessions was solved as long as policy makers followed the rules and made rational choices of inflation-unemployment combinations. The Phillips curve was seen as a constraint, which policy makers had to acknowledge and incorporate into their strategy for managing aggregate demand. The menu offered by the Phillips curve said that for a given structure of the labor market and for given external factors, such as the rate of change of price on import goods, the government could choose combinations of inflation and unemployment which lay along the Phillips curve. During the 1950s and 1960s the inflation/unemployment combination in Sweden was around 4/1.5. The experiences in these years formed a consensus in Sweden that full employment meant an unemployment rate of less than 2%. An unemployment passing 2% was a signal of the existence of unused capacity in the economy.

The stabile and high growth rate, full employment and moderate inflation in the 1950's and 1960s were taken as evidence that Keynes' theory was true. The Keynesian paradigm evolved into becoming the dominant paradigm. There seemed to be no need for alternative paradigms. From the point of view of economic research the unemployment problem was solved. Now was it up to policy makers to formulate adequate policies based on the dominant paradigm.

A Crazy World

A few years after economic researchers and policy makers agreed that the unemployment problem was solved something unexpected happened. In the last year of the 1960s price increases departed significantly from the relationship between inflation and unemployment identified in the empirical studies made by Phillips and others. Now rising unemployment rates were associated with accelerating rates of inflation in many industrialized countries. When policy makers tried to manage the balance between inflation and unemployment both inflation and unemployment increased. The Keynesian interpretation of the situation was that the Phillips curve had shifted to a less favorable position. The actual inflation-unemployment combination in the OECD-countries moved from 2.8/1.9 in 1964 to 5.9/1.7 in 1970.

In this situation with a less favorable and unstable Phillips curve the food and oil prices exploded and the system of pegged exchange rates broke down. Inflation in the seven major OECD countries rose to 12% while unemployment rose to 5.8%. This unhealthy combination of high inflation and high unemployment combined with low growth became known as stagflation. In the Keynesian paradigm there was no room for stagflation. From a Keynesian perspective the economic conditions was abnormal. Public confidence in the ability of government to manage the situation waned. The reality seemed to blow the framework of the theory.

The policy makers were now facing three different problems – unemployment, inflation and balance of trade - of which the Keynesian approach was suitable only for one. Demand management should according to the textbook be used to control rising unemployment. Keynes' theory gave no room for a combination of raising unemployment and raising inflation and gave therefore no hints of how to manage the raising rate of inflation. The policy makers' solution to the new stagflation problem became a treatment of the symptoms in the form of wage and price controls. President Nixon imposed price controls in the U.S in 1971 when rate of inflation persisted above 4%. Many other nations like Canada, United Kingdom, Italy, The Netherlands and Belgium followed. The third problem was large deficit in the balance of trade. The quadrupled oil price in 1973-1974 made this problem acute in many industrialized countries. The problem was not completely new to some industrial countries. Britain and Denmark had periodic large deficits in the balance of trade in the 1950s and 1960s, which were partly caused by an overheating economy.

A proper Keynesian reaction to such an overheating problem would be to reduce aggregate demand. However, the political cost of such a reduction, in terms of raising unemployment, was considered too high. The solution chosen by the policy makers was instead to introduce import restrictions, which directly reduced the import and indirectly the growth rate. France, that had similar problems, chose a devaluation strategy. In the 1950s France devalued her currency no less than seven times. Besides from that inflation as a consequence was raising the French strategy did not act as a serious brake on the domestic economy.

In the 1970s it became obvious that the economic problem was more complex than in the 1930s when Keynes developed the general theory. In the first stage the situation was considered as abnormal. The abnormal situation got OECD to appoint a group of independent international experts to study and report on alternative policies countries might follow to regain full employment and price stability. The group consisted of five distinguished scholars from the academy, two high level civil officials from international organizations and one representative from the business community. All the members were caught in the Keynesian paradigm and therefore sought the solution inside the framework of this paradigm.

The expert group concluded that some historical accidents had temporarily made the economy crazy. In their view the stagflation represented a temporary deviation from the normal caused by *an unusual bunching of unfortunate disturbances unlikely to be repeated on the same scale, the impact of which was compounded by some avoidable errors in economic policy* (McCracken et al. 1977 p.14). The most important among these unfortunate disturbances were the food and oil price explosions. The food price explosion was the result of a sequence of poor harvest, which resulted in a decline in world grain reserves. The oil price explosion was caused by unilateral decisions by OPEC. The major error of policy was that the policy was too expansionary in the beginning of the 1970s. The expansive policy strengthened the boom in 1972-73 and the build-up of an inflationary pressure.

The experts concluded that beacuse the problem was caused by some historical accidents unlikely to be repeated and reinforced by some unhappy errors in economic policy the situation could be restored to what it was before stagflation. Consequently the expert group concluded that the deterioration in the trade-offs between unemployment and inflation should not be interpreted, as if demand management no longer was effective tool in reducing inflation. The conclusion opened up for an obvious policy recommendation. The recommended solution to the stagflation problem was a careful active demand policy.

Despite careful optimism of the export group concerning the relevance of the Keynesian tools the general trust in the Keynesian approach was weakened. Sweden's leading daily newspaper published in April 1975 a symbolic obituary over *the economic ideas that were created by John Maynard Keynes has now got to the eternal rest, leaving us in anxiety and lacking in a sound economic policy* (Dagens Nyheter 1975). Finance ministers, directors of central banks, economists, members of parliaments and other experts and admirers signed the obituary. The obituary signalled the start of the search for options to the Keynesian approach. The eyes were again directed back to the 1930s. Keynes' principal rival from the 1930s was back on stage.

THE HAYEKIAN COUNTERREVOLUTION

Friedrich von Hayek was in the 1930s the principal rival of the new theories of Keynes. Hayek was a member of the Austrian School of Economics that originated in the late 19th and early 20th in Vienna. Hayek and the Austrian School applied a micro approach focusing on motivations and actions of individuals. Their approach differs from the Keynesian macro approach that focuses on aggregate variables. From the pont if view of the Austrian School of Economics business cycles are caused by distortion in interest rates due to the government's attempt to control money. When governments keep interest rates artificially low high misallocation of capital take place. The misallocation of capital forces the economy to go through a recession in order to restore the natural progress. The Austrian School of Economics holds that inflation is caused by money supply not supported by an increase in the production. But members of the school underline that inflation does not mean that all prices increase simultaneously. Prices of some goods and services may increase faster than others, leading to changes in the relative prices of goods and services. Based on this approach the Austrian School of Economics blame the Great Depression in the 1930s on the massive unsustainable credit expansion during the 1920s and argue that depression was perpetuated by attempts to resist the liquidation of unprofitable investments.

As one of Keynes' leading professional adversaries von Hayek was expected to provide a full refutation of the general theory, but he never did. Hayek later explained that he saw no point in working out a detailed critique of the general theory because Keynes was constantly changing his theoretical framework. Instead he chose to devote his energies to elaborate Böhm-Bawerk's, a distinguished member in the "first wave" of the Austrian School of Economics, capital theory. The result of his work was an academic book of 410 pages of text and three appendixes containing a highly abstract study of a pure theoretical problem (Hayek 1941). Besides the fact that Hayek's book could not compete with Keynes' popular versions of the general theory his book was not published until in 1941 when Keynes' theory already had become firmly established. Hayek's theory of the business cycle was swept aside by the emerging Keynesian revolution.

Hayek's critique of the Keynesian approach was fundamental. He was critical to Keynes' top-down perspective on economics. Hayek applied a bottom-up perspective on the economy looking upon the economy as the sum of the behavior of myriads of individuals, acting based on their self-interest, in a constantly changing context. The economy was like a wild djungle and not like a planned park. The economy is a system too complex to be encapsulated in an arithmetic formula. Consequently Hayek considered it foolish to believe that any fixed relation between consumption and income should exist. In the Keynesian approach consumption and saving are determined quite mechanical by past income.

Based on the Keynesian view two predictions can be made. First, rich people will save a higher proportion of their income than will poor people. Second when society gets richer the proportion of the national income saved will tend to rise. The first prediction has been found to be true while empirical studies by Simon Kuznets have falsified the second prediction (Kuznets 1966). Hayek also had objections to Keynes' tendency to ascribe a real existence to arbitrary statistical aggregates such as the wage level and capital. Finally Hayek criticized that Keynes treated capital as a homogenous entity, thereby ignoring its complex structure reflecting long and complex production chains. In Keynes' theory there was no room for variations in the demand-supply balances between different industries.

No interest was devoted to Hayek's ideas during the Keynesian era. The Keynesian paradigm was the conventional wisdom that dominated the teaching at the universities. University students were not taught about economic schools like the Austrian School of Economics with Hayek and the Chicago School of Economics with Milton Friedman that both were critically to the Keynesian paradigm. The room for critical thinking outside the dominating paradigm was restricted. Keynes' theory was too convincing and too attractive to be false. We tend to believe what we want to believe and Keynes told the policy makers something they wanted to believe in, while the other two schools highlighted an uncomfortable dilemma. The higher the real wage stipulated by workers the fewer will be employed.

Hayek's approach received renewed topicality in the wake of the 1970s economic crisis when the shortcomings of the Keynesian approach became visible. The interest and influence of Hayek's ideas was given a further boost in 1974 when he was awarded the Nobel Prize for economics. However, Hayek has to share the prize with Gunnar Myrdal, a Swedish Keynesian economist and social democratic politician. The motivation for awarding this odd couple, an Austrian School of Economics member and a Keynesian, was *for their pioneering work in the theory of money and economic fluctuations and for their penetrating analysis of the interdependence of economic, social and institutional phenomena.*[1] In his Nobel address Hayek described Keynes' general theory as "fundamentally false" and 'charlatanism' and he explained stagflation as a self-inflicted wound that was brought about by policies recommended by the economist to pursue. He concluded that curing stagflation would require painful readjustments, such as higher unemployment and widespread bankruptcies. He disagreed with the Keynesian belief that policy makers could offer a solution to the problem. Myrdal in his Nobel address focused on the eguality issue in world development.

Two years after Hayek received the Nobel Price Milton Friedman, one of the prominent representatives of the Chicago School of Economics, was awarded the Nobel Prize for economics. The Nobel committee's motivation

---

[1] https://www.nobelprize.org/nobel_prizes/economic-sciences/laureates/1974/.

was; *for his achievements in the fields of consumption analysis, monetary history and theory and for his demonstration of the complexity of stabilisation policy*[2]. Milton Friedman's Nobel Price marked the end of the Keynesian era in academics. The University of Chicago, the home of the Chicago School of Economics, became the new centre for economic research. However, Friedman's economic analysis owed little to Hayek and was closer to Keynes. He joined the Keynesians in his disbelief in Hayek's interpretation of the Great Depression, which the Austrian School of Economics blamed the massive unsustainable credit expansion in the 1920s.

Defying Keynes and most of the academic establishment at the time, Friedman argued that price level depends on the money supply. In the long run, he argued, increased money supply increases prices, but has only negligible effect on output. On the other hand, in the short run increased monetary growth cause employment and output to increase. Correspondingly, will a reduced supply of money results in lower employment and lower growth rate. In a study of the monetary history of the United States he and his co-author argued that the great depression was the result of Federal Reserve's monetary policy (Friedman & Schwartz 1963). Federal Reserve tightened the money supply when they should have loosened it.

However, when it came to politics Friedman was close to Hayek. While Keynes believed state intervention was a suitable means for improving the lives of citizens, Friedman and Hayek both argued that whenever the state intervene in the economy, it hamper the ability of the free market to create wealth. Consequently Hayek and Friedman both disliked state intervention and were in favor of cutting taxes because, according to them, individuals knew better than politicians how their money best are spent.

The Keynesian approach reformulated after the oil crisis in 1973/74 is much less cheerful than it appeared to be in its glad dawn of 1936. It could no longer tell the statesman that she will be right to do just what she would like to do and it will earn her popularity if she does it. In the new situation of the 1970s when the industrial countries experienced high unemployment,

---

[2] https://www.nobelprize.org/nobel_prizes/economic-sciences/laureates/1976/.

high inflation and a large deficit in balance of trade simultaneously governments were forced to make a priority order among these three problems. Just to control aggregate demand was no longer enough.

A Period of Structural Changes

The 1970s represents the end of the Keynesian era. When Keynesian economists based on the experiences in the 1970s were looking forward they saw a need for the state to add new instruments for controlling the economy. In their view there was a need for an incremental expansion of the state's control over the economy.

It will be a gradual, unheralded, perhaps even largely unnoticed process, because what we are going through is a slow process shifting the boundaries of both permissible and mandatory action by the state, morally justified in terms of an ambiguous and changing 'national interest'. But at some stage, in a crude sense, the economic initiative will have transferred from private groups to the state and we shall thereby have crossed over that conceptual line between a Keynesian variant of capitalism to its aftermath, corporatism (Winkler 1977 p. 86-87).

An incremental expansion of the state's control over the economy above described as a transformation from capitalism to corporatism was for Hayek a road to serfdom (Hayek 1944). His solution to economic problems was radical different. He was in favor of less government and more private initiatives and not more government and more public initiatives. From Hayek's point of view, a growing governmental influence over the economy would result in a loss of freedom and prosperity. He had presented his view in his bestselling book "The Road to Serfdom". The book had made strong impression on Margaret Thatcher who became prime minister in UK in 1979. She had studied it as a student in Oxford in the 1940s and found the book newly relevant in the mid-1970s. After her election she wrote a letter to Hayek telling him *I am very proud to have learned so much from you over the past few years. I am determined that we should succeed. If we do so, your contribution to our ultimate victory will have been immense* (Wapshott 2011 p. 259).

When Thatcher took over as prime minister she made a radical redirection of economic policy. The new policy was a combination of a Hayekian structural policy, shrinking the size of government, freeing business from regulations, privatization of state assets and cutting taxes, and a Friedman inspired monetarist policy aiming reducing the rate of inflation. Thatcher's economic counterrevolution met considerable resistance, not least from members of her own government, who took growing unemployment and violence in the streets as evidence that the policy was wrong. But Thatcher was convinced that her Hayek/Friedman based policy was right and she insisted that there was no going back to Keynesianism. The monetarists saw no other way to fight inflation other than by monetary contraction. The monetarists were aware of that such a contraction undoubtedly is followed by a temporary recession. That was seen as the inevitable price for successfully combating inflation.

Thatcher's economic policy had a significant impact on inflation, which decreased from 18% in 1980 to 3.4% in 1986. However, this change had a high price tag in terms of raising unemployment, which raised from 6.8% in 1980 to 11.3% in 1986. In the same period growth in GDP accelerated making UK's growth rate higher than the declining growth rate in the Euro area in 1986. For those who prioritized inflation control, politics proved successful while for Keynesians the trade-off between inflation and unemployment was unacceptable high.

Thatcher's economic policy was a source of inspiration for Ronald Reagan in his presidential campaign 1980. Reagan campaigned on tax cuts, a smaller federal government and strong defence. When being elected as president invited Ronald Reagan Milton Friedman to join the president's Economic Policy Advisory Board. The board resisted tax increases, strongly urged further cuts in federal spending and pushed for deregulation (Anderson 1990).

Federal Reserve had already in 1980 imposed a tight monetary policy by sharply raising interest rates. This monetary squeeze got inflation to fall from 11.8% in 1980 to 3.7% in 1983. But again the price tag in terms of unemployment was high. Unemployment rate rose from 7.1% in 1980 to 9.7% in 1982. Reagan's monetary policy caused a deep recession in 1981-1982. However, the tight monetary policy, advocated by Friedman, was only one out of four pillars in Reagan's economic policy. The other three was reduction of growth in government spending, reduction of the federal tax and capital gains tax and reduction of government regulations.

Under Reagan's presidency the tax system was reformed leading to lower taxes. The focus in tax policy was to reduce marginal tax and corporate tax. Tax rates for the highest earners were reduced from 70% in 1980 to 28% in 1988. Corporate tax was reduced from 28% to 20%. However, government spending continued to grow, mainly due to increased military spending. In fact Reagan spent more, measured as annual average percent of gross domestic product, than any recent president. The combination of reduced taxes and increased government spending resulted in a growing national debt. During Reagan's presidency the U.S. moved from being the world's largest international creditor to be the world's largest debtor nation with a debt reaching 40.9 per cent of the GDP in 1988. In this way Reagan combined in a pragmatic way a contradictory policy combining tight monetary policy with an expansionary fiscal policy. Reagan continued the economic deregulation that started in the Carter administration, but at a slower rate. Price controls were eased or eliminated on oil and natural gas, cable TV, long-distance telephone service and interstate bus service. Banks were allowed to invest in a broader set of assets and the scope of antitrust laws was reduced. In addition the number new regulations under the existing laws were reduced (Niskanen 1988).

Thatcher's and Reagan's policies were both followed by a period of raising growth in GDP 1982-1990. U.K. and the U.S stood out with raising growth rates in a period when growth rates was declining in the Euro area as well as in Japan. Economists belonging to the two camps disputed about how policy contributed to this boom. Reagan's pragmatic combination of a tight monetary policy and an expansionary fiscal policy gives arguments for the Monetarists as well as the Keynesians.

The monetarists argue the policy purged inflation from the economic system and the deregulations and tax reforms released the free forces of capitalism. Milton Friedman had no doubts.

There's no doubt in my mind that those actions of Reagan, lowering tax rates plus his emphasis on deregulating, unleashed the basic constructive forces of the free market, and from 1983 on; it has been almost entirely up.[3]

Keynesians naturally focused on other aspects of the economy. One eminent Keynesian, Robert Solow, agreed upon the impact of Reagan's policy but he put attention to the growing budget deficit.

The boom that lasted from 1982 to 1990 was engineered by the Reagan administration in a straightforward Keynesian way by rising spending and lowered taxes, a classic case of an expansionary budget deficit (Noble 2006).

These two contradictory assessments of Reagan's economic policy illustrate the schizophrenic nature of the policy. A tight monetary policy, as a tool to combat inflation, was combined with an expansive fiscal policy, as a result of reforms in the tax system combined with large efforts to strengthen defence.

Thatcher and Reagan both faced similar situations and had exposure to similar ideas and they reinforced each other. The coincidence that Thatcher and Reagan was in office at the same time and the boom that followed the policy was important for the worldwide public acceptance of a new non-Keynesian approach to economic policy. Tax reforms focusing on reducing marginal taxes and corporate taxes were conducted in many European countries during the following years. Similarly, deregulation became a dominant theme worldwide. Liberalization of international air transport, telecommunication markets and energy markets are examples of this. The establishment of the EU's internal market with its free flow of people, capital and goods and services implied further deregulation for EU member states.

The tax reforms and the deregulations not only spread to many countries, but they also contributed to a change in conversational topics. While economics conversation in the 1960s centred on what kind of production

[3] Milton Friedman in *Commanding Heights*, PBS, http//www..pbs.org/wgbh/commanding heights/shared/minitext/tr_show01.html.

government should nationalize and how to expand the welfare state the conversation in the 1990s shifted to how much should be deregulated, and what the optimal tax policy would be.

Not all researchers were satisfied with these changes. This so-called counter-revolution gave rise to strong reactions from among many social scientists, which started to use the term neoliberalism as a catchphrase for the new market-oriented policy. They talked about a new neoliberal paradigm that constituted a paradigm shift away from the post-war Keynesian consensus (Harvey 2005). Neoliberalism was seen as an ideology associated with the rise of a global financial capitalism that replaced Keynesianism, which was associated with a national capitalism. The role of the state in a neoliberal era is restricted to create and preserve an institutional framework based on strong property rights, free markets and free trade.

THE SCHUMPETERIAN REBIRTH

Christopher Freeman, a British economist specialized in the economics of industrial innovation, was one of those individuals who was critical to the neoliberal turn. To him the Austrian School of Economics assigned the state an overly passive role in the economy. Although Keynes seemed out-dated, it must, he thought, in some way be room for governments to play an active role. In his search for a new role for governments he focused on the role government could play to manage long-term structural change and technical innovation. These were aspects neglected by both Keynes and Hayek. Freeman saw similarities between the economic situation in the 1980s and 1930s and he was worried about the harmful social and political effects of unemployment.

Freeman took the point of departure in the Austrian economist Joseph A. Schumpeter's theory of the role on innovations in economic development and combined it with the Russian economist Nikolai Kondratieff's theory, mediated by Schumpeter, of long waves in economic development. For Schumpeter, who shared the bottom-up perspective on the economy with the Austrian School of Economics, it was innovations made by entrepreneurs that secured long-term economic growth. He combined his theory of innovations with Kondratieff's empirical research of long waves. Kondratieff studied price levels statistics for four developed economies and found a pattern of long waves. Based on his data he identified two waves with a length the varying between 47 and 60 years and a third still ongoing that started in 1896 (Kondratieff 1926). Schumpeter made a follow up analysis and based on this he argued for the existence of a longn wave of about 50 years, which he referred to as Kondratieff's long waves (Schumpeter 1939).

Schumpeter's main contribution to the research about long waves was that he identified significant technological changes as the main cause of long waves. In Schumpeter's interpretation of capitalism the entrepreneur is placed in the centre. Entrepreneurs are actors who innovate and apply new combinations of factors of production that displace old ones. These technological changes result in the emergence of new industries, which have a gradually growing impact on economic growth. The other side of the coin was that the industries based on innovations outcompeted old industries. Thus structural changes caused by innovations have a strong element of "creative destruction". Schumpeter considered this "creative destruction" to be far more important for economic development than price competition among existing firms.

Schumpeter saw innovation activity as an endogenous process: the action of the first entrepreneur was followed by a herd-like swarm of imitations. As a consequence innovations tend to come in "bunches". Radical innovations cause a large swarm of incremental innovations that will drive economic development for a long time. These radical innovations and the following swarm of incremental innovations was, according to Schumpeter, the main cause of Kondratieff's long waves. Schumpeter presented steam power and innovations in cotton textile industry as the engine of the first wave and innovations in railway and steel production as the cause of the second. Electrical engineering and chemistry caused the third wave. The notion of long waves was rejected and ignored by most economists during the boom decades when the Keynesian paradigm dominated. In the Keynesian paradigm focusing on the short business cycle there was no room for long-term cycles.

During the 1970s, when the belief in Keynes theory was weakened, there was a notable quickening of interest in Kondratieff's long waves. Researchers at the Science Policy Research Unit, lead by Christopher Freeman, became the centre for this research. Freeman's contribution was that he offered a more elaborate explanation of the causes of the long waves. Freeman, like Schumpeter, placed focus on radical innovations, which in turn generated a multitude of other innovations leading to the creation of new industries and new markets (Freeman, Clark & Soete 1982). In this way the upswing was caused by an extensive use of some generic technologies that became the foundation for a swarm of new industries, which grew rapidly as their markets grew. After some decades when these new industries are firmly established their growth rate decline and the competitive pressure within the industries grow stronger. The upswing of the long wave is weakening and growth is slowing down. The upswing is gradually transformed to a downswing.

In the beginning of the downswing investment continues but change character from being mainly investment in new capacity to be investment in labor saving and material saving technologies in order the meet the growing competitive pressure. As a result capital intensity grows and the profitability decline. Freeman concluded that the Keynesian framework offered no appropriate tools to revive the economy in the structural crisis that followed a downswing in the long wave. Most economists agree upon that cyclical trends in economy are related to the role of capital accumulation in economy. Freeman's contribution was that he linked the size of capital accumulation to investments generated by radical innovations and the swarm of incremental innovations that follow.

The upswing in the long wave is based on high investment rate generating a fast growing capital producing sector. The fast growing investment commodity industry needs to make investments themselves in order to satisfy their growing demand. Demand for investment goods become self-reinforcing when companies in the investment commodity sector themselves requires new investments in order to increase their production capacity. Thus additional demand on firms in the investment commodity sector is generated. This accelerator effect seems to be the prime causal factor in a cyclical over- and under-expansion of the capital-producing sector. It creates a long powerful regenerative process that drives the expansion of the investment commodity sector that ends up in a situation when the capacity of the sector exceeds demand. As a result, the downturn in the long wave will plague the investment commodity industry with an inconvenient overcapacity that it takes decades to decommission.

A neo-schumpeterian interpretation of the long post-war boom is that it reflects a simultaneous explosive growth of new technologies and industries like synthetic materials, drugs, electronics, petro-chemicals and vehicles. When the upswing of the long wave is over a long period of over-capacity in different parts of the investment commodity sector - steel, heavy engineering, construction etc. – follows. That was what happened in the 1970s with an emerging overcapacity in the global steel industry and other investment goods industries as a result. Excess capacity in the investment commodity sector has to be physically worn out and work force fired with raising unemployment as result. The accelerator effect is disconnected making the impact of efforts to increase aggregate demand short-lived and small. Recessions tend to grow longer and deeper while boom periods are shorter sand weaker. This process of industrial destruction continues until the stage has been cleared for a new era of rebuilding based on new technologies (Forrester 1981).

Keynes stipulated stimulation of aggregate demand when economy has unused resources. The problem is that aggregate demand is the sum of the demand of a large number of persons and companies demanding a huge number of different products and services. In cases when the existence of unused resources reflects structural problems in certain industries stimulation of aggregate demand will primarily stimulate growth in small expanding industries, which already experience a lack of labor with relevant skills, while large declining industries, which are in a process of downsizing, are affected only marginally. As result Keynesian stimulation would make the lack of resources in the new growing industries grow more than unused resources are shrinking. Increased public spending will in such a situation at best reduce the speed of the downsizing and extend the duration of the ongoing structural crisis. This describes the situation in the downswing of the Kondratieff wave. Thus, when the economy is in such a phase, Keynes' approach is ineffective.

Researchers that applied a long wave perspective agreed upon that the Keynesian approach offered no appropriate tools to revive the economy. However, as researchers educated in the Keynesian tradition they were, in contrast to Joseph Schumpeter, convinced that policy makers must have an important role also in the Kondratieff framework. For them the new situation illustrated the need for an incremental expansion of the state's control over the economy. The question was only which role public policy makers could play in order to prevent the downswing or manage the consequences of the "creative destruction" that follows by the downswing? Therefore, most researchers applying the Kondratieff perspective saw a need for a long-term policy dealing with technological changes.

In their search for such a policy their eyes fell on Japan. The reason was that Japan in the 1970s and 1980s appeared as a shining exception in a world characterized by weak economic growth and high unemployment. During these two decades, Japan's economic growth was 35% higher than growth in the OECD countries and 45% higher than in the EU countries. Researchers studying the "Japanese miracle" paid special attention to the role of the Ministry of Industry and Trade (MITI) and the Japanese industrial policy, which were assigned a central role in the explanations of the phenomena (Johnson 1982), MITI played a central role in identifying and support new technologies that could have extensive structural impact on Japan's economy.

Christopher Freeman did visit Japan to study the "Japanese miracle" (Freeman 1982). His conclusion was that Japan's success reflected the fact that the country's national system of innovation was more efficient than the national system of innovations in Europe. What Freeman called national system of innovations was the network of organizations in public and private sector that interact and in collaboration initiate, modify, import and spread new technology. Freeman brought home two important conclusions from his visit to Japan. First, radical innovations are quite few and are therefore developed on few places. From as policy point of view the focus should therefore not be on creating radical technologies but on importing, modifying and spreading such new technologies. Second, the Japanese case underlined the importance of tight cooperation between business and state with a flow of labor moving between the two spheres. In many European countries business and state is two separate spheres with restricted cooperation.

Most researchers that applied the Kondratieff perspective saw a need for a long-term policy dealing with technological changes. Freeman's definition of the national system of innovation and his focusing on modifying and spreading of new technology was challenged. The concept was gradually broadened. In this process focus was moved from the cooperation of organizations and spreading of new technologies to learning, searching and exploring (Lundvall 1992). A new broader definition of national system of innovations that include all parts of the national economic structure and the institutional set up that affects learning as well as searching and exploring was introduced. The focus on national systems reflected that national economies differ regarding the economic structure and the institutional set up. The differences was assumed to be reflected in national idiosyncrasies in internal organization of firms, inter-firm relationships, role of the public sector, institutional set up of the financial sector and R&D organization. Bengt-Åke Lundvall introduced this broad concept national system of innovation as a new theory with roots in the German economist Friedrich List's analysis of the political economy of national systems (List 1841).

Characteristic of the system of innovation concept is that it from the very beginning was developed to serve as a tool that prescribes what measures national public policy makers should take. The concept of national system of innovation is therefore primarily a policy concept dressed in scientific apparel. Researchers belonging to the "system of innovation school" share a strong confidence in policy makers' ability to control development through active efforts with Keynesianism. The message is that government should take a proactive part in the restructuring of the economy primarily through stimulating institutional learning (Lundvall 1992).

INNOVATION POLICY – THE LONG TERM ALTERNATIVE

Christopher Freeman introduced the concept national system of innovation in OECD who adopted the concept. The system of innovation concept became central to OECD's Technology/Economy Program (OECD 1992). It quickly became a success among participating policy makers. The Finnish government was the pioneer. The Science and Technology Policy Council of Finland, presided over by the prime minister, adopted the term national system of innovation as an organizing concept for their 1990 Review of the Science and Technology Policy (Science and Technology Council of Finland 1990). The review took place before the outcome of the Technology/Economy Programme was summed up.

One reason for the fast response from the Finnish government was that the Great Depression in Finland, caused by the breakdown of Soviet Union, demanded some new policy initiatives. GDP in Finland was reduced by 7 percentages in 1991 and unemployment rose from 3.5% in 1990 to 17.5% in 1993. The government's new strategy was a mix inspired of Hayek and Schumpeter's ideas. A strict monetary and fiscal policy was combined with an ambitious innovation policy, being in line with Schumpeterian ideas of competitiveness. As a result of this policy mix reductions in health and social services was matched by increased investments in public R&D. Highest priority was given to increase funding of technology programs that, in line with the system of innovation perspective, included collaboration between universities, state research institutes and firms. The National Technology Agency (TEKES), that was responsible for these programs, grew and become the most important R&D funding organization in Finland. Its share of the total R&D funding in the state budget almost doubled between 1990 and 1998. The tight fiscal policy, aimed at improving public finances and supporting the economic recovery, was applied until 1997. Within seven years, 1994-2000, a budget deficit of 6% turned into a surplus of 7%.

The Great Depression initiated a "Schumpeterian" transformation of Finnish industry. The Finnish economy's traditional centre of gravity resource-based heavy industry was increasingly challenged by the knowledge-based Information Communication Technology (ICT) sector.

The growth of ICT industries significantly increased their contribution to the Finnish GDP and exports. Large investment in Research and Development combined with the long - term approach in building a national system of innovation supported this process. NOKIA, at the time an international champion in the telecom industry, became the engine of growth and innovation of Finish ICT industries. NOKIA's R&D expenditures grow and became about one third of the total Finnish R&D spending. NOKIA became a flagship for the new Finland and, due to its large R&D investments, a key component in Finland's innovation system. NOKIA's success was partly made possible thanks to public investments in R&D, education and the provision of telecommunication infrastructure. Along with the national policy EU contributed via the Cohesion Policy to the formation of a regional innovation system policy. The Finnish system of innovation policy in these years had tangible similarities with the Japanese model as Christopher Freeman presented it in his lessons from Japan (Freeman 1987).

Since its emergence in the late 1980s the system of innovation concept rapidly attracted the interest of policy makers and the concept diffused among national governments, regional authorities as well as among international organization such as the OECD, the European Union, UNCTAD and UNIDO. This rapid diffusion was facilitated by the fact that the concept originally was formulated in a policy analysis aimed at providing policies to promote economic growth. In the diffusion process focus did gradually changed from a system of innovation policy to a broader innovation policy. This process peaked when the European Union made innovation the core of the Europe 2020 strategy (European Commission 2010). The strategy intended to represent a new beginning for Europe out of which a stronger Europe should emerge. The 2020 Flagship initiative "Innovation Union" was one of seven flagship initiatives announced in the Europe 2020 strategy. The aim of this flagship initiative was to create a true "Innovation Union" in 2020 by collectively taking *responsibility for a strategic, inclusive and business oriented research and innovation policy to tackle major societal challenges, raise competitiveness and generate new jobs* (European Commission 2011). EU's approach was, in the Keynesian tradition, based on the idea that policy makers can control the economy and therefore innovation was transformed into a tool that policy makers can use to solve concrete societal challenges like climate change, energy supply and the scarcity of resources. As a consequence the Innovation Union initiative did focus on innovations that addressed the major societal challenges identified in Europe 2020. This top-down perspective on innovation as policy tool was far from Schumpeter's focus on individual entrepreneurs who innovate through applying new combinations of factors of production that displace old ones.

A Keynesian Heaven

Keynes' reputation had languished for twenty years when President Bush rediscovered and rehabilitated him in 2001 thanks to Al-Qaeda leader Bin Laden. Bin Laden's stated aim was to bankrupt the U.S. through terror and the attack on World Trade Centre and Pentagon was a first step. Bush's response to this threat was a large Keynesian stimulus that combined massive new federal spending to strengthen America's borders with pork barrel projects that had nothing to do with keeping America safe. Federal Reserve followed by reducing interest rates to 1% and to pump money into the economy. Yet this massive Keynesian stimulus to bolster the economy did not appear to work. By the end of 2002, growth was sluggish, unemployment was on the rise, and the budget deficit had reached $158 billion. Inflation was falling from 3.2% before 9/11 2001 to 1.6% in 2003. Policy makers were concerned that America was facing the Japanese syndrome. The Japanse economy was, after the success in the 1970s and 1980, in the 1990s characterized by a combination of interest rates at zero and lavish public spending being unable to reignite the economy. I was a strong Japanese evidence for Keynes' theory still being dead.

The next attempt to rehabilitate Keynes was as a response to the financial crisis in 2008. The Keynesian stimulus in 2001 created a flood of liquidity in the economy creating an abundance of cheap money that became an easy prey for in restless bankers and restless households of which some had no income, no job and no assets. These subprime borrowers wanted to realize their dream of acquiring a home. The trouble started when the Fed started raising interest rates in 2004. Home prizes began to fall and many subprime borrowers could not withstand the higher interest rates and started defaulting on their loans, forcing subprime lenders to file for bankruptcy. The problems in the subprime market spread to financial firms and hedge funds that owned enough securities backed by failing subprime mortgages. The size of the subprime mortgages was enough to create a global financial tsunami.

The cross-border transmission was extremely rapid, due to the tight connections within the financial system itself and also the strongly integrated supply chains in global product markets. Initially most observers were not yet alerted that systemic crisis would be a threat, but this began to change with the failures of Bear Stearns in the United States and the European banks Northern Rock and Landesbank Sachsen. Now observers started to realize that it was a systemic crisis representing a global threat. In autumn, the list of (almost) failed banks had grown long enough to ring the alarm bells that systemic meltdown was around the corner: Lehman Brothers, Fannie May and Freddie Mac, AIG, Washington Mutual, Wachovia, Fortis, Bradford & Bingley, Dexia, ABN-AMRO, Hypo Real Estate and the three Icelandic commercial banks Kaupthing, Landsbanki and Glitnir. The damage would have been devastating had it not been for the numerous rescue operations that were initiated by the governments in several countries.

President Bush suggested in the initial stage of the crisis a large Keynesian economic stimulus in the form of an income tax rebate. American banks were given money outright to save them from bankruptcy. President Obama followed in Bush's footstep and urged the following year congress to pass a 787 billion stimulus bill, in tax breaks and spending on unemployment benefits and infrastructure. In Europe policy makers responded to the crisis with an aggressive easing of monetary policy and a wave of debt guarantees. The surprising revival of Keynes got Robert Lucas, the Nobel Prize winner in 1995, who had done more than most other economist to bury Keynes, to declare: *I guess everyone is Keynesian in a foxhole* (Lucas 2008).

The short-term success of the Keynesian spending can be discussed. Unemployment in The U.S. rose from 5.8% in 2008 to 9.6% in 2010 after which it start sinking back towards the figure of 2008. Unemployment in the Euro-area was 7.6% when it started to rise in 2008 and it peaked at 12% in 2012. Then it started to fall slowly and is now back on the level of 2010, 10%. Based in the figure for GDP a more positive interpretation of the effect of the Keynesian policy can be made. GDP in the U.S. fall by 3.1% in the years 2008/09 but recovered by growing 2.5% in 2010. The European Union shows a similar pattern. A decline in GDP by 4.3% in 2009 was followed by 2.1% growth in 2010. If the time horizon is extended the Keynesian policy seems less effective. The accumulated growth rate in the period 2010-2016 is 40% lower in the European Union than in seven years before the financial crisis. Corresponding figure for the U.S. is 14%. The fact that America recovered better from the crisis reflects other factors than differences in public spending.

The recovery after the financial crisis was slower than after the recession in the beginning of 1990s. Growth rate was about fifty per cent lower in Europe and about one third lower in the U.S compared to the situation in the early 90s. On the other hand, the inflation rate was also lower, about 40 per cent lower in Europe and 60 per cent lower in America. The critical question is how to interpret this new economic situation. Neo-classical economists argue that the austerity policy of the early 1990s has reduced inflation expectations and the recovery was deterred by "rational expectations" of those who believed that extra government spending and borrowing would lead to higher taxes and less gentle conditions for business. Keynesian economists argue that the combination of low growth and stable prices indicate a too low aggregate demand. The Phillips curve has, if it still exists, moved closer to origo giving room for a more expansionary policy than before.

Paul Krugman, the Nobel Prize winner in economics 2008 was like other Keynesians demanding a larger injection of cash and credit into the economy (Krugman 2010). His argument was that policy makers were caught in the history preaching the need for austerity when the real problem was inadequate spending. They were fighting a non-existent inflation and thereby increasing the risk for the real threat, which according to Krugman, was deflation. In an economy with no inflation there seems to be no limits for government spending. This is a Keynesian dream world in which the room for easy money and public spending is almost unlimited.

Policy makers in many countries followed the Keynesian trail with easy money and public spending without any disturbing inflationary effects happened. Initial hopes that stimulus measures could be designed to create long-term growth turned out to be too ambitious in most countries. The impact of the spending on growth rate has been smaller than its impact on public dept. Government debt as a percentage of GDP rose in most industrialized countries. The U.S public debt as a percentage of GDP rose from 73% in 2008 to 105% in 2016, corresponding figures for the members of European Union was 60% and 83%. As a result only eleven member states in EU, compared to 19 in 2008, managed to fulfil the EU stability criteria of public debt, less than 60% of GDP, for membership in the Euro area. Ironically only one of the member states of the Euro area, Luxembourg, managed to fulfil the criteria. In five of the member states public debt exceeded 100% of GDP, with Greece in the front with 181%. The only member state to reduce its public debt in this period was Malta. A handful member states – Luxembourg, Denmark, Estonia and Sweden – show a rather stable public debt below 60% of GDP. The Keynesian policy with its low interest rates implies that large public debt so far have been an easy financial burden. This is a situation that will change with raising interest rates.

The absence of inflationary pressure in the economy strengthened the expansive bias of the Keynesian approach. The consequences of stimulus in a recession and contraction in a boom are quite different. While stimulus measures are enjoyed directly by the residents in the form a lower taxes, further public service or more public transfers they must imagine the possible positive long-term effects of contraction measures. The gains of contraction measures take the form of avoiding a hypothetical future situation of uncontrolled inflation, which would lead to even worse economic problem. This is a gain that, by its very nature, cannot be experienced, but can only be imagined in the mind of the individual person

(Buchanan & Wagner 1977). Direct experiences beat abstract imaginations. As a result contraction measures will have weaker political support that stimulus measures. People may not agree upon description of the actual economic situation as a boom. Those still unemployed have no reason to accept the description. Persons belonging to the group whose taxes will be increased or who benefits from goods and services supplied by the government that are reduced have reasons to oppose the contraction. Also persons who consider their own economic situation to be vulnerable to a downward shift in aggregate demand may react. Workers and investors will be worried about the consequences for their jobs and investment. Those anticipating the prospect of making economic gains from inflation will lose an opportunity.

The fact that Keynesian stimulus measures have direct positive impact on citizen's wellbeing creates strong political support for such policy in all democratic societies. Deficit finance will generate political support, even in a non-Keynesian economy, first of all among persons whose real taxes will be reduced or those who expect an increased flow of benefits from the government. Those who consider their own economic position likely to be improved due ro increased aggregate demand may also support a deficit policy.

In other words, the strong political support for stimulus measures make policy makers tempted to initiate stimulus measures also in situations when it is unnecessary. The other side of the coin is that policy makers try as long as possibly to avoid fiscal austerity measures. Difficulties in real time to determine where in the business cycle the economy is give room for subjective interpretations of the situation. The attractiveness of the stimulus policy makes it tempting for policy makers to go for that alternative at least in the absence of a bothersome high inflation pressure. The recovery after the financial crisis in 2008 illustrates the strength in this temptation.

The Keynesian reaction to the financial crisis was efforts to increase aggregate demand. Increased public spending combined with extremely low interest rates and an increase in the amount of money was the policy mix used. This was a relevant first reaction to a financial crisis that resulted in negative growth in 2009 in both the US and the EU. From 2010 on growth rate in the U.S. has been around 2% and in EU about 1,4%. Certainly the growth rate is lower than before the crisis, but it is still a stable recovery with a continually lower unemployment rate. Governments concluded, based on that unemployment was still higher than before the financial crisis, that the economies had unused resources. Efforts to stimulate aggregate demand have been made all the years since the financial crisis despite the fact that the economy showed sign of having reached a boom phase, although the boom was weaker than boom phases before the financial crisis. How the situation is interpreted depends on which perspective one uses. Keynesians focus on the supply of unused resources, Schumpeterians pay attention to the structural dynamics of the economy and Hayekians look at the public deficit.

By using a Schumpeterian perspective you can argue that the fact that growth rate is lower after the financial crisis than before reflect that the economy is in the downswing of the Kondratieff wave. If we apply the Schumpeter/Kondratieff perspective the accelerator effect does not function making the Keynesian approach inefficient. From an Schumpeter/ Kondratieff perspective what policy makers now interpret as a mild recession may in fact be a boom. The size of the unused resources in the US and some larger EU countries indicates that this could be the case. The attractiveness of the Keynesian approach is that it offers a solution that is attractive for the population although it may not be effective in the actual situation. Schumpeter tells us that the economy is in a period of structural change that short-term policies only marginally can affect. For policy makers the choices between Schumpeter's wait and see alternative and Keynes' stimulation policy is simple.

As a result public spending, low interest rates and increased money volume has been used in a period that looks like a boom period. The absence of inflation has made it possible. Why inflation hasn't returned when the economy has recovered is a topic open for speculations. From a Keynesian perspective the most attractive answer would be that institutional changes have permanently changed the conditions for inflation. Globalization has made inflation a global force. Most countries are open for import from other countries making it possible to import goods and services from low cost countries. An ongoing a shift of production from high cost countries to low cost countries is pushing back inflation. The process is strengthened by digitalization that increases productivity and displaces the power in negotiations to the employer's advantage. The room for wage inflation decreases. Many economists argue based on experiences from Japan that an ageing population also contributes to lower inflation.

The present situation with a Keynesian stimulation policy in an economic boom represents an unknown territory and the long-term implications of the policy are unclear. However, it seems clear that a high and growing public debt will reduce the room for further Keynesian stimulus policy next time the economy turns into a recession. Interest rates are now so low, in some countries even negative, that a further lowering of them seems difficult. On the other hand, public debt in many countries is so high that further growth in debt or raise in interest rates could threat the welfare state, unless a period of high inflation will solve the debt problem. In a situation when annual growth in GDP is lower than interest rate the servicing of the public debt will demand reductions in welfare expenditures and/or higher taxes. In EU where tax rate as a percentage of GDP in average is 45 per cent, and with six member states have a tax rate above 50 per cent, the room for further tax raises are restricted. The Keynesian celestial kingdom will not last forever and policy makers will face some problems beyond the two paradigms.

THE KEYNESIAN VS. THE AUSTRIAN APPROACH

Schumpeter's cyclical perspective has visible touch points with the perspective of the Austrian School of Economics. The point of departure for both of them is that economic development is formed by a large number of actors that act based of their self-interest as consumers, entrepreneurs, investors, borrowers etc. Both argue that credit expansion plays a crucial role and public policy makers are assigned to have no opportunity to control the evolution. Policy makers' main task is to avoid mistakes that exacerbate existing problems. Based on these similarities I combine these two theoretical perspectives into a common approach called the Austrian approach. The Austrian approach is compared with the Keynesian approach in order to illustrate why policy makers prefer the latter.

Keynes' theory applies a short-term macro approach on the economy with policy makers in the driver seat. In the Keynesian world policy making is in the hand of a small group of educated and intellectual bureaucrats inspired by a disinterested concern for the public good. Wrong decisions are reflecting intellectual error that would be corrected if the correct ideas were promulgated with clarity and vigor. Decision-making is seen as an efficient learning process according to which empirical experiences gradually improve the theory's solutions. These rational decision makers are thought to combine the necessary stimulus measures during periods of recession with contraction measures in periods of economic boom in such a way that the budget balance is maintained over the business cycle. In the Keynesian approach policy makers' role is primarily to control aggregate demand in order to fine-tune the economy aiming at reaching an acceptable balance between unemployment and inflation.

In contrast to Keynes top-down perspective, the Austrian approach has a bottom-up perspective that emphasized the importance of individual actors and thus the complexity of reality. According to the Austrian approach all economic phenomena is caused by subjective choices of individuals made in their different roles. Therefore the focus of the Austrian approach is on examining the social ramifications of individual choices and not on aggregates and societal groups. The approach emphasizes the organising power of the marked. Policy makers' interference in the economy creates distortions, which result in misallocation of resources. The complex nature of political decision-making increases the risk for distorting policy interventions. From the point of view of the Austrian approach political decision-making processes are characterized by different groups' pursuit of self-interest. In a situation where personal-budget constraints are absent different groups can easily demand financial support from the government without being concerned over who are supposed to pay for it. Somebody else than the group who benefit from the support, whether met through taxation or inflation, will normally pay the cost of the gifts. The pursuit of self-interest makes it easier to make decision about new public gifts than to decide about financing them. Thus, the Keynesian approach has a bias toward deficit spending leading to increasing public debt.

The Keynesian bias toward deficit spending has some serious long-term consequences. It produces a bias toward growth in the provision of services and transfers through government while deficit financing sends a signal to taxpayers that public services have become relatively cheaper. Because public services are paid by the tax collective, the impression for the individual is that they are free. As a consequence citizens' demand of public service and transfers will grow when the opportunity cost of public goods relative to private goods is not visible for the citizens. Hayek warned, based on his view that opportunity cost is a basis for individuals' rational choices, that such a distortion in demand could threaten citizens' economic freedom.

The existence of strict rules, such as the balanced-budget principle, or standards, such as the gold-standard limits on money creation, established some limits on the bias toward government overspending. Without such strict rules deficits will be created to a greater extent than justified by the Keynesian principles. In cases when public debt grows faster than GDP the Keynesian short-term solution may accumulate to a long-term public debt problem. In the Austrian approach this is a serious offense because according to this approiach public policy makers primarily are controllers responsible for the budget balance.

The Keynesian approach and the Austrian approach represent two distinctly different views on the economy and, as a consequence, also two different perspectives on the role of politics in the economy. With his top-down perspective, Keynes assumed that rational politicians governed by their concern for the public good could control aggregated demand and thus secure full employment. In situations when unemployment rose there was a need to increase aggregate demand why the population should be offered gifts in the form of increased public services or lower taxes. In Hayek's bottom-up approach politicians is only one among many actors belonging to different kinds of groups acting based on their self interest. Economic development is shaped by the collected actions of all these actors. The complexity of political decision making combined with the importance of involved groups self-interest make it difficult to predict the result of such a process. The outcome will more reflect the relative strengths of different groups than the policy makers' concern for the public good. As result political interventions to actively try to reduce unemployment leads to harmful economic distortions. With the starting point of the Austrian School of Economics the role of politicians is reduced to adjust the public finances according to the current economic situation.

For policy makers the choice between the Keynesian approach, where policy makers through economic stimulus can ensure full employment, and the Austrian approach according to which policy makers' top priority is to manage public finances through austerity policy is easy. A theory that assumes policy makers are sitting in the driver seat and that the unemployment problem can be solved by offering inhabitants more public service or lower taxes is each policy maker's dream. Which policy maker will argue against an approach that postulate that policy makers are able to manage the economy by offering gifts to the citizens when unemployment is unacceptable high? History tells us that only politicians with a strong, almost religious, conviction of being right make such a choice. Because most politicians are pragmatic and tend to follow the electorates wishes rather than their own personal conviction public policy making get a Keynesian bias. The new Keynesianism reflects that we again are living in a period when the Keynesian approach seems to be useful. How long today's Keynesian celestial kingdom will survive remains to be seen.

References

Anderson, M. (1990) *Revolution. The Reagan Legacy.* Hartcourt Brace Jovanovich, San Diego

Buchanan, J. M. & Wagner, R. E, (1977) *Democracy in Deficit. The Political Legacy of Lord Keynes.* Academic Press, New York

Dagens Nyheter 8 April 1975

European Commission (2010) *Europe 2020. A European strategy for smart, sustainable and inclusive growth.* Brussels

European Commission (2011) *Europé 2020 Flagship Initiative Innovation Union.* Luxembourg

Forrester, J. W. (1981) "Innovation and Economic Change" *FUTURES* Vol. 13 Issue 4 August 1981 p. 323-331.

Freeman, C., Clark, J. & Soete, L. (1982) *Unemployment and Technical Innovation. A Study of Long Waves and Economic Development.* Frances Pinter, London

Freeman, C. (1987) *Technology, Policy, and Economic Performance:; Lessons from Japan.* Pinter Publisher, London

Friedman, M. & Schwartz, S. (1963) *Monetary History of the United States 1867-1960.* Princeton University Press, Princeton

Harvey, D. (2005) *A Brief History of Neoliberalism.* Oxford University Press, Oxford

Hayek, F. A. (1941) *The Pure Theory of Capital* Auburn, Alabama

Hayek. F. A. (1944) *The Road to Serfdom.* Routledge, London

Johnson, C. A. (1982) *MITI and the Japanes Miracle. The Growth of Industrial Policy 1952-1975.* Stanford University Press, Stanford

Keynes, J. M (1923) *A Tract on Monetary Reform.* Macmillan and Co., London

Keynes, J M. (1936)*The General Theory of Employment, Interest and Money.* Macmillan, London

Keynes, J. M. (2010) "Can Lloyd George Do It? "1929. Published in J. M. Keynes *Essays in Persuasion* Palgrave, London

Keynes, J. M. (2012) *Collected Writings vol. 19. Activities 1922-1929. The End of Reparations.* Cambridge University Press, Cambridge

Kondratieff, N. D. (1926) "Die Langen Wallen der Konjunktur" *Archiv für Sozialwissenschaft und Sozialpolitik* Vol. 56, No. 3

Kuznets, S. (1966) *Modern Economic Growth. Rate, Structure and Spread.* Yale University Press, New Haven

Krugman, P. (2010) "The Third Depression" *The New York Times* June 27.

List, F. (1841) *Das Nationale System der Politischen Oekonomie. [The National System of Political Economy].* Kyklos-Verlag, Basel.

Lucas, R. (2008) "The Comeback Keynes" *Time* October 23.

Lundberg, E. (1968) *Instability and Economic Growth.* Yale University Press, New Haven

Lundvall, B-Å. (ed.) (1992) *National Systems of Innovation. Towards a Theory of Innovation and Interactive Learning*. London, Pinter Publisher

Magid, J. (2012) "The Marshall plan" *Advances in Historical Studies*, Vol. 1, No. 1-7

McCracken, P. (1977) et. al. *Towards Full Employment and Price Stability.* OECD, Paris

Myrdal, G (1944) *Varning för fredsoptimism. [Warning for peace optimism].* Bonniers, Stockholm 1944

Niskanen, W. A. (1988) *Reaganomics: An Insider's Account of the Policies and the People.* Oxford University Press, New York

Noble, H. B "Milton Friedman, Free Market's Theorist, Dies at 94" *New York Times*, November 16, 2006

OECD (1992) *Technology and the Economy The Key Relationship*. OECD, Paris

Phillips, A. W. H. (1958) "The Relation Between Unemployment and the Rate of Change of Money Wage Rates in the United Kingdom, 1861–1957." *Economica,* 25, No. 2: p. 283–299.

Say, J-B (1834) *A Treatise on Political Economy* Grigg & Elliot, Philadelphia.

Schumpeter, J. A. (1939) *Business Cycles: a theoretical, historical, and statistical analysis of the capitalist process.* Mansfield Centre, Connecticut

Science and Technology Council of Finland (1990) *Guidelines for science and technology policy in the 1990s*. Helsinki

Wapshott, N. (2011) *Keynes Hayek. The Clash That Defined Modern Economics.* Norton & Co, New York.

Winkler, J. T. (1977) "The Coming of Corporatism". In Robert Skidelsky (ed.) *The End of the Keynesian Era. Essays on the disintegration of the Keynesian political economy.* Macmillan, London

In: Keynesian Policies
Editor: Noralv Veggeland

ISBN: 978-1-53614-026-2

Chapter 2

FRANKLIN D. ROOSEVELT: THE RELUCTANT KEYNESIAN

David B. Woolner, PhD*
Marist College, Poughkeepsie, NY, US

ABSTRACT

"Franklin Roosevelt: The Reluctant Keynesian" examines US President Franklin Roosevelt's ambivalent relationship to John Maynard Keynes. In light of the policies pursued by Franklin Roosevelt under the New Deal, one might assume that FDR was an ardent follower of Keynesian economics. Many of the policies that Keynes' advocated, such as massive expenditures on public works and the use of deficit financing to revive the economy, were in line with what happened during the course of the New Deal. But in fact FDR is perhaps best described as a "reluctant Keynesian," as his frequent calls for a balanced budget and rhetorical adherence to economic orthodoxy stood in sharp contrast to the policies his administration pursued to meet the crisis of the Great Depression. Given the policies pursued by Franklin Roosevelt during the New Deal, one might assume that FDR was an ardent and early follower of Keynesian

* Professor Dr. of History, Marist College, Senior Fellow and Resident Historian, the Franklin and Eleanor Roosevelt Institute, New York, US

economics. Many of the policies that Keynes' advocated in his direct communication with Roosevelt, such as massive expenditures on public works and the use of deficit financing, are in line with what happened during the course of the New Deal. But in fact FDR is perhaps best described as a "reluctant Keynesian." Indeed, if we look at the rhetoric and policies pursued by FDR in his first few months and years as President, we might come to the opposite conclusion about Roosevelt's willingness to embrace Keynes' ideas. For the early FDR was much more inclined to tilt towards fiscal orthodoxy than the economic policies promoted by Keynes. FDR repeatedly called for a balanced federal budget and of his first moves as President was to push through the Economy Act, a relatively obscure piece of legislation that called for a cut of a half billion dollars from a federal budget and gave the President broad powers to cut and reorganize the federal government and to slash federal salaries by up to 15 percent. Yet by the end of the 1930s and early 1940s it was clear to all concerned that many of the economic policies his administration had adopted—including the use of massive government borrowing and spending—were essentially those advocated by Keynes.

Keywords: Keynes, Keynesian economics, New Deal economic policy, FDR and Keynes, deficit spending, Great Depression, New Deal

> The economic experiments of President Roosevelt may prove, I think, to be of extraordinary importance in economic history, because for the first time—at least I cannot recall a comparable case—theoretical advice is being taken by one of the rulers of the world as the basis of large-scale action. The possibility of such a remarkable event has arisen out of the utter and complete discredit of every variety of orthodox advice. The state of mind in America which lies behind this willingness to try unorthodox experiments arises out of an economic situation desperate beyond precedent. — John Maynard Keynes, January 1934.[1]

On December 16, 1933, US President Franklin D. Roosevelt received a letter from his friend, Felix Frankfurter, a Harvard Law Professor who was then at Oxford, noting that at the request of the New York Times, the British

[1] "Roosevelt's Economic Experiments," by J.M. Keynes in *The Listener*, January 17, 1934, John Maynard Keynes Papers, A/33/34, Kings College, Cambridge. For more on Keynes impact on the New Deal and on twentieth century economics see: Robert Skidelsky, *Keynes: The Return of the Master* (New York: Public Affairs, 2009).

economist John Maynard Keynes had written an "Open Letter to the President" which was scheduled to appear on December 31, 1933. Keynes (who had been urged to write the letter by Frankfurter) had given Frankfurter an advance copy of the letter and Frankfurter enclosed a copy for the President. Keynes was very interested in what was happening in Washington and had written the letter in part because the immediate up-tick in the US economy that followed FDR's inauguration appeared to be at an end, which was a real concern for the British economist. Impressed by the bold moves the President had taken to date, Keynes observed that FDR had made himself "the trustee for those in every country who seek to mend the evils of our condition by reasoned experiment within the framework of the existing social system. If you fail," he went on, "rational change will be greatly prejudiced throughout the world, leaving orthodoxy and revolution to fight it out. But if you succeed, new and bolder methods will be tried everywhere, and we may date the first chapter of a new economic era from your succession in office."[2]

KEYNESIANISM

Keynes then went on to note that the Roosevelt Administration was engaged in a double task of recovery and reform—recovery from the slump, and the passage of those business and social reforms that are long overdue. But he also warned that "wise and necessary" as reform may be, it might also impede recovery. Keynes advised that it would be better initially to work towards recovery with all speed, as success here will provide the prestige needed to accomplish long-range reform[3] Keynes also addressed some of the specific aspects of the 100 days. Here, for example, he suggested dropping the National Industrial Recovery Act (NRA), as he could "not detect any material aid to recovery in the NRA," while insisting that "the vast administrative task set by this act has seemed to represent a wrong

---

[2] "An Open Letter to the President," John Maynard Keynes to FDR, December 31, 1933, Felix Frankfurter, Copies of Correspondence with Franklin D. Roosevelt, Box 1, Franklin D. Roosevelt Presidential Library (hereafter cited as FDRL), Hyde Park, New York.

[3] Ibid.

choice in the order of urgencies." As such, Keynes suggested that even though the act is on the books, and even though a considerable amount of effort had gone into implementing it, "it might be better …to allow [more] experience to accumulate before trying to force through all of its details."[4] In lieu of the NRA, Keynes argued that the Roosevelt Administration should place a far greater emphasis on public expenditures, both to put people to work and to increase the purchasing power of the worker—and that this effort should be financed *not* through increased taxation but through borrowing. Keynes also argued for an increase in the money supply (inflation) and noted that government investment in capital projects is better than the "involuntary idleness of millions."[5]

In light of many of the policies pursued by Franklin Roosevelt under the auspices of the New Deal, one might assume that FDR was an ardent and early follower of Keynesian economics. After all, many of the policies that Keynes' advocated in this, his first direct communication with Roosevelt, such as massive expenditures on public works and the use of deficit financing, are in line with what happened during the course of the New Deal. But in fact FDR is perhaps best described as a "reluctant Keynesian," for it would take many years and much hard experience, before he would admit to following policies similar to those advocated by the famous British economist.

Indeed, if we look at the rhetoric and policies pursued by FDR in his first few months and years as President, we might come to quite the opposite conclusion about Roosevelt's willingness to embrace Keynes' ideas. For the early FDR was much more inclined to tilt towards fiscal orthodoxy than the economic policies promoted by Keynes. During the 1932 campaign, for example, FDR repeatedly called for a balanced federal budget and even went so far as to sharply criticize President Hoover for his failure to meet this objective during his last years in office. To be fair, we must acknowledge that part of what drove FDR to take this line of attack was his sense that it would gain him political points among the large section of the American population that viewed—and still views—balanced budgets as a sacred

[4] Ibid.
[5] Ibid.

obligation. But we should not let this or FDR's strong belief in government action to secure greater economic security for the average American obscure the fact on the whole he remained something of a fiscal conservative.

Once elected, there is ample evidence to suggest that FDR fully intended to make good on his promise to cut federal spending by 25 percent and balance the budget. One of his first moves as President, for instance, was to push through the Economy Act, a relatively obscure piece of legislation that stands in sharp contrast to the many other programs and laws launched during FDR's famous 100 Days. Among other things the Economy Act called for a cut of a half billion dollars from a federal budget of $3.6 million, including major cuts in veterans benefits, even in the wake of the Bonus Army fiasco of 1932 that did so much damage to President Hoover's reputation. It also gave the President broad powers to cut and reorganize the federal government and to slash federal salaries by up to 15 percent.[6]

The Economy Act was signed into law on March 15, 1933, just eleven days after FDR's inauguration. To carry out its provisions, Roosevelt appointed former Arizona Congressman Lewis Douglas as his Budget Director. Douglas regarded balancing the budget as absolutely essential and during his brief tenure in Congress had introduced a resolution establishing a Congressional Committee on government economy. Thrilled at the power invested in the Executive to cut federal spending, Douglas met with FDR virtually every day during the latter's first year in office. Together the two men cut government salaries; abolished and/or consolidated federal agencies; reduced expenditures on veterans by over 30 percent, and carried out a host of other cuts to the 1934 budget.[7]

BUDGET MATTERS

Given FDR's strong support for both the Economy Act and for Douglas, there is little doubt that the President's belief in the efficacy and desirability

---

[6] Anthony J. Badger, *FDR: The First Hundred Days,* (New York: Hill and Wang, 2008) 51-54.

[7] Ibid; Elliot A. Rosen, *Roosevelt, The Great Depression and the Economics of Recovery* (Charlottesville, VA: 2005), 75-77.

of a balanced budget was sincere. But as noted, FDR was also a strong believer in progressive government and in the need to provide relief to the millions who were suffering under the scourge of poverty and unemployment during the Great Depression. He was also quite willing to engage in what he famously called "bold persistent experimentation" to meet the economic challenges of his day.[8] As such, FDR was far more willing to look to new as opposed to old remedies to meet the needs of the nation than his predecessors, and while he respected Douglas and like Hoover had been schooled in the tenets of economic orthodoxy as a young man, he was not a slave to any particular ideology. Above all, FDR placed the highest priority on the need for government to provide adequate relief to the poor, even if this meant that the government must engage in borrowing to do so. To square FDR's strong belief in the need for government action—and spending—to meet the economic crisis with his equally strong belief in the need for a balanced budget, Roosevelt devised a two tiered budget formula that help him reconcile—in his own mind at least—these two competing impulses. Under this formula FDR drew a distinction between what he referred to as the "normal budget," which he hoped to balance, versus the need for emergency spending; emergency spending that supported the myriad of programs that made up much of the New Deal and which in effect meant that as President FDR never actually produced a balanced federal budget.[9]

As in all of FDR's actions, there was a political dimension to this two-tiered budget structure as FDR could claim to his more conservative constituents that he was taking steps to cut government spending while at the same time responding to the very real needs of the millions of unemployed. But it is important not to read too much into this. Like his struggle with polio and his belief that through persistent effort and exercise he would one day regain the use of his legs, FDR never fully abandoned his hope that he would at some point be able to produce a balanced budget.

---

[8] FDR first made reference to this concept in a commencement address he delivered at Oglethorpe University in Atlanta, Georgia, on May 22 1932, Master Speech File, FDRL.

[9] Ronald Edsforth, *The New Deal: America's Response to the Great Depression* (Malden, MA: Blackwell, 2000), 56-57.

SECOND NEW DEAL

Thanks to this inherent fiscal conservatism, the seemingly massive federal spending and borrowing that FDR engaged in during the New Deal years is actually quite small. In fact, there were only two occasions between 1933 and 1939 when the federal deficit, as a percentage of gross national product, exceeded the 4.6 percent of President Hoover's last year in office.[10] It should come as no surprise then, that in spite of his ever-increasing international reputation, and growing legion of followers within the US economic community, FDR was not particularly taken with Keynes or his ideas. At the time of their first and only meeting during the 1930s, for example, FDR hinted at a certain ambivalence about Keynes when he quipped that with all of his "numbers" Keynes struck him as more of a mathematician than an economist. Keynes for his part also remarked after the meeting that FDR did not seem to know much about economics.[11] Nevertheless, Keynes remained deeply interested in FDR's New Deal, and before leaving the United States (where he had traveled to receive an honorary degree from Columbia University) for his return to England, drafted a twelve page "Agenda for the President" that included nine major observations and/or recommendations about how best to consolidate "economic and business recovery." Here, Keynes reiterated his earlier recommendation that the president scrap the NRA, in large part because of the act's "excessive complexity and regimentation." He also observed that he could see no likelihood that business "of its own initiative, will invest in durable goods on a sufficient scale for many months to some," and as such, regarded the conservative argument that the government should retire from the economic field, based on the notion that "business left to itself would soon work out its own salvation," as inherently foolish. The only solution to the economic crisis, in Keynes view, was for the government to engage in direct stimulus of the economy for at least the next six months to a year. Here, Keynes recommended that the Roosevelt Administration focus its

---

[10] David M. Kennedy, "What the New Deal Did," *Political Science Quarterly*, Volume 124, Number 2, 2009, 251-268.

[11] Frances Perkins, *The Roosevelt I Knew* (New York: Penguin, 2011), 215-216.

spending on housing and the railroads. He also urged the president to pressure the Treasury and Federal Reserve to bring down long-term interest rates, and insisted that it would be a mistake for the government to try to balance its expenditures with revenue (i.e., raise taxes) during the course of the next two years.[12]

Shortly after Keynes delivered his Agenda to FDR he published another major article in the *New York Times* that followed the same arguments. For the next two years, however, Keynes direct contact with FDR more or less ceased. FDR, in the meantime, launched what is sometimes referred to as "the Second Hundred Days" or "Second New Deal"—a flurry of legislative activity in 1935 and 1936 aimed at providing the American people with a basic measure of social and economic security. In contravention to Keynes persistent arguments in favor of stimulus over reform, the key provisions of the Second New Deal included the National Labor Relations Act, which granted unions the right to organize and engage in collective bargaining and established the National Labor Relations Board to determine bargaining unit jurisdictions, hold elections, and certify those unions that had received a majority vote as the legally binding representative of the workers involved. The Second New Deal also saw the passage of the Social Security Act, which provided old age pensions, unemployment insurance, and welfare aid to dependent mothers, the blind and the physically handicapped. Other measures of the Second New Deal included stricter regulations for private utilities, higher taxes for the rich, further banking legislation, and a major rural electrification program.

THE ROOSEVELT RECESSION

The one major economic stimulus measure in the Second New Deal involved the establishment of the Works Progress Administration or WPA. Created by Executive Order on May 5, 1935, the WPA pumped more than

---

[12] "Agenda for the President, " by John Maynard Keynes, June 5, 1934, President's Personal Files (PPF) 5235, FDRL, Hyde Park, NY.

$10 billion dollars into the Depression economy and employed approximately 8.5 million people. By the time it ended in 1943, it had also built much of the economic infrastructure of country, including over 650,000 miles of roads, 78,000 new bridges and viaducts, and 350 airports, all of which greatly facilitated the movement of goods and people across the country. The WPA also built roughly 40,000 buildings, created 8,000 parks and vastly improved the nation's supply of clean drinking water through an array of large and small water and sewage disposal projects.[13]

Thanks to these and the earlier provisions of the New Deal, the U.S. economy performed quite well during FDR's first term in office. Indeed, we sometimes forget that since 1933, when FDR took over at the height of the Great Depression, the economy had been expanding steadily, at an average rate of 14 percent per year. Keynes was clearly impressed by these developments and in a conversation he had in London with a senior official in the US Department of Agriculture in May of 1936, insisted that the Roosevelt Administration should continue to ignore any claims by Wall Street bankers and others that whatever economic recovery had occurred "would have come more quickly had the government not interfered. They will use that argument," Keynes cautioned, "as an excuse to going back to complete anarchy." This "false argument" had to be avoided at all costs, Keynes insisted, because "the recovery in very large measure is a result of what the administration has done, and further government action is desirable" to maintain its momentum. In the same conversation, Keynes also noted that he saw little risk of inflation.[14]

Unfortunately for FDR, many of the presidents more conservative economic advisors, including Treasury Secretary Henry Morgenthau Jr., did not share Keynes' views about the risk of inflation. Schooled as most of these advisors were in the tenets of economic orthodoxy (which called for cuts in spending during an economic downturn), and unsure of the effects of the Keynesian-style deficit spending that the administration had been

[13] For more on the New Deal see: William E. Leuchtenburg, *Franklin D. Roosevelt and the New Deal* (New York: Harper, 2009); and David M. Kennedy, *Freedom from Fear: The American People in Peace and War* (New York: Oxford, 2005).

[14] "Abstract of conversation with John Maynard Keynes," submitted to the President by Henry A. Wallace, May 8, 1936, FDRL, Hyde Park, NY.

engaged in under the terms of the early New Deal, they advised President in the spring of 1937 to cut the budget, reduce deficit spending and tighten the money supply as a means to stave off inflation. Heeding their word, and no economist himself, FDR did just that. The results were an unmitigated disaster.

Thanks to this decision to move away from the increasingly Keynesian policies the Roosevelt Administration had been following; policies that saw the unemployment rate fall from a high of 25% in 1933 to 14% by 1937—the largest single drop in unemployment in American history—FDR launched one of the sharpest economic downturns in American history—the so-called "Roosevelt Recession" of 1937-38. In just a few short months the GDP declined by 13 percent; industrial production by 33 percent; wages by 35 percent and an estimated four million people lost their jobs. No fool, FDR quickly reversed himself and went back to Congress to seek a massive stimulus bill to put people back to work and repair the damage to the Depression-era economy. Within three months growth had returned and the economy was back on track.

The sharp economic downturn that took place in the wake of the Roosevelt Administration's attempts to balance the budget in the spring of 1937 did not go unnoticed on the other side of the Atlantic. As the situation deteriorated, Keynes felt compelled to write directly to the President from his distant vantage point at Kings College, Cambridge; to offer FDR what Keynes called his "bird's eye impressions" about the situation in the United States. Keynes attributed the downturn in the US economy to what he termed "an error of optimism" about its current state, and to a number of specific underlying causes that Keynes found quite troublesome, including the tightening of the money supply, and most especially, the curtailment of government spending on public works and other facets of the economy.[15] In reviewing all of the factors that contributed to both the post 1933 recovery, and to subsequent downturn, Keynes insisted "the present slump could have been predicted with absolute certainty." He also endorsed FDR's efforts to push through minimum wage and maximum hour legislation—which would

[15] John Maynard Keynes to Franklin Roosevelt, February 1, 1938, PPF 5235, FDRL, Hyde Park, NY.

culminate in the passage of the Fair Labor Standards Act in June—and urged the president to return to large-scale public expenditures, which he viewed as critical to "maintain prosperity at a reasonable level."[16]

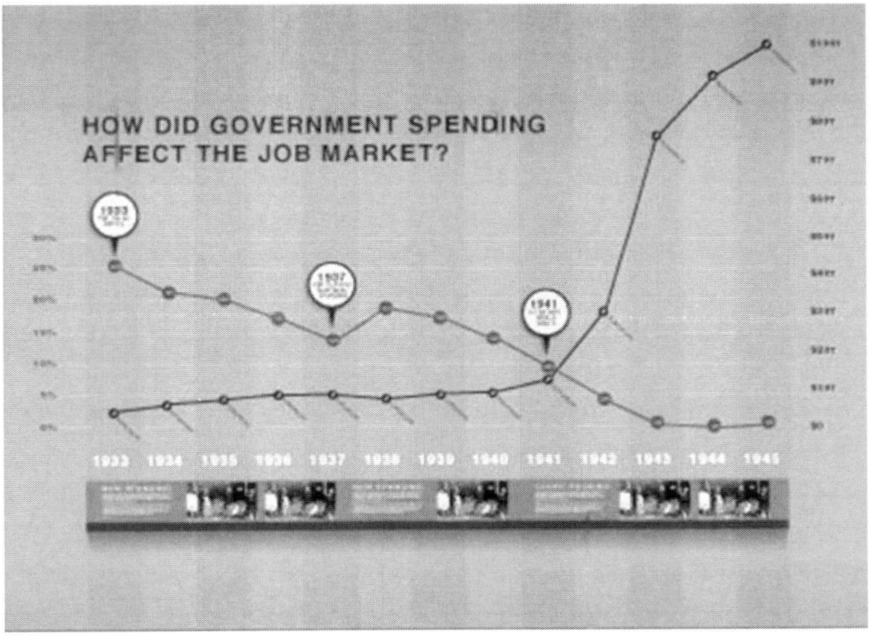

Figure 1. Graph depicting the relationship between government spending and employment between 1933 and 1945. Courtesy of the FDR Presidential Library and Museum.

Keynes's observations may have been accurate, but the "I told-you-so" tenor of his missive did not sit well with the president, who, in a conversation with Merriman Eccles (perhaps the most Keynesian of all of his economic advisors), appeared 'rather piqued by the tone of certain passages." FDR sent Keynes a polite reply that highlighted his pleasure at seeing that Keynes was "in agreement with so much of the administrations economic program." Given the state of affairs in Europe in 1938, FDR also observed that he was sure Keynes would appreciate "that prosperity in the United States will be

---

[16] Ibid.

more potent in obtaining the ends we are all interested in if other democracies strive persistently for similar objectives."[17]

Even though the "Roosevelt recession" was brought to a swift end through a massive federal program of spending and lending, the downturn nevertheless shook the confidence of the administration and led the President to call upon Congress to establish a "Temporary National Economic Committee" to conduct a "thorough review" of the American economy. The Temporary National Economic Committee or TNEC, held Congressional hearings from December 1938 until March of 1941. Unlike today's focus on government borrowing, however, the primary concern of TNEC was not the deficit (although there were those, within the Roosevelt Administration, such as Henry Morgenthau Jr., who still clung to the fiscal orthodoxy that demanded balanced budgets and an end to deficit spending) but rather "the concentration of economic power in American industry," and the perplexing problem of "why we have not had full employment and full utilization of our magnificent resources."[18]

Over the course of the next three years the committee (which included Congressional representatives from both parties and officials from within the administration appointed by the President) heard from hundreds of witnesses, and compiled an enormous set of data on the US economy that has proved to be an invaluable resource to economic historians. Even before the committee finished its work in 1941, three main points of view emerged about how best to revive a stagnant economy. One view argued that trusts and monopolies were inevitable and that the best way to deal with these large concentrations of economic power was through federal regulation; a second view held that monopolistic practices, such as the setting of prices and wages, inhibited economic growth by creating a climate of under consumption and that the best means to counteract this was for the government to pursue the breakup of large trusts and monopolies; while the

---

[17] Franklin Roosevelt to John Maynard Keynes, March 3, 19398, PPF 5235, FDRL, Hyde Park, NY.

[18] Franklin D. Roosevelt Message to Congress on Curbing Monopolies, April 29, 1938, Master Speech File, FDRL, Hyde Park, NY.

third view held that the best means by which the government could have the greatest impact on the economy was through taxation and spending, in other words, a compensatory fiscal policy.[19]

The Third Way

In the end it was this third view—which essentially endorsed Keynesian economics—that eventually emerged as the predominant message from the hearings and from the Committees recommendations. Part of this was due to the clear observation that FDR's decision for the government to spend its way out of the recession in the spring of 1938 was the right one, as the 1937-38 recession came to a rapid end in the wake of FDR's increase in economic stimulus. Keynes's ideas were also given a boost by the 1938 publication of the widely read book *An Economic Program for American Democracy* that placed Keynes's ideas in more layman's terms, and added further sanction to the idea that government spending—even deficit spending—was a legitimate and effective tool with which to combat the twin miseries of recession and unemployment. And finally, by 1941, there was the overwhelmingly empirical evidence provided by the massive federal spending that went into the emerging war effort, which ultimately brought unemployment down to less than 1% and would lead to the enormous wartime and postwar expansion of the US economy. In essence, then, the entire focus of FDR's committee was not on how to reduce the size of the federal debt, but rather on how *government* might take direct measures to restore the economy and put people back to work.[20]

---

[19] Alan Brinkley, "The New Deal and the Idea of the State," in The Rise and Fall of the New Deal Order, 1930-1980, ed. by. Steve Fraser and Gary Gerstle (Princeton: Princeton University Press, 1989), 89-91; *Franklin Roosevelt: His Life and Times,* ed. by Otis L. Graham and Meghan Robinson Wander (New York: DA Capo Press, 1985), 419-420.

[20] Ibid.

CONCLUSION

To many New Dealers, the power of these fiscal and monetary instruments was a revelation. Indeed, it seemed as if it would no longer be necessary to search for ways to reform capitalist institutions in order to revive the economy and produce economic growth. Even unreformed institutions could be helped to work better through the intelligent application of fiscal and monetary policies. To the most exuberant Keynesians, this discovery meant that the greatest dilemma of the modern industrial world had been resolved, that the problem of monopoly—the problem that had preoccupied and frustrated more than two generations of reform efforts—need no longer preoccupy modern society; that it would be possible to lead the way to economic growth not by focusing on producers but by helping consumers—by pumping money into the hands of the millions of men and women who created the market demand for what capitalists produced.[21]

As we have seen, FDR may never have publically embraced Keynes's theories, and in fact preferred to call his subsequent use of massive government borrowing and spending "compensatory fiscal policy," but the two concepts were virtually identical. Spurred along by this change of heart and by the growing demands to increase defense spending to meet the challenges of World War II, the federal government borrowed 100s of billions of dollars in the late 1930s and early 40s, while at the same time government expenditures—i.e., stimulus—reached record levels. By the time the United States was fully engaged in the war, federal spending accounted for more than half of the country's Gross National Product, business was booming and the scourge of unemployment had all but disappeared.

And what were the long-term consequences of all of this borrowing and spending? Economic chaos? A sovereign debt and default crisis? No, what followed was more than three decades of postwar economic expansion and the creation of perhaps the best paid and best educated work-force America

[21] "Franklin Roosevelt and the Progressive Tradition, by Alan Brinkley and David B. Woolner in *Progressivism in America: Past, Present and Future*, ed. by David B. Woolner and John M. Thompson (New York: Oxford University Press, 2016), 22.

had ever seen—in short the birth of the modern middle class. FDR may have been a reluctant convert to Keynesian, but his willingness to embrace bold persistent experimentation, and his absolute refusal to abandon the American people to their fate meant that for intents and purposes, his policies mirrored much of what Keynes had to say in the open letter he penned to the President in 1933. Perhaps the closest FDR ever came to admitting that he was in fact a Keynesian, can be found in a speech he made at Forbes Filed in Pittsburgh in October 1936, when, reflecting on the terrible state of the economy he inherited in 1933 he said:

> "Something had to be done. A national choice had to be made. We could do one of two things. Some people who sat across my desk in those days urged me to let Nature take its course and to continue a policy of doing nothing. I rejected that advice because Nature was in an angry mood…
>
> To have accepted that advice would have been to offer breadlines again to the American people, knowing this time, however, that in many places the lines would last far longer than the bread. In those dark days, between us and a balanced budget stood millions of needy Americans, denied the promise of a decent American life.
>
> To balance our budget in 1933 or 1934 or 1935 would have been a crime against the American people. To do so we should have had to make a capital levy [tax on wealth] that would have been confiscatory, or we would have had to set out face against human suffering with callous indifference. When Americans suffered, we refused to pass by on the other side. Humanity came first".[22]

References

Alan Brinkley, "The New Deal and the Idea of the State," in *The Rise and Fall of the New Deal Order, 1930-1980*, ed. by. Steve Fraser and Gary Gerstle (Princeton: Princeton University Press, 1989).

[22] FDR Address at Forbes Field, October 1, 1936, Master Speech File, FDRL, Hyde Park, NY.

Alan Brinkley and David B. Woolner, "Franklin Roosevelt and the Progressive Tradition," in *Progressivism in America: Past, Present and Future*, ed. by David B. Woolner and John M. Thompson (New York: Oxford University Press, 2016).

Anthony J. Badger, *FDR: The First Hundred Days,* (New York: Hill and Wang, 2008).

David B. Woolner, *The Last 100 Days: FDR at War and at Peace* (New York: Basic Books, 2017).

David M. Kennedy, *Freedom from Fear: The American People in Peace and War* (New York: Oxford, 2005).

David M. Kennedy, "What the New Deal Did," *Political Science Quarterly*, Volume 124, Number 2, 2009.

Elliot A. Rosen, Roosevelt, *The Great Depression and the Economics of Recovery* (Charlottesville, VA: 2005).

Frances Perkins, *The Roosevelt I Knew* (New York: Penguin, 2011).

Robert Skidelsky, *Keynes: The Return of the Master* (New York: Public Affairs, 2009).

Ronald Edsforth, *The New Deal: America's Response to the Great Depression* (Malden, MA: Blackwell, 2000).

William E. Leuchtenburg, *Franklin D. Roosevelt and the New Deal* (New York: Harper, 2009).

In: Keynesian Policies
Editor: Noralv Veggeland ISBN: 978-1-53614-026-2

Chapter 3

FINANCIAL STABILITY AND ECONOMIC GROWTH

Bjørn Skogstad Aamo*
University of Agder, Kristiansand, Norway

ABSTRACT

Economic growth has in the last decade been close to zero in large parts of the developed world following the Financial Crisis of 2007/2008. We discuss the reasons for the crisis and the impacts on economic developments in various regions.

What can we learn from a longer view of the history of the causes of financial crises? It seems that housing booms have been a major cause for many of the banking crises.

Financial crises recessions are more costly than normal recessions in terms of lost output. What can be done to ensure a high degree of Financial Stability with an environment where stable economic growth can be achieved?

* Professor II Emeritus, University of Agder, Kristiansand, and former Director General, the Financial Supervisory Authority of Norway bjorn.aamo@outlook.com.

Keywords: the financial crisis, sub-prime loans, CDO's, credit markets, the sovereign debt crisis, banking crises in history, lessons from the crises, financial stability and economic growth

INTRODUCTION

Discussions on economic growth have both in academic and political circles in most of the post-war period focused on demand, productivity and employment. The International Financial Crisis in 2007/2008 did however in a dramatic way remind us of the importance of financial stability as a precondition for stable economic growth. This is also supported by a longer view of economic history.

Financial stability is a broad concept which cover both the financial institutions, the financial markets and the infrastructure for payments. Financial stability requires a financial system that is resilient to shocks and thus capable of channelling credit and execute payments. It is dependent on a legal framework, which sets basic requirements for the participants and public institutions with powers for supervising the operations and ensure that rules are obeyed. A key definition of financial stability is the absence of crises in the financial system.

The threats to financial stability are developments and vulnerabilities which may ultimately lead to a financial crisis. Strong lending growth may produce debt levels which households and/or companies are unable to serve by paying interests and paying back the loans. Banks have normally margins and financial capital to bear some losses on lending. Large losses will in the event however prevent banks from performing their normal services to society. Credit will be restricted both for new investments and for servicing normal trading operations. A negative vicious circle may be started where the problems of the banking sector leads to stagnation and even decline in economic activity and rising unemployment, adding to further problems for the banks themselves.

We shall first look at the financial crisis of 2007/2008 and the following years and the impacts on economic growth of various regions. We shall further discuss the interaction between the functioning of the credit markets and other features of financial stability and the economic performance of different countries during and after the crisis. We shall then discuss a longer historic view of banking crises and the economy and what lessons we may learn.

THE FINANCIAL CRISIS OF 2007/2008

There is broad agreement that this recent financial crisis was set off by the collapse of the markets for sub-prime housing loans in the US. Millions of Americans got loans with low interest rates and no repayments. When house prices were increasing, refinancing was easy. When prices stopped increasing and started to fall, refinancing became very difficult. People who could not serve their loans left the houses and gave the keys to the banks or other lenders in accordance with the Non-recourse principle. This principle makes the lender responsible for the loan when the borrower cannot serve a mortgage loan. The bank will sell the house to cover the loan. When house prices had started to decline, this would push the prices further down into a vicious downward spiral.

The development of house prices in the US is shown in Figure 1.

Several economic developments had made western economies vulnerable to the collapse of housing prices in the US and the sub-prime-loans. There had been a period of strong increases in spending in the US, based on borrowing from abroad and strong expansion of US financial markets, stimulated by very low interest rates. From the second quarter 2001 to the same period in 2003, the Federal Funds rate was reduced from 3.75 per cent to 1 per cent and was kept at a low level for several years. Half of the US credit market lacked legal requirements for adequate capital and financial supervision, including the leading investment banks. The two federal housing agencies, Fannie Mae and Freddie Mac, had supplied loans for millions of house-buyers as part of policies for affordable housing, however with inadequate standards for the buyers to serve and repay loans.

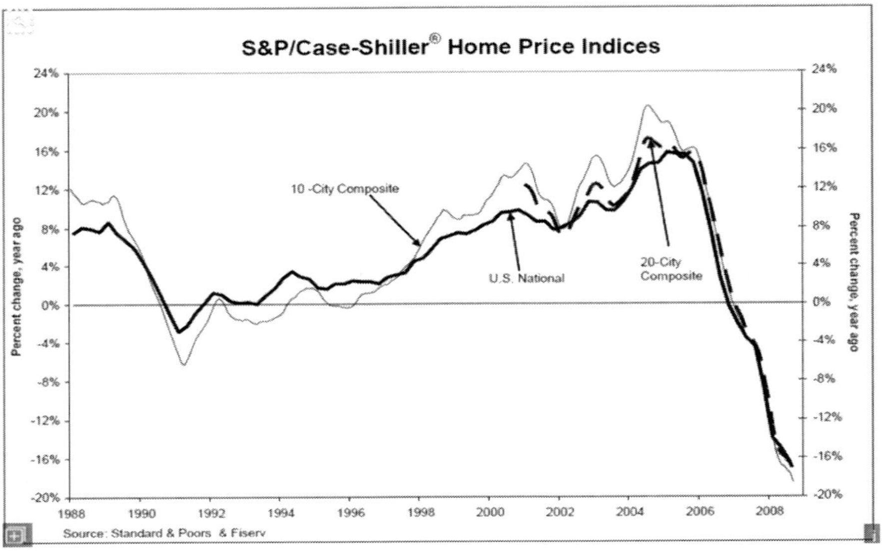

Figure 1. Housing prices in the United States.

The sub-prime loans were "packed and sold" as securities to investors all over the world, known as ABS (Asset Backed Securities), MBS (Mortgage Backed Securities) or CDO (Collateralized Debt Obligations). The number of CDO-contracts had been around 100.000 annually until 2004-2005 and exploded with close to 500.000 in each of the years 2006 and 2007. Rating agencies approved of these instruments as increasing house prices had prevented direct losses. The US investment banks were highly exposed, both as traders and investors. Banks in most European countries invested substantially in such securities. Other financial institutions, hedge funds, mutual funds and pension funds also bought large quantities of these securities. They were expected to give higher returns than many other types of securities.

In Europe BNP Parisbas 9th August 2007 had to freeze three of their funds as they found it difficult to value their holdings of CDO's. The British bank, Northern Rock, had borrowed a lot of money to fund mortgagers for customers. As the problems of CDOs and other Asset Backed Securities made securities markets more nervous, the bank was not able to sell its securities in the market, and it asked British authorities for liquidity loans.

This in turn sparked fears that the bank would shortly go bankrupt, prompting customers in the thousands to queue to withdraw their savings. It was the first run on a British bank for 150 years. The reaction of the customers should be seen against the inadequate UK deposit-insurance scheme where only the first 2000 pounds of a deposit were fully covered.

When the fifth biggest investment bank, Bear Sterns, was rescued by US authorities in the spring of 2008, there was a feeling of relief as a possible financial crisis was seen to have been avoided. However, on September 15th 2008, the fourth largest investment bank, Lehman Brothers, went bankrupt without any intervention by US authorities.

The bank was left to conduct normal bankruptcy procedures managed by a private lawyer in New York. Financial markets all over the world were influenced, and normal bank-to-bank lending came to a standstill in many markets. Most banks were dependent on such loans for their liquidity supply.

Lehman Brothers had substantial operations in more than 60 countries, not at least as a broker and lender in the securities markets. To illustrate, in Norway some 20.000 deals at the Stock Exchange were stopped following the Lehman Brothers bankruptcy.

The day after the bankruptcy, 16. September, the Committee of European Banking Supervisors (CEBS) had a telephone-meeting. Our Belgian colleague Peter Praet expressed the general feeling when he stated: *"There is no one in charge over there."* US Investment banks were only regulated by legislation for security firms without any banking supervision. US authorities could not take a lead. It was left to national authorities all over the world to clean up the mess, with some contacts with private lawyers in New York.

Banks in North America and Europe suffered heavy losses both on the sub-prime-based bonds and their relations with Lehman Brothers. The losses reduced the general ability of banks to serve industry and society. Banks also play a key role for exports. Japan, Germany and other exporters of industrial goods, saw production and employment suffer from the international financial crisis.

Several major banks had significant losses threatening their very existence and were given government support or were taken over by national authorities. Banks in Greece, Portugal, Ireland, Spain and Cyprus had problems also for domestic reasons, and needed direct government assistance.

For Greece the problems were primarily caused by general heavy fiscal expansion over years. Loans extended to the Greek government or bonds bought by private European banks thus became part of the crisis for the European banking industry. The international assistance to Greece was of great importance to limit the problems of European banks.

In many countries little room of manoeuvre in government finance prevented fiscal measures for encouraging economic growth. Lack of cooperation between the social partners made it difficult for several countries to remain competitive in trade of goods and services.

ECONOMIC DEVELOPMENTS AFTER THE CRISIS – THE GREAT RECESSION

The decline in economic activity was most significant in the Eurozone countries of the European Union. Other European and North American countries were also impacted. The difference between countries may to a large degree be explained by differences in the resilience of their banks and their financial systems in general. For many Eurozone countries, the negative impacts of the financial crisis came in a situation where both the problems of weak government finances and high levels of private debt made them very vulnerable.

The countries of the Eurozone thus suffered a steep decline in GDP and thereafter a slow and weak recovery. The GDP-level of 2007 was not regained before 2017. GDP of the European Union in total declined by more than 4 per cent in 2009 alone. In the Eurozone the problems of the banks dominated in the first years of the crisis, as credit for the private sector became limited. When governments intervened with supply of capital to assist the banks, they soon ran out funds. Governments borrowed heavily and soon met limits for what the markets were able and willing to supply.

This set out a *sovereign debt crisis* which marked the second phase of the financial crisis for economic developments in Europe.

The problems of the Eurozone were closely linked to the highly diverse development of competitive position and current accounts among members. While Germany was running a surplus in their current account of some 6 – 8 per cent of GNP in the years 2006 – 2008; Spain, Portugal and Greece had deficits of some 10 to 15 per cent of GNP.

The strict rules for common Exchange rates in a Monetary Union, made it difficult for the weaker countries to improve competitiveness and deal with the economic decline as they could not devaluate their currencies. Restrictive demand policies became the main instrument for reducing inflation and wage increases, thus producing more decline and higher unemployment. The flexibility of exchange rates in European countries outside the Euro-area, made it easier for these countries to maintain and improve competitiveness and restart economic growth. A series of deliberate or indirect competitive devaluations among the core of European countries might however also have had some negative impacts in the form of higher inflation and economic instability.

Many Eurozone members payed a high price for keeping fixed exchange rates. It was typical that the GDP of Finland in 2017 was not higher than in 2007, while neighbouring Sweden, which had not adopted the Euro, grew by more than 10 per cent in the same period.

The GDP of Japan fell sharply in 2008 and 2009 and recovered only slowly in 2010 and the following years. The exports of machinery and other industrial goods were severely hit by the lack of credits and other banking services.

The US experienced a significant decline in GDP the first year of the crisis. Demand and production was however relatively soon stabilized and started growing. It seems the US had more resilience and flexibility it its economy, than did the countries of the Eurozone. The strong position of the Federal Reserve and that the markets were able and willing to finance an expansionary budget under President Obama, are elements that explain the better performance of the US economy.

Sweden is dependent on exporting manufacturing goods and suffered a significant decline in production as credit facilities weakened. Production soon bounced back when finance again became available and domestic demand was stimulated. Norway was less effected by the financial crisis than most other countries. One reason was that Norway had learned from its own banking crisis in 1990-93. Banks had since then improved the quality of credit processes and had low losses. Authorities had set higher requirements for bank capital than in other countries. Norwegian banks were thus able to continue to offer credit to private businesses and households and increase total credit significantly. The Norwegian banking crisis is described in an article I wrote for an anthology in honour of Thore Johnsen, (2017). The lessons learned are discussed in a book *"Læring fra kriser"("Learning from crises")* – 2016 (Norwegian only).

A *recession* is defined by a declining GDP in two consequent quarters. This definition is used by OECD and other international organizations. Based on OECD Statistics, the recession lasted for 33 months in the Eurozone, first for 15 months from Q2 in 2008 and then 18 months from Q4 2011 to Q1 2013. Within the zone France was on the lower end with 21 months of recession. Italy experienced 60 months, Finland 54 months, Spain 48 months and Portugal 51 months. These countries suffered most. Unemployment in Spain and Greece passed 25 per cent in 2012-2014, while Portugal and Italy experienced rates of 12-15 per cent. German unemployment on the other hand declined from 10 per cent in 2005 to 5 per cent after 2012.

The US had a quick decline and a relative rapid recovery which made the recession last for only 12 months. The recession of Canada lasted only 9 months. In Europe Sweden, with a steep declines and rapid recovery had one of the shortest recessions, 15 months. The recession in Norway was relative shallow and came in three periods of each six months, altogether 18 months. An improvement of terms of trade connected with higher oil prices was helpful. Norway was the first country in Europe where GDP passed the previous peak level of 2007/2008, as shown in Figure 2.

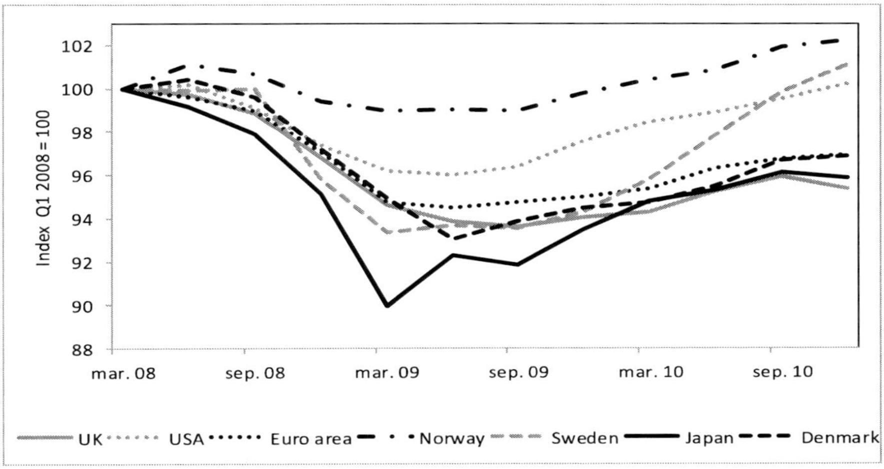

Figure 2. Development of GDP in the first years following the Financial Crisis of 2007-2008. (Based on OECD Statistics.).

Comparisons of economic developments between countries are not always easy because of variations in exchange rates and estimates for developments in GDP. The World Bank recommends the "Atlas method" whereby *Gross National Income (GNI)* in local currency is converted into US dollars by a three years average of exchange rates and adjusting for differences in inflation rates. On this basis the following table which covers most of the period after the crisis, is extracted from the World Development Indicators:

The three Scandinavian countries, Denmark, Norway and Sweden, stand out with high levels of GNI pr. capita and positive developments from 2007, the year prior to the financial crisis, to 2015. These three countries seem to have been less effected by the financial crisis than other European countries, indicating a more robust financial sector and more room of maneuver in economic policies.

The financial crisis of Iceland was mainly self-made, due to the hyper-expansion of their banks to some 20 other countries. The timing of the Icelandic crisis was however influenced by the liquidity problems created by the global financial crisis.

Table 1. GNI per capita, Atlas method (current USD) in 2007 and 2015, World Bank 2017

Country	*GNI per capita 2007*	*GNI per capita 2015*
Norway	78.400	93.600
Iceland	61.900	50.300
Denmark	55.700	60.300
Sweden	52.000	57.800
United States	48.600	56.100
UK	47.800	43.700
Finland	46.000	46.600
Germany	40.700	45.800
France	40.300	40.500
Euro-area	36.800	37.500
Italy	35.800	32.900
Spain	29.900	28.400

France, Italy and Spain suffered from a mix of both vulnerabilities in the financial sector and limited general room of manoeuvre in economic policies. The developments in these countries explain much of the rather dismal developments of the Euro-area as a whole, while Germany had a better performance.

The US had a relative quick recovery, actively using the room of manoeuvre in both monetary and fiscal policies. UK banks were severely hit by the crisis, and several of them needed substantial Government capital to make them able to continue in business.

CREDIT MARKETS

In the Eurozone total credit stagnated in the years after 2008. As the graph below are based on credit in nominal numbers (source: Bank for International Settlements, BIS), they imply a decline in real terms of total credit supply for this area. This reflects an interplay between the restrictive lending praxis enforced on the banks by the crisis and few initiatives and weak demand from industry. Lending in Norway and Sweden continued at a normal rate. Denmark, with stronger links to the Eurozone and its largest bank involved in the special domestic crisis of Ireland, experienced credit growth clearly below its Scandinavian neighbours, but higher than the Euro-countries.

The decline in credit in the Eurozone was caused by a mixture of elements. Low levels of capital in the banks made them highly vulnerable to the losses on sub-prime-linked securities. The banks thus had to restrict lending which then added to the problems of private industry. New losses came as demand and production were reduced and companies could no longer serve their loans. In many countries housing prices fell significantly, producing a vicious circle where lower prices reduced the ability of banks to give new mortgage loans for buying new or old residences.

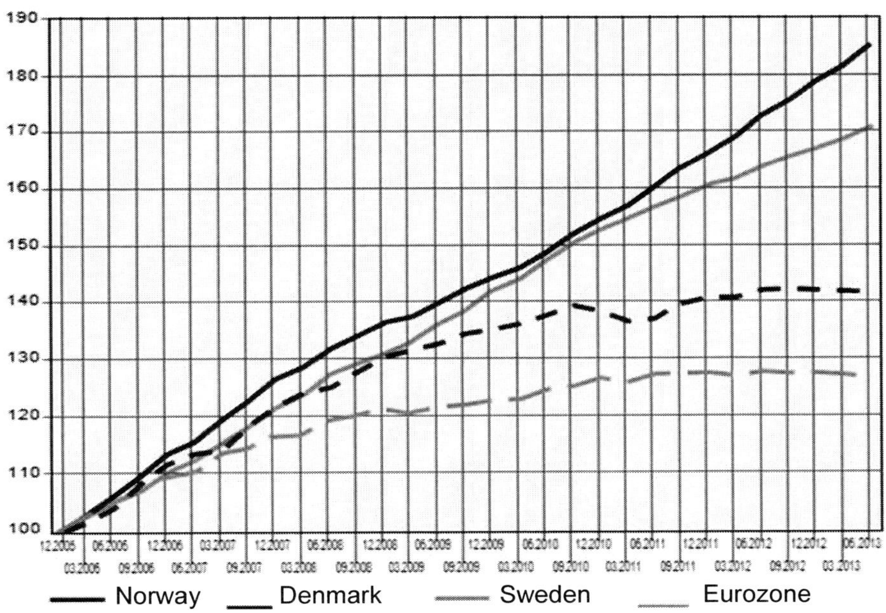

Figure 3. Nominal credit growth, during and after the Financial Crisis (Source BIS), in Norway, Denmark, Sweden and the Eurozone.

Prior to the financial crisis, private debt had been growing fast in many countries. The level of household debt in Portugal in 2008 were 20 times the level of 1980, in Greece 15 times, in Spain 8 times and in Italy 5 times. These four countries saw a clear decline in debt levels in the years after 2008, reflecting restrictive policies and negative developments in employment and housing markets.

The similar level of household debt in Germany was only twice the 1980 level. France and Sweden were at moderate levels, some 3-4 times the 1980 level, while Norway was on the high side with household debt close to 5 times the 1980-level in 2008.

After 2008 the household debt level in Germany stayed roughly constant, while debt levels had to be reduced in southern Eurozone countries. France and Sweden saw a moderate increase in household debts, while Norway entered a new period of fast growth in household debts. If household debt is measured against income, Norway is at the top of the list with levels which are twice annual disposable income. Norway is followed by Sweden, while average household debt levels in Germany and France are roughly on the same level as annual disposable income. (Source for the figures above: BIS and IMF, in *"Finansielle kriser og resesjoner" (Financial crises and recessions)* by Jens Henrik Larsen. – in Norwegian only).

Both the markets which supply banks with liquidity and the authorities require that banks keep capital, own funds, of a reasonable size related to the operations of the banks. Capital requirements are a *fraction* where own funds are the *numerator* and loans and credits are the main items of the *denominator.* As banks after the crisis of 2007/2008 were unable to attract private capital to maintain or increase the numerator, the only way to maintain or increase the value of the capital fraction was to keep the denominator low, through restrictive credit practices.

In several countries supply of government capital was necessary to make banks able to fulfill their role and supply credits.

For *Ireland* overexpansion of the private banks was the main reason for the crisis, closely linked to the financing of a housing bubble which burst in 2007. Six banks required substantial Government support. The Government budget went from a surplus in 2007 to a deficit on more than 30 per cent of GDP in 2010.

Spain was also hit by a housing bubble. When housing prices were increasing, the building boom and high employment contributed positively to the public finances. When the bubble burst, the government of Spain had to spend billions of euros on rescuing banks and public finances went into deep deficits.

The problems in *Italy* developed more gradually, with a long period of negative or weak growth of production. The nonperforming loans rose from 6 per cent of total loans in 2008 to 18 per cent in 2014. Several major banks had to be rescued by public funds in 2016-2017.

Statistics on bank capital or own funds are somewhat fragmented. The World Bank does not give comparable figures for all countries. The general impression however, is that banks in most European countries had a weak capital position, which forced them to pursue restrictive credit policies which than again contributed to stagnating production and rising unemployment. The BIS (Bank for International Settlements) found in their 80th Annual report (2010) that banks with a solid capital coverage (Tier 1 capital ratio) in 2006 had mastered the crisis better than banks with a low capital ratio.

In an interview with *Central Banking Journal,* October 2017, Jaime Caruana, Head of the BIS for eight years, summarized key observations by saying:

> "There is empirical evidence that within the range of capital we are talking about in these regulations, it is the well-capitalized banks that provide lending. It is the well-capitalized banks that contributed to growth. Probably, we could have done more in terms of conveying this positive message."

This statement is in striking contrast to claims from private banking organizations that higher capital requirements make lending more difficult.

OECD has made indebt studies on reasons for the default of banks. An article by Adrian Blundell-Wignall and Caroline Roulet, presented in the

OECD Journal on Financial Market Trends, Volume 2012/2, studies the process of the distance-to-default in a panel sample of 94 banks. They found that the Basel Tier 1 ratio found no support as a predictor of default risk. This ratio is based on refined rules where different loans are given weights depending on either the Standard rules or by models developed by the banks themselves. The unweighted leverage ratio, on the other hand found however strong support. Banks with low levels of own funds compared to the banks total levels of loans, had a significantly higher risk for default than banks with more solid levels of own funds.

The own funds are of great importance, but most clearly when seen in relation to banks total activity, called - *The leverage ratio.* The article is very critical to the complexity of the Basel capital requirements, which makes it difficult both for the banks themselves, the authorities and the markets to detect the lack of sufficient capital. The authors thus clearly support more focus on the leverage ratio.

GOVERNMENT FUNDS FOR THE BANKS – THE SOVEREIGN DEBT CRISIS

The period after 2010 was marked by the problems of Eurozone national governments having lost the fiscal room of maneuver, often called *The Sovereign Debt Crisis,* causing a prolonged period of economic stagnation. They had to cut back public expenditures or raise taxes or both, thus reducing demand and economic growth.

The financial crisis had a strong negative impact on Eurozone countries for several reasons:

1. Many countries had experienced booms in housing or other markets and had high debt levels.
2. Systems and methods for macro-prudential surveillance was poorly developed, and no warning signals were issued for investments in CDO's or other Asset Backed Securities.

3. International cooperation was underdeveloped, and countries in the first years of the crisis generally left to themselves. At the same time Eurozone rules gave countries little room of maneuver in monetary policies and no room to devalue exchange rates.
4. Many banks had a low level of own funds compared to total bank activity, - and capital to total exposure was weak.
5. The assistance governments had to render private banks because of the international financial crisis, added significantly to the problems of their public finances.

The governments of Greece, Cyprus, Ireland, Portugal, Spain, and to some extent also Italy, could not deal with the problems on their own. They had no room of manoeuvre in their public budgets. They were forced to reduce expenditures or raise taxes or some combinations of the two. From 2010 actions and policies were moved to a European and International level with several new measures, such as the European Financial Stability Facility (EFSF) and European Stability Mechanism (ESM).

The European Central Bank took on a more active role in coordinating measures as part of crisis management. For Greece and some other countries that required significant assistance, the ECB and other EU institutions would also coordinate activities with the International Monetary Fund. As mentioned before, assistance for Greece was also indirectly an assistance to European banks who had lent to the Greek Government or bought their bonds.

The high degree of integration of the economies of the Eurozone countries, where both trade, investment, capital and labour markets were heavily influenced by developments in other Eurozone countries, contributed to negative developments being spread to most members of the group.

The stagnation of the Eurozone countries lasted well into 2015 and 2016, when some positive economic developments became visible. 2017 was the first year since 2007 were the whole group could show clear positive economic developments in both increasing production and reduced employment.

BANKING CRISES IN HISTORY

The international financial crisis of 2007/2008 came as a surprise to leading economists and politicians in both North America and Europe. Ben Bernanke was the chairman of the Federal Reserve from 2006 to 2014. He and other economists had played down the risks to the financial system prior to the developments which gradually became visible in 2006/2007. He used the term *"The Great Moderation"* to describe a change in the economic system which reduced volatility and created greater stability. (Used in a speech early 2004 in the Easter Economic Association.) Both he and other leading economists were later connected with the phrase *"This time is different"* as a description of why the economies could grow further with little risk of a crisis.

This phrase was used by Carmen M. Reinhart and Kenneth S. Rogoff as title for their book *"This time is different. Eight Centuries of Financial Folly."* The book was issued in late 2009 and has become the classic analytical summary of financial crises throughout history, admired by academics and others all over the world (Reinhart C. Carmen & Kenneth S. Rogoff: 2009).

Reinhart and Rogoff studied banking crises in sixty-six countries starting in 1800. Most countries have since then had several banking crises throughout this long period. The single most important event to explain a coming banking crisis, is a boom in the prices of housing or real estate. Banks may get into trouble also for other reasons, like rapid expansion of government activity and deficits on current accounts. More often history has shown examples of expansion in private property and debt which create trouble both for the current accounts, as consumption grow faster than production and for governments as tax income decreases when a banking crisis strikes.

The banks finance their operations by borrowing short, including from their depositors, and lend on longer terms for the building of houses, factories and for other purposes. Banks are thus highly exposed to the general trust of people and businesses. The book discusses several banking crises in history, which have been triggered by a collapse in the trust of the banks, leading to a run to retrieve deposits. The crisis of Northern Rock in 2007 is a recent example of this. Both in the book and in recent banking regulation, the protection of depositors by institutions, which cover normal deposits for most depositors, are described as important for reducing risks for banking crises.

The book gives a reference to a study of Kaminsky and Reinhart (1999) on twenty-six banking crises after 1970. In eighteen of the countries covered, the financial sector had been liberalized within the preceding five years. In only a handful of countries (for instance in Canada) did liberalizing of the financial sector proceed smoothly. Rapid liberalization would often produce a boom in housing and real estate.

Reinhart and Rogoff do *not* mention the lack of own funds or *weak bank solvency* as important elements for explaining the occurrence of banking crises. They have focused their studies on large files of statistics on lending and GDP. Statistics on banks own funds are only available in recent years and not easily comparable between countries. There may thus be reason to think that banks with solid own funds could be less exposed to banking crises than others. As mentioned in section 4 above, OECD-research has found clear links between low levels of capital in relations to banks total lending, the leverage ratio, and the risk for banks to get into trouble.

In the Nordic countries several individual banks with solid own funds survived the crises of late 1980's and early 1990's, while banks which lacked such funds went bankrupt. Denmark, which had higher levels of own funds and where the financial supervisor had forced the banks to make higher provisions for possible losses, escaped the banking crises which hit Norway, Sweden and Finland during this period.

The Great Depression of the 1930's is seen by Reinhart and Rogoff as a reflection of the many deep banking crises of the 1920's, and the government policies of restricting imports and public spending afterwards. The long period after 1945 with few and moderate banking crises is reflecting the many regulations which continued for decades after the Second World War. Some of the regulations prevented the kind of booms in housing markets and real estate which produced banking crises in both earlier and later years.

The authors carefully study the so-called "Big five" banking crises of the post-war period (Spain 1977, Norway 1987, Finland and Sweden 1991 and Japan 1992) and find that all these crises occurred after booms in real housing prices. In Norway, the full banking crisis came in 1990-93, while the authors use the peak of the housing boom in 1987 for their international comparisons. For the big five, the decline in real housing prices from their peaks varied between 32 per cent (Sweden) and 52 per cent (Finland). Norway with 42 per cent were in the middle. All the five countries suffered a decline of GDP connected with the banking crisis, although this decline was more severe in Sweden and Finland than in Norway, Spain and Japan.

Reinhart and Rogoff summarize the observations on banking crises (Chapter 10) by "*Thus what we have really shown here is that severe banking crises are associated with deep and prolonged recessions and that further work is needed to establish causality and, more important, to help prioritize policy responses. Nevertheless, the fact that recessions associated with severe banking crises are so consistently deep and share so many characteristics has to serve as a key starting point for future researchers as they attempt to untangle these difficult episodes.*"

In another study on financial crises and economic growth, Jorda, Schularik and Taylor studied over 200 recession periods in 14 advanced counties between 1870 and 2008. In their article *"When Credit Bites Back: Leverage, Business Cycles and Crises"* they concluded that financial crises recessions cost more than "normal" recessions in terms of lost output. More credit-intensive expansions tend to be followed by deeper recessions and slower recoveries.

LESSONS FROM THE RECENT CRISIS AND PREVIOUS CRISES. FINANCIAL STABILITY AND ECONOMIC GROWTH

The Financial crisis of 2007/2008 gave the most severe economic setback for industrialised countries since the 1930'ies. The Eurozone countries experienced a decade of economic stagnation. High debt levels, weak capital levels of banks and weak government finances made these countries highly vulnerable to negative developments in international financial markets. The lack of financial stability was negative for economic growth.

The Financial crisis of 2007/2008 was also a crisis for the regulatory authorities, having failed to prevent the crisis:

- Large parts of financial activity were without regulation, capital requirements and supervision.
- Little or no macro-prudential supervision which could have detected risks following the expansion of CDO's and other Asset Backed Securities.
- Lack of international coordination, not at least in Europe.
- Some of the bank capital, like subordinated debt, could not carry losses.
- Bonuses and other economic rewards increased risk-taking by the banks.
- Complex instruments in non-liquid markets.
- Private credit ratings and use of internal models gave a too positive picture of the resilience of credit institutions.

In view of the crisis, Government leaders in the larger countries, the G20 group, asked the Basel Committee to revise international regulations to reduce risks of new crises. The Basel Committee is a group of representatives from Central Banks and Financial Supervisors who meet regularly on the premises of Bank of International Settlements, in Basel Switzerland. It has been in operation since the 1970'ies. The rules produced have been adopted by EU and other major countries. The first version of regulations, Basel I, was released in 1988. A more refined version, including the use of internal models in banks, Basel II, was published in a final version in 2006, to enter into force in 2007/2008.

The financial crisis of 2007/2008 made it clear that a fundamental strengthening of these relative new rules was required. The banking sector entered the crisis with too little capital and inadequate liquidity buffers. The new version of regulations, Basel III, was endorsed by the G20 leaders in November 2010 and formally agreed at the December 2010 Basel Committee meeting. In several areas the final rules were left open for further discussions and negotiations.

The basic requirements were that common equity should be above 4.5 per cent of the risk weighted balance as of 2013. An additional capital conservation buffer of 2.5 per cent should be faced in from 2019. Both in Basel II and Basel III, banks may calculate the risks with their own, internal models.

The banks want to keep costs of capital as low as possible. Methods which leave a substantial part of the responsibility for judging the required level of capital to the banks themselves, create a high risk for the capital to be too low to meet future challenges. As the OECD-study shows, the link between risk weighted capital of the Basel type and the probability for default is not clear.

To make the system more robust, two methods have been discussed:

- A separate leverage requirement, were capital should be at least 3 per cent of total exposure.
- Adding a floor linked to the Standard method, below which risk weighted capital should not be reduced as shown by the models.

The leverage requirement was discussed for some time until an implementation date was fixed for 1. January 2018. A revised exposure measure and special requirements for Global Systemic Important Banks were fixed for 1 January 2022 at the Committee Meeting in December 2017 (Press Release 7. December from BIS).

Total loans and other assets exposed by the banks compared to own funds, the leverage, in European banks are still at a high level. Core Tier 1 Capital as a per cent of total exposure was only 4.7 per cent at the end of 2016. In Norway the similar rate was 7.6 per cent, reflecting that Norwegian authorities have been pushing for higher capital coverage than in other European countries. Norwegian banks have nevertheless been able to finance higher growth than achieved in most other European countries.

The capital floor has been discussed for years and was finally included in the Basel rules in December 2017. (Press release 7. December from BIS.) The minimum requirements linked to the new standardized approach will start softly at 50% of the capital required in 2022, and then the floor will increase gradually and slowly to 72.5% in 2027. In Norway and some other countries, a similar floor of 80 per cent has been applied for many years.

The EBA (European Banking Authority) has calculated that the sum of the new regulations agreed by the Basel Committee in December 2017 applied to 88 European financial institutions, gave a net reduction of capital requirements of some 0.6 per cent.

It should be mentioned that early in the process after the crisis, the EU passed a new capital directive CRR/CRD IV and decided that minimum capital requirements should be at least 9 per cent from 2011. At that time this was of importance to speed up the process of strengthening bank capital in European banks. Similar initiatives for pushing capital formation in the banks have not, however, been taken more recently.

The new Basel III Accord also gave countries an opportunity to add requirements for countercyclical buffers. This instrument has however not been used by any of the Eurozone countries, and only by a few other countries, like Switzerland, Norway, Sweden and, more recently, the UK.

It remains highly uncertain whether the political initiatives following the financial crisis of 2007/2008 will be sufficient. The process for strengthening the banks own funds has been slow and some of the results are not convincing. International cooperation has however been developed, and the exchange of information between relevant bodies, central banks and supervisors are better organized both internationally and in Europe, then before the crisis. The new crisis-resolution arrangements, based on the Bank Recovery and Resolution Directive, give authorities better instruments for containing risks leading to new banking crises in Europe.

History has shown many cases where economic growth has been disrupted for years by financial instability and banking crises. Reinhart and Rogoff have underlined the many housing and real estate booms which have led to banking crises, followed by years of economic stagnation.

Building a more robust financial system to safeguard economic growth in years to come, should motivate further action in several areas. Some of them should be:

1. Developments in the housing and property markets should be carefully monitored. Many years of low interest rates have stimulated borrowing. If risks of excessive growth in prices and debt are not contained through monetary policies, other regulatory measures should be introduced to prevent excessive growth of debt. As an example, the Norwegian Government has passed regulations that limit the amount of housing loans to five times the annual income and 85 per cent of the value of the property. It seems that the regulation which became effective 1 January 2017, has contained further growth in loans and housing prices.
2. Banks should be better capitalized than has been required so far, with special weight on the leverage ratio. Financial institutions with access to provide services in the financial market, should have sufficient own funds to cover possible losses following adverse developments.
3. Financial supervisors and other public authorities should cooperate closely in monitoring international financial developments and prepare possible actions to contain excessive risks.
4. Depositors in banks should be covered by a guarantee covering normal deposits, which prevent a loss of confidence in banks in the case of market disruptions.

There are many challenges ahead which give good reasons for building a more robust financial system with solid banks and macro-prudential policies at national and international level. Such policies should include surveillance and regulatory measures for containing disturbances in the financial markets and active supervision of the financial institutions. Preventing new booms in housing and property will be of key importance to avoid new crises.

The world has endured the longest period of very low interest rates in history. Both households and industry have high levels of debt and have become vulnerable to higher interest rates or a shortfall of incomes. Expectations of higher interest rates may have strong negative impacts on the stock markets. There are also risks connected with environmental and political/military developments, which may have significant economic impacts. Robust banks and financial systems will be of key importance to limit recessions and encourage economic growth in the future.

REFERENCES

Aamo, Bjørn Skogstad (2017); "The Norwegian Banking Crisis in the Early Nineties." Article in *"Finance in Society – An Anthology in Honour of Thore Johnsen,"* Oslo: Cappelen Damm AS.

Aamo, Bjørn Skogstad (2016): "*Læring fra kriser*" (Norwegian only, - "Learning from Crises" in English.), Bergen: Fagbokforlaget.

Blundell-Wignall, Adrian & Caroline Roulet (2012): "Business models of banks, leverage and the distance-to-default." *OECD Journal on Financial Market Trends*, Vol. 2012/2.

Jorda, Oscar, Moritz Schularick & Alan M. Taylor (2013): "When Credit Bites Back: Leverage, Business Cycles and Crises." *Journal of Money, Credit and Banking,* Vol. 45 Dec. 2013.

Kaminsky, Graciela L. & Carmen M. Reinhart (1999): "The Twin crises: The Causes of Banking and Balance-of-Payments problems," *American Economic Review* 89 (3): 473-500.

Larsen, Jens Henrik (2015): "Finansielle kriser og resesjoner" (Norwegian only – *"Financial Crises and Recessions"* in English), Oslo: Cappelen Damm AS.

Reinhart, Carmen M. & Kenneth S. Rogoff (2009), "*This time is different – Eight Centuries of Financial Folly,"* Princeton and Oxford: Princeton University Press.

World Development Indicators, *The World Bank* 2017.

In: Keynesian Policies
Editor: Noralv Veggeland

ISBN: 978-1-53614-026-2

Chapter 4

ECONOMIC CRISES: A KEYNESIAN NEW DEAL PERSPECTIVE

Noralv Veggeland*
Inland Norway University of Applied Sciences,
Lillehammer, Norway

ABSTRACT

History is filled with examples of how economy has been affected by shifting political conditions. The Keynesian state's macro-economic form of intervention, which developed just after the Second World War, was a clear answer to the structural economic crisis of the inter-war period of the 1920s and 1930s. The Keynesian economic theory was, in many senses, deduced from classical economic theories. Correspondingly, nowadays we see the Keynesian principles being transformed, yet having fundamentally survived despite a change of framework. The ongoing financial and debt crisis needs a solution, and the answer seems to be found in principles that could be identified as neo-Keynesianism and neo-interventionism. This

* Corresponding author: Professor of Public Policy. Currently professor at Massachusetts State University, Amherst and EUI, Florence. Earlier Member of the Norwegian Research Council. He owns a long list of national and international publications. noralv.veggeland@inn.no.

chapter is tracing back and analyzing the political economy of the historical capitalism.

Keywords: political-economy, classical economists, economic crises, interventionism, keynesianism, neo-keynesianism

NEO-INTERVENTIONISM AND NEO-KEYNESIANISM OF TODAY

There is an ongoing crisis in Europe, characterized by being both a credit and a financial crisis. Measures are needed, causing the EU to act as an interventionist state in the sense of what John Maynard Keynes recommended (1936). However, principally, the framework has changed into a new one, thus the introduction of the concepts of neo-interventionism and neo-Keynesianism.

The EU – together with the European Central Bank (ECB) and the International Monetary Fund (IMF) – has taken important interventionist steps giving loans to counteract the crisis, experienced in particular in member states like Greece, Italy, Spain, Portugal, Ireland and Hungary, by claiming wide-ranging reduction in public spending, reducing salaries and lowering pensions. On the other hand, the EU established a stability fund of nearly 1000 billion euro to help states in trouble. In December 2011 the ECB presented an intermediary but long-term solution to heal the actual debt problems of certain states – the Long-Term Refinancing Operation (LTRO). The aim of the operation was to support the banks with money by an exchange procedure: banks sell expensive old bonds and gilts – turned over in the market with 6% - 9% interest rate – to the ECB, and get fresh money in return. The banks agreed on paying the money back in three years' times at the same price. For the money, the banks need to pay an interest rate of only 1% in return. The measure was meant to secure the bank's liquids. The common understanding is that the banks use their money to buy new state bonds and gilts to secure access to financial assets for those countries. In the first round of exchanging money, euro 500 billion were taken over from the

ECB by the national banks, and the amount has more than doubled since then. The problem with this measure, which makes it intermediary, is that the debt as such has not disappeared. What is needed is real economic growth and creation of jobs. High unemployment rates continued in 2014 as a huge social and economic problem for many EU member states.

The supranational EU interventionism of the ongoing crisis also aims to lower the degree of devolution and national independence. Europe took a major step towards full fiscal union a few years ago, as every EU member state – except the UK and the Czech Republic – vowed to cut budget deficits and submit themselves to greater scrutiny from the European Commission.

The majority of EU member states – 25 out of 28 states – voted for the so-called "Financial Pact," which gives the EU and its institutions the authority to control member states' ability and political will to keep their national budgets in accordance with EU economic and financial rules and regulations. The agreement is seen as a significant victory for German Chancellor Angela Merkel, who spent months pushing for Eurozone members to agree on tighter budgetary constraints. Under the treaty, signatories have agreed to cut budget deficits and reduce national debts as a proportion of their economic output or face "automatic" fines, likely to stand at 0.5% of GNP. Sanctions will be put in place if the national debt exceeds 3% of the GNP. National interventionism is losing adequate rendering, and governing democratic authorities are becoming emptied of power.

The political scientist Wolfgang Streeck writes in 'Le Monde diplomatique' January 2012, which "Markets dictate what supposed sovereign democratic states may and may not do for their citizens. Consequently, the citizens do not respect their elected representatives as their own, but identify them as representatives for interests of other states and international organizations." Streeck is right, but one of his words should be replaced by another word. It is not the market but supranational regulations, which dictate sovereign states. To be dictated is the price to pay for overcoming the contemporary; the regulations generate new forms of supranational interventionism and adequate ideas. However, the neo-interventionist and neo-Keynesianism thinking is differently executed, seen in contrast to Keynes' interventionism, which was directed at the promotion of economic stability and national effective demand. The latter interventionism was steering national market regulation by economic demand interventions (Shonfield 1969), rather than debt reduction; Keynes recommended the raising of public loan in order to realize effective demand objectives.

Table 1 sketches the structure of this paper. International economic crises of our time have their history. Before the Second World War, in the 1920s, there occurred a pre-Keynesian demand crisis causing threatening unemployment in Western states. The state reacted passively, and its policy was shaped accordingly, relying on classical liberal economic theories. In the chapter I will review some of the classical economists associated with these theories; Adam Smith, Davis Ricardo and Thomas Robert Malthus – leading up to Karl Marx and Keynes. In the 1930s John Maynard Keynes wrote his "General Theory of Employment, Interest and Money" (1936), which introduced the principle of the interventionist state. The theory argued for the necessity of an active state to secure effective demand in order to overcome the ongoing pre-war demand crisis.

Keynesianism as a political strategy succeeded until the 1970s, when the stagflation crisis undermined the previous enduring economic stability. The intermediary solution to the stagflation crisis was to politically leave Keynesian principles behind, and during the 1980s-1990s to establish a monetary, supply-side economy. The theory was deduced from ideas promoted by the so-called Vienna School of monetary economists, which rejected a dominant state function as adequate for the creation of economic growth and stability (Friedman 1980, Veggeland 2009, 2010). The monetary economic policy turned bankruptcy. In the late 2000s the international financial and debt crises occurred and became a grave challenge for Western governments.

The contemporary crisis is a double crisis caused by both public and private dysfunctional debt and loans. What is clear is that this double crisis has prompted governments and the EU to become active and stick to interventionism in the sense of what John Maynard Keynes recommended (1936).

Table 1. Solutions for international economic crises, 1), 2), 3) promote changes in state orders and choices of predominant economic theories. Different theories get transformed to ideology when not valid any longer as solutions

Crises:	**Demand shortage**		**Stagflation**	**Financial shortage**
State order:		**Interventionist**	**Regulatory**	**Neo-Interventionist**
Theories:		**Keynesianism**	**Monetarism**	**Neo-Keynesianism**
Intermediary solutions:		**1)**	**2)**	**3)**
Years:	**1920s-1930s**	**1930-1960s**	**1970- 1990s**	**2000 – 2010s**

Consequently, we may talk about the occurrence of neo-interventionism as a new state order rooted in neo-Keynesianism theory. Important contributor to this neo-Keynesianism turn is the Nobel Prize winner in economics Paul R. Krugman (Krugman 2012). See also Table 1.

PRINCIPLES OF THE PRE-KEYNESIAN STATE

The interventionist state's macro-economic form of central planning actions, which developed just after the Second World War, was a clear answer to the structural economic crisis of the interwar period of the 1920s and 1930s, see Table 1. The legitimacy to intervene in the market, which this form of planning gave the government, is primarily connected with the work of John Maynard Keynes (1883 – 1946), the English economist. In 'The General theory of Employment, Interest and Money' from 1935, parts of which had already been published elsewhere, Keynes elaborated on a new foundation for the understanding of economic growth and its conditions in the market economy. This entailed studies of the causes behind economic fluctuations, and what determines the level of national income and employment. Even though Keynes was a liberal economist, he opposed the laissez-faire perspective, and marked the clear need for state intervention to tame the market and to escape and avoid economic crises. For these reasons there has been talk of the 'the Keynesian Revolution.' In this context Andrew Shonfield (1969: 3) puts forward an essential question:

> "What was it that converted capitalism from cataclysmic failure which it appeared to be in the 1930s into the great engine of prosperity of the post war Western World? There is no simple answer, which rests on a denial of the validity of the question itself. The economic order under which we now live and the social structure that goes with it are so different from what preceded them that it is misleading – so it is alleged – to use the word 'capitalism' to describe them."

Through his work, Shonfield (1969: 3-39) provides answers to the 'conversion' question, which could be summed up as follows: Keynes' General Theory provided the rationale for state interventions, effective demand, and spending to achieve recovery and full employment. It revolutionized business-cycle theory and established the framework for modern macro-economic analysis including growth economics. In terms of references, the effects of this work could aptly be called the 'Keynesian Revolution,' Schonfield suggests.

As always happens along lines of ideas, historically they emerge before an actual revolution, which biases evolution of socio-economic theories and political ideologies. This was also the case regarding the ideas that shaped the 'Keynesian Revolution.' A number of predecessors contributed as founding fathers of the economic ideas and legitimated government intervention into the market which led up to Keynesianism. The ideas were all colored by the social setting for which they were innovatively designed, and inspired by the political ideas and ideological approaches of their time, such as liberalism, utilitarianism, and socialism. Let us look more closely into some of these 'founding fathers' (Stewart 1972, Schumpeter 1939):

Adam Smith

History is filled with examples of how economy has been affected by shifting political conditions. Adam Smith, who published 'The Wealth of

Nations' in 1776, can be taken as the founder of modern economics. Despite his concern with what we call conditions for 'economic growth,' the book contains no real discussion of why the level of employment is what it is and how markets should be intervened in, and regulated. At the time, agriculture was still by far the most important economic activity, and in an agricultural society the notions of being employed and being unemployed were not really distinctive; the whole family worked, but might have been seasonally underemployed. Smith simply assumed that there was always full employment. Regarding regulation, he was in line with the liberal political thinking and classic economic theory of the time; he believed in the 'invisible hand' as the regulatory and taming principle of the market. He noted merely one thing limiting the free market approach. The comment was that of course 'landlords talk together' and they make their decisions and agreements and intervene in regard to prices when they unavoidably meet now and then. This phenomenon he recognized as a negative externality that might disturb the rule and efficiency of the 'invisible hand,' and thereby the balance of the economy. It represented a socio-economic risk that should be avoided. He never put forward the idea that such personal 'decisions and agreements' were indeed a corporate way of taming the actual markets.

Adam Smith took over the idea that the economic sphere was a sort of nature, and therefore stable and structured by 'natural law.' With this view he elaborated upon the contributions of the great founders of political liberalism at the time – especially John Locke (1632-1704). For Locke, a state of nature existed before the occurrence of a social contract conducted by the political state. In that pre-organized state each individual was facing nature and free interaction. They had to deal with work, the products and utility of the work, and property rights, therefore each man was a *homo economicus*. The social contract and the government interventions emerged only in reaction to outside threats and with the obligation to protect the natural law and private property. Adam Smith took the idea of the 'natural man' as the 'economic man' and made it fundamental in his theory. He reaffirmed the liberal view that the economic sphere should remain free and have historical and ideological precedence over other spheres of social life.

David Ricardo

The next founding economist of major importance is David Ricardo, who published the first edition of his 'Principles of Political Economy and Taxation' in 1817. Like many other nineteenth century economists his main interest lay in the factors steering the distribution of a nation's income between the major social classes – landowners, capitalists, and workers – i.e., rent, profits and wages, respectively. The capitalists must make large profits and accumulate money, he states, because they would invest these in new machinery; this will create more employment and enable increased production. This belief is a fundamental approach in the economic neo-liberalism theory of today, 200 years later. Ricardo operated in the optimism of the dawn of the industrial society. The suggestion of the spokesmen of anti-government neo-liberalism claim validity in the pessimism of the aftermath of the industrial period. The issue of government interventions was not in the focus of Ricardo. Instead, liberation of industrial potentiality and ability was his concern. Present neo-liberalism, with roots in the thinking of Ricardo, makes the government interventions explicitly the cause for unliberated industrial potentials, both nationally and in a global perspective.

Thomas Robert Malthus

Thomas Robert Malthus, another economist of the early 1800s, is best known for his theory of population growth and food shortage. According to him, there is a tendency for the population to increase exponentially, while the supply of food only increases linearly. This represents the number one of natural socio-economic risks in the contemporary economy, as Malthus saw it.

The theory had its background in the actual population explosion in Europe at the time, and the occurrence of extensive emigration waves to America. With this part of Malthus' work Ricardo did not disagree. However, there was another part he opposed. Against Ricardo's theory of profits and investment in production machinery, Malthus pointed out that there was a danger that the investment would raise the production capacity at a faster rate than the ability of the society to consume. Of the wages received by the workers only a part would be used to buy goods, which are produced because of the investment. Investment increases the production, but the nation state would find itself with a 'general glut of commodities,' which cannot be sold. This will lead to unemployment, he argued. He went on arguing that, in fact, there is a large class of landowners and capitalists that do not invest their money; they tend to save their money, producing nothing, but consuming a lot, Malthus recognized. Malthus pointed out calamities, but no principles or means to avoid them through government involvement.

Ricardo seems, to some extent, to have accepted the logic of Malthus' thinking, but his answer was that an economy might suffer from shortage of what he called 'effective demand' on occasion but not in the long run. Actually, Ricardo was more or less right at the time when he elaborated his long-run effective demand proposition. During the early nineteenth century, the only way most industrialists could finance new buildings and machinery needed for expanding their business was out of their own profits. In the long run the market would create effective demand without involving the government. Keynes said later on that 'Ricardo conquered England as completely as the Holy Inquisition conquered Spain' (quotation from Stewart 1972: 27).[1] His influence is prevalent in certain approaches today in the shadow of the neo-liberal supply-side economics, i.e., the belief in a government policy that excludes central state interventions. Instead, the government should promote deregulation and tax cut in order to increase the inclination of industrial economic investments and thereof consumer demand. This belief still rules the rightwing economic-political approach of the dominating OECD member states (Sachs 2006).

---

[1] In terms of reference and in the framework of contemporary neo-liberal economic theory and policies, it might be stated that the profit-investment logic of Ricardo at the end of the nineteenth century conquered the whole of the Western world.

Karl Marx (1818-1883)

As an economist, Karl Marx was clearly indebted to Smith and Ricardo. He took over much of their framework and gave it a new view. Marx published his main work, 'Das Kapital,' in 1867. He was the first leading economist to notice that by the middle of the nineteenth century, heavy unemployment was quite common in the developing industrial European states. He tried to find the reason for why Ricardo was wrong in his proposition on effective demand. Marx reasoned that competition forces capitalists to invest their profits in labor-saving machinery, for if they do not, their profit rate and efficiency will fall, and they will be forced out of business. Out of self-interest they will continue to do so. But when doing it, there will also be a drop in work places and the unemployment will rise. For those who still have jobs, the alternative is to accept lower wages, forced upon them by the capitalists.

According to Marx, a fall in employment also meant a fall in profits because only work creates economic values. The clue in the view of Marx is that when this happened, and contrary to what Ricardo had assumed, capitalists would – in the long run – have little incentive to invest their profits. And since only a small part of the capitalists' profits can be spent on consumption, the general surplus of commodities that Malthus had been afraid of would become a reality. Marx elaborated a theory of capitalism that concludes that capitalism will necessarily end in a deep-rooted crisis and revolution: The crisis will occur as a result of unemployment growth which will get heavier and heavier. The basic reason for this is *the relentless fall of the profits*, which inevitably leads to a general economic crisis. The suffering working class will revolt and rise to power. The new society will become classless and a central state authority will become unnecessary. Marx identified an institutional dysfunction inherent to the capitalist system, and saw the government as part of this system. He foreshadowed the breakdown of the capitalist system as a whole; the ultimate solution was a revolution of the working class and a stateless communist economy.

On the one hand, Marx's theory was colored by the strong tension between social classes in the developing industrial society in Europe at the time, between the repressed working class and the exploding class of capitalists. On the other hand, it was colored by a strong technological belief, a belief in the liberation power of the promising productivity of the new machinery, and the ways to organize it. These production forces of the working class embedded the ability to free them from the serfdom of wage-work, and would make them economically and politically free as two sides of the same coin. Nevertheless, in spite of the historical fact that his theory about the relentless fall of the profits, the impossibility of balance in trade cycle, and the economic development in general, had limited validity. Marx did represent a significant figure in the evolution of economic theory, and indirectly the belief in government intervention principles to stabilize the economic circle were deduced from this theory, despite his vision of a stateless communist society. As for his theory on capitalism and a market economy, if left to itself, the theory made clear that such an economy would become dysfunctional in the long run. This aspect of Marxian theory inspired John Maynard Keynes. Michael Stewart writes (1972: 33):

> "It was much more difficult, after what he (Marx) had written, to believe that the capitalist economy, if left to itself, would necessarily function satisfactorily. In particular, it was more difficult to accept Ricardo's view that profits were always invested in new machinery".

Certainly, Keynes learned from Marx's lesson about market failures and the logic of capitalism (Veggeland 2009). Actually, Marx created a new framework for political economic thinking. Despite being a liberal economist, and different from Marx's vision about the stateless society, Keynes accepted that the capitalist economy would not function satisfactorily if left to itself. Government interventions were needed. Unlike Marx, Keynes' theoretical approach was to find means to make the market economy survive.

The Political Economy of the Interventionist Keynesian State

John Maynard Keynes' great contribution to economics – General Theory of Employment, Interest and Money (1936) – was to define the modern economy and reveal that this economy did not work the way classical liberalists had supposed. Further, he provided a new and completely convincing explanation of how balance could be achieved in a (national) market economy. With the interwar economic crisis as background, he innovatively demonstrated that heavy unemployment was not a temporary deviation from the normal state of development, but could represent an equilibrium situation, which could go on forever (see Table 1 of today's situation of unemployment). If full employment was desired, it was no good following the recommendation proclaimed by classic liberal economic theory – making the government sit back and hope for the best, i.e., laissez-faire policy. The government must ensure, through interventions, that there is enough *effective demand* in the national economy to create full employment.

Hence 'effective demand' is a key notion in the Keynesian theory. As already pointed out, this notion was essential also in the dispute between Malthus and Ricardo more than a century earlier. Malthus suggested that an economy might suffer from disturbance, namely the shortage of what he called 'effective demand,' while Ricardo more or less denied this assumption. Michael Stewart (1972: 30) indicates that Keynes was perhaps reading too much or too little into Malthus when he wrote, in his *Essay on Malthus*:

> "One cannot rise from a perusal of this correspondence (between Malthus and Ricardo) without a feeling that the almost total obliteration of Malthus' line of approach and the complete domination of Ricardo's for a period of a hundred years has been a disaster to the progress of economics".

Nevertheless, reading too much or not into what Malthus had grasped rather intuitively, Keynes founded a 'revolutionary' theory on the disputed notion of effective demand. Contrasting a monetary perspective, in his theory effective demand simply means 'demand backed by money' – in other words actual expenditure. The crucial question is then: what determines effective demand? In order to answer this, Keynes broke down aggregated effective demand into two components – consumption and investment. He claimed it is necessary to study each in turn, and how they could interact in the economy for the purpose of creating full employment.

According to Keynes:

Consumption: Aggregated consumption in an economy relies on wages and income; the latter represents purchasing power.[2] Purchasing power may give variable expenditures as output, depending on the size of the wages. Besides, it depends quite a lot on how the National Income is distributed, socially and geographically. Consumption might be more than just private consumption; it might also be investment if the consumption is part of running businesses. And further, buying a car might be private consumption, but used by the firm for transport, it turns out to be an investment. Increasing consumption of any kind expands the effective demand in the economy.

Investment: Money spent on investment is determined by two things: the amount the investment will yield – the profit – and by the variable cost of borrowing the money needed to finance the investment. The cost is variable because of changing interest rates,[3] though it seems fairly obvious. No one is going to borrow money in order to finance a factory machine or an accommodation facility if the interest payments exceed the profits made by the factory and the facility.[4] But the other way around, if profits exceed the costs, while not certain, does the chance of investments being made increase?

---

[2] Before consumption wages and income are needed.

[3] For the monetarists the interest rate is a steering instrument.

[4] Well, in the ongoing basically loan-driven international crisis, foregoing borrowing behavior deviates from this norm.

What challenged Keynes then as an economist believing in liberal economic principles, was how to stabilize consumption and investment, and thereby the market economy, on a level of full employment. Neoliberal thinking of today has almost forgotten this Keynesian stabilization strategy. Full employment and full utilization of the production forces in general, were essential for Keynes; neither more nor less than full utilization was the goal. 'More' would mean pressure in the aggregated economy with rising prices and increasing inflation as a negative consequence.

What then could be the proper measure, to balance full employment and stable low inflation rate, as part of his effective demand concept of consumption and investment?

Keynes did not believe in Ricardo's view that profits were always invested in new machinery, nor did he believe in Marx's thesis about the relentless fall of the profits. In his theory he introduced an idea with the greatest political implications of the time: the advantage of *state (government) interventions* in the market in order to balance employment and inflation, see Figure 2 below, through using public consumption and investment as regulatory measures, and planning and centralized administration as steering instruments. This is what Majone (1994: 77) calls the 'dirigiste state of the past', which in our time has been replaced by the "regulatory state" which is denying Keynesian economic government intervention.

The interventionist state as an instrument to counteract risk in a market economy is a theoretical as well as a practical concept. But according to Keynes, the interventions should only be temporary, to overcome the international economic crisis of the 1930s. This he promised, as the liberal economist he was. It should turn out differently. Keynesianism became the theoretical foundation of the flourishing modern interventionist state – in fact, the post war social democratic welfare state lasting until the 1970s and 1980s, see Table 1 [Veggeland 2007, Flora et al. (eds.) 1999].

Let us try to illustrate some of the Keynesian principles by formalizing the structure.

What is important here (Figure 1) is the way Keynes provided legitimacy for the central government to initiate basic central planning, and to intervene and make consumption and investment adjustments according to the national masterplan of economics and sector developments. This meant regulating market mechanisms for the purpose of long-term effective demand, and thereby full employment and low inflation. In return, the domain of politics gained legitimacy because of economic stability and growth success as results of the interventions.

The advancement of the post war welfare state and its framework might be said to be the height for general acceptance of Keynesian policies with broad lasting legitimacy [Flora et al. (eds.) 1999]. Optimistically, some scholars pointed out that a new international economic crisis would probably never occur again because of the balancing effect of the interventionist state (Shonfield 1969). They were wrong.

What measures made the interventionist state strong? The Keynesian approach to macro-economic crises created a new bunch of conceptual tools for economic policy and central planning by the government. After the Second World War, these conceptual tools were widened to include sector planning, regional planning, environmental planning, and connected extensive social and regional distributive policies. The success of this type of planning and governance rested upon the assumption that the national economy was relatively closed and protected from external impacts. That situation changed during the 1970s-1980s. The markets were enlarged globally in order to allow businesses to gain access to new markets, and the Keynesian classical principles for effective demand failed.

Keynesianism represented a top-down rational form of planning and decision-making – "the dirigiste state." Means-ends strategies were recommended to make both growth developments and distributive policies work (Friedman 1987, Amdam and Veggeland 1998:26-27). Politically, this type of planning fitted the social democratic ideology at the time, and its insistence on market control, state ownership and monopolies and an active income and cost policy. Economic government intervention and a planned society were considered desirable.

Giandemico Majone (1997: 139-167) has argued that the Keynesian interventionist state had three main tasks: 1) macro-economic stabilization, 2) the distribution of income and 3) the regulation of the market. The goal of macro-economic Keynesian intervention was to achieve economic growth and the principle of full employment. The instruments for this were financial and monetary policy, together with active employment and industrial policy. In this setting, public monopolies should dominate as executives of the infrastructure service policies.

Figure 1. The structure of the Keynesian political economy.

Keynesian income distribution policy included the redistribution of resources from one social group, region and economic sector to another, as well as educational goods, supplementary benefits and health services. The goal was to level-out inequalities for social reasons but also for the objective of securing market demand for goods and thereof full employment and economic growth (Einhorn and Logue 2003, Veggeland 1998). The Keynesian interventionist policy of judicial regulation aimed to redress and avoid 'market imperfections' such as monopolies, unfair competitive advantages, incomplete market information and incomplete access to public goods.

The state interventionist policy, together with its distribution policy implication, is what has been called the 'social democratic welfare state,' or even the 'Keynesian welfare state' [Ferrera and Rhodes (eds.) 2000]. Macro-economic planning to sustain effective demand in the interventionist state was based upon complex mathematical models developed by the Norwegian economist, Ragnar Frisch, who won the Nobel Prize in 1969. Models used have been known under the term "Eco-Circ," MSG and MODIS (Amdam and Veggeland 1998: 27).

The mode of governance was democratic in the sense that the Western national parliamentary government system combined the monopoly position of being Lawmaker (the Parliament) with the monopoly position (the Government) as executive of public policy, besides acting as a gatekeeper in international affairs. The state budget, the national accounts, sector policy, welfare policy, distributive policy and other areas became the subject of parliamentary policy. Furthermore, public planning acts were democratic but only in the sense that political top-down "hearings" were arranged before leading to the formulation of goals for the development of regions, municipalities and sectors. Politically, this was the most popular form of state in the post-war period until the 1970s-1980s. From this point in time, doubt crept into the social democratic consensus on the advantages of the Keynesian interventionist state mode of governance, i.e., the national state monopoly of being an economist, politician, planning actor, producer of infra-structural and social goods and services, and employer (Giddens 1998).

IN THE SHADOW OF THE INTERNATIONAL STAGFLATION CRISIS

In the 1970s the international economy entered a crisis, the so-called "stagflation" crisis, see Table 1 above. The crisis became the fundamental causal factor in subsequent changes of the Keynesian state order (Veggeland 1998, 2009). Unemployment in the Western industrial states arose to 10% - 15% on average, and the inflation reached dangerously high levels. This represented a fundamental brake in the stable economic development formed on the basis of the Keynesian principles of state intervention believed to be a lasting stabilizing factor.

At the time it was difficult to imagine that the balance in economic circulation would once again reach the crisis dimensions which could be compared with the interwar great Depression of the 1920s-1930s. Andrew Shonfield, the great English economist, in his prominent work from 1969, 'Modern Capitalism,' argued optimistically from a Keynesian perspective, that a lasting economic stability for the future had been accomplished:

> "The central thesis of this book is that there is no reason to suppose that the patterns of the past, which have been ingeniously unraveled by historians of trade cycles, will reassert themselves in the future." (1969:62).

Andrew Shonfield was wrong in his expectation. In the 1970s the crisis arrived. The crisis manifested as a stagflation crisis, i.e., stagnation and increasing unemployment occurred, with a corresponding increase in inflation and stagnation as parallel processes.

The disputed 'Phillips curve'[5] is showing the empirically based relation between inflation and unemployment in the Keynesian period. The curves are also illustrating the failing of the Keynesian principles from the 1970s, see Figure 2. A fundamental change occurred in the Western economies. Despite of Keynesian government intervention polices, the "Phillips curve" moved upward and designed both increasing unemployment and inflation rates as empirical facts. In other words, the Keynesian economic tools did not work any longer.

In Figure 2 the rate of inflation is plotted on the vertical axis, the unemployment on the horizontal axis. Reduced governmental effective demand in order to lessen the pressure in the national economy with the intention to lower the inflation did not work. The opposite effect occurred. Despite the fact the effective demand was lowered, an unwanted race of the inflation rate upwards was observed (Cumes 1984). The arrow illustrates the

---

[5] Alban William Phillips, an economist, wrote a paper in 1958 titled '*The relationship between unemployment and the rate of change of money wages in the United Kingdom 1861-1957*', which was published in the quarterly journal *Economica.* In the paper Phillips describes how he observed an inverse relationship between money wage changes and unemployment in the British economy over the period examined. Similar patterns were found in other countries in 1960. Phillips' work made explicit the empirical link between inflation and unemployment: when inflation was high, unemployment was low, and vice-versa. But empirical correlation does not necessarily indicate causality, therefore a disputed work.

movement of the curve in the national economies at the time. The curves display a development from a trade-cycle in balance from the 1950s until the 1970s with both low inflation and unemployment – it was, in fact, called "an after war period of full employment". It was the consequence of the Keynesian economic policy. Then, the economy got into a stage of imbalance at the end of the 1970s until the 1980s, with both increasing high inflation and unemployment as the prevailing situation. The curves show the tradeoffs at different stages between inflation and employment. From the 1990s until the new crisis of 2007-2008, the Western national economies became stabilized, but with a high level of unemployment. Classical market liberal principles became reformulated to neoliberal principles. Monetary and supply-side economic policy replaced the traditional Keynesian policy. The new economic policy was deduced from theories developed by neoliberal economists like the Nobel Prize winner in economy, Milton Friedman. Less state and freer market movements was the message. During this period the economies were stabilized, in a way, but with a high level of unemployment, see Figure 2. From 2007, an economic crisis of a new kind emerged – the financial crisis – with its origin in the USA.

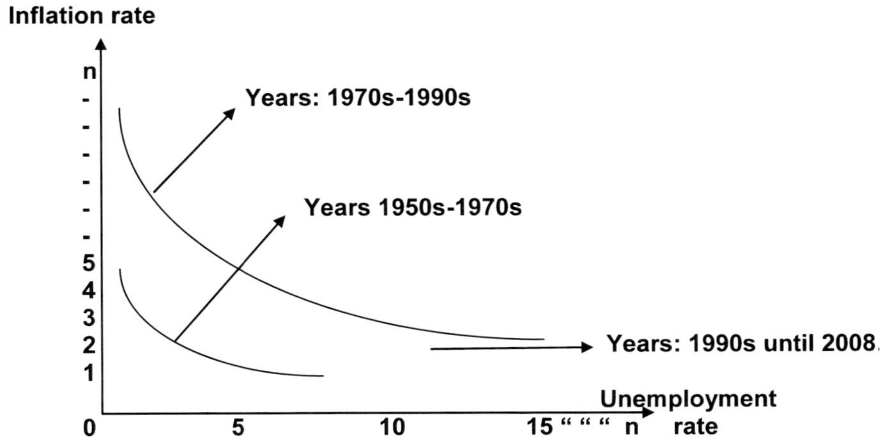

Figure 2. Curves illustrating the development of crisis tradeoffs affecting the Keynesian state: Changing stability levels for inflation – unemployment relations and growing rates of unemployment from the mid-1900s until the early 2000s.

What happened in the 1970s was that old methods of balancing employment and inflation were no longer effective, or to be more precise, they did not work as expected. Theories and models of state interventions built upon the Keynesian General Theory were now found ineffective in most OECD member states. Measures introduced by governments to reduce the rising unemployment rate only resulted in the empirical fact that, even doing so, the level of inflation spiraled upwards. New technology in certain industrial sectors increased productivity and competitiveness and contributed to inflation, while businesses using old technology were closed down and made unemployment rise (Cumes 1984). The principle of effective demand failed. "Effective demand" as the main stabilizing factor of the economic circle, was first pointed out by Riccardo, 200 years earlier, as a natural thing in a market economy; production and consumption belonged to an order of nature that assured mankind's survival. Keynes, in the 1930s, rejected Riccardo's natural approach, and asserted state intervention as necessary for economic stabilization. Besides that, the Keynesian theory was followed by a new reformulated neoliberal theory, based on the classical liberal economists, i.e., Milton Friedman's anti-state and supply-side monetarism in the 1960s. Indeed, confusion about the reason for the economic crisis of the 1970s dominated the academic literature at the time (Veggeland 1998).

Confusion was also reflected in OECD reports written under the intention of providing advice to member governments. They were unable to decide which remedies were most appropriate (McCracken et al. 1977). A quotation (1977:14) may shed some light on the confusion:

> "To summon up, the immediate causes of the severe problems of 1971-75 can largely be understood in terms of conventional economic analysis. There have been underlying changes in behavior patterns and in power relationships internationally and within countries. But our reading of recent history is that the most important feature was an unusual bunching of unfortunate disturbances unlikely to be repeated on the same scale, the impact of which was compounded by some *avoidable errors in economic policy*. The continuing legacy of 1971-75 makes for unusual difficulties in framing policies for the years immediately ahead. We reject, however, the

> view that existing market-oriented economic systems and democratic political institutions have failed. What is needed is *better use of existing instruments of economic policy*, and better functioning and management of existing market mechanisms." [SIC!]

Later on, in the 1980s, the OECD got out of its confusion and made a choice; Keynesian theory and measures were overruled by neoliberal theory and measures. Now the OECD recommended anti-inflation measures and policies which might create new markets and effective demand nationally and internationally. Consequently, the unemployment rate increased to a high level in most OECD-countries, as Figure 2 illustrates. Two things should have been done, according to the OECD: (1) Pick up and implement the principle of "creative destruction" to forward innovation, a term coined by Joseph A. Schumpeter (1939). Innovation became the keyword. That meant letting old industries be closed down and letting the market decide which innovative and competitive industries had the capacity to survive, a theory outlet by the classical economist Joseph Schumpeter in the 1930s. Outranged industries should be closed down and state subsidies forbidden, in order to stimulate innovation and the growth of new competitive business based on new technology and organization. Free market competition was basically the fundamental condition for the realization of the creative destruction principle, according to Schumpeter, and the OECD experts' belief in his thinking. (2) This neoliberal approach should be followed by comprehensive reforms in order to modernize the public sector. New Public Management (NPM) principles took over from Max Weber's mode of bureaucratic management as the main steering principle. The public sector should be diminished, save for its role as reflecting the private sector mode of organizational order. Accordingly, the public sector should become more competitive in the setting of the new market economy (OECD 2002, 2005). The principles of the New Public Management (NPM) promised such a solution.

Great Britain and the United States grasped the inflation-fighting strategy early on, and deeply reformed the economic policy to a supply-side economy under the umbrella of neoliberal ideology, an ideology with roots in classical liberal market thinking [Storper and Scott (eds.) 1992]. Other Anglo-Saxon states followed the same policy-inflation to get out of the stagflation crisis, but with a critical rise of unemployment. Normally, the unemployment rate rose to an average of 15% - 20%. The consequences of one-sided fighting of the stagflation crisis were noticeable globally.

New Public Management (NPM) reforms entered the political scene in the 1980s. In line with classical market liberalism, but reformulated by neoclassical economists like Milton Friedman, central planning and state intervention became defined as negative strategies to achieve innovation and effective demand. Neoliberal market thinking, with its focus on privatization, innovation, and the creation of new markets, took over as the ruling strategy. The policy of the World Trade Organization (WTO) and the EU implemented more free market movements. The objective was reestablishment of effective demand in member states and the stabilization of the international economic circle. The appearance of new technology and the arising globalization of markets were viewed as developments that had triggered the stagflation crisis, and at the same time outdated the Keynesian national interventionist economic order. According to the neoliberal economists, in a new global perspective, the national markets and institutions of the Keynesian interventionist state are too narrow, regulated, and dominated by government initiatives. Classical liberal economic theory, back to Malthus and Ricardo, was revitalized and reformulated (Friedman 1980). The neo-liberalists recommended strategies for international free trade agreements and deregulatory initiatives on the one hand, and a more decentralized, competitive and innovation-oriented public policy on the other. Privatization and less government interventions became the keywords for such a policy. Governments responded with initiating public reforms to implement a new institutional order for the promotion of innovation and functional networking cooperation, both nationally and internationally (Amin and Thrift 1995, Jessop 1994). In fact, in Europe, it was the arrival of the Multi-Level Governance (MLG) of the EU besides NPM structures that expanded, and became dominant at the time [Hayward and Menon (eds.) 2003].

Hereby, constitutionally, the ground was prepared for the institutionalization of the new regulatory state, replacing the Keynesian interventionist state, as noted by G. Majone (Majone 1994, 2007). This implied commitment to a global free market economy that stressed the virtues of competition and greater efficiencies through reregulation, specialization, and economies of scale (Egan 2004). The new regulatory state developed as a national principal of power. The National Central Banks were reorganized to become independent arm's length bodies regarding steering each country's monetary policy. It was this regulatory state that got into the grave financial and debt crisis that occurred in 2007. This latest crisis seems to have restored the principles of Keynesianism and the state interventionism but in another framework, called neo-Keynesianism and neo-interventionism, as Table 1 above indicates.

Explanation Approaches to the Keynesian Economics in Crisis

It has been said by many scholars that the Keynesian policies adopted by the advanced economies in the West carried with them the seeds for their own demise, and created the basic conditions for the regulatory state formation (Cumes 1984, Friedman 1962). The so called Keynesian state period, mid 1940s-1970s, was an era of exceptionally persistent economic growth, stability, and the building of the modern welfare state. It happened in accordance with different national social models and administrative traditions (Knill 2001, Veggeland 2007).

When the international economic crisis arrived in the 1970s, the Western governments applied the widely accepted and well-tried Keynesian remedies and political instruments, which they would have used in the 1950s and 1960s. They believed the crisis to be a short-term incident to be overcome swiftly (OECD 1977). This was a wrong belief. The crisis lasted, and as we have observed, the Keynesian remedies and instruments did not work as a response, see Figure 2. The governments initially assumed that the fault lay in their domestic management, and not in the validity of the Keynesian economic principles.

However, as the problems continued and deepened, talks about a short-term fluctuation were heard less and less among politicians and classical economists. The crisis then became increasingly recognized as a long-term, deep-rooted structural crisis, which required new remedies in order to be resolved. Economists began to say that Keynesian economics had 'failed' as such.

The monetarist Milton Friedman (1980) stood up and said that Keynesianism had all along been doomed to failure, because of too little market and too much state. His view was that policies, which were regulating production, productivity, demand and employment through state interventions, had not worked properly, nor would they in the future.

As elaborated earlier, governments applied Keynesian policies with great success as long as they effectively had the capacity and political will to implement aggregated effective demand. However, this capacity declined in the 1970s. Why has this occurred?

Explanation Approach 1

The capacity to balance the economy, Figure 2, declined because of a variety of reasons. One of the main reasons was that the building of the welfare state had reached a mature level, meaning transfer of money to welfare services and social arrangements could not be reduced, in order to preserve the legitimacy of national politics. Further, the abolishment of allocating money to social groups and individuals in need was out of the question. Attitudes towards manifestations of welfare and social security such as schools, health care, social care for elderly people, disabled individuals and others who could not look after themselves, etc., had become too deeply embedded in Western polity (Arter 1999). The impact on the economy of holding up the welfare consumption expenditure while stagnation continued was recognized, and it stimulated the cry for privatization – more market and less state.

Explanation Approach 2

Gender policy also influenced the capacity of the governments. Generally speaking, women's liberation had been made possible by the economic progress of the post-war period. The entry of females into the labor market had in our context two effects (OECD 2005). Firstly, the entry enormously increased the volume of available labor force for employment. The labor market could not offer jobs to them all. The number of people employed might have increased but statistically, it also contributed to the growing of unemployment, Figure 2.2. Secondly, the entry of wives into the labor market meant that unemployment was less destructive of individual and family consumption levels than it had been previously. Saving or investment by family units could be reduced as economic activity decreased but a certain level of consumption persisted. If their incomes were relatively maintained, their consumption was maintained. It disturbed the economy through reducing the effective demand (Cumes 1984). This contributed to the failure of the Keynesian remedies.

Explanation Approach 3

Related to international trade, it is a fact that a high-valued currency, leading to high import exposure, is anti-inflationary, and low-valued currency increases the export exposure, which leads to greater inflation. During the post-war period free-trade exposure of goods and services dominated intergovernmental negotiations. The European Community (EC) was established, and so was the European Free Trade Association (EFTA). In general, globalization of economic transactions had its start, resulting in free trade economies.

One of the Keynesian remedies was using revaluation of national currency, up or down, in order to balance inflation and employment. In an open economy, and in the framework of the free-trade concept of integrated international markets, the economic and political capacity to use this instrument declined [Bratton et al. (eds.) 1996]. It contributed little to help adjusting the effective demand. Therefore, in Europe, it started the process of creating the European Single Market (ESM) in the 1980s, and the European Monetary Union (EMU) in the late 1990s, which introduced supranational surveillance and rules for trade and monetary policy (Woolcock 1996). The goal was to 'create markets' but also to 'correct markets' by powerful regulation and control, across borders (Scharpf 1999).

Explanation Approach 4

Lastly, there is a *change of technology* explanation, building upon, among others, the economist W. E. G. Salter. He argued (1969) that an industry may be viewed as a number of plants embodying techniques, ranging between the most modern plants embodying the current best-practice technique, and the oldest plants still in use which embody the best-practice technique of an earlier date, and which is now outmoded. The consequences of this competition between old techniques, which generate what he terms '*extensive growth*' – growth, which merely reproduces a given situation but ultimately fails – and new techniques that generate '*growth in debt*,' create winners.

He writes (Salter 1969: 65):

> "The appearance of a best-practice technique has the following effects: first, the output of the industry is expanded until price falls to equality with the total costs of plants employing the new technique; secondly, some of the older existing plants are scrapped or replaced until the operating of the oldest plant (or plants) equal the new level of price and best-practice costs. A flow of new best-practice techniques leads to a series of such equilibrium (which combine both short- and long-run elements) and so trace out the path over time of output, costs, prices and productivity."

In the 1970s, and especially in the 1980s, a new technology innovation was introduced in economic production, in manufactory industries and in service production, and in the polity in general – the Information and Communication Technology (ICT).

The supply-side economy viewed ICT as a new factor to boost the Keynesian economy in stagnation. In sector after sector and firm by firm, the ICT replaced the old technology and machinery. Investments went to this new sector, and the demand for highly skilled labor forces grew rapidly – and so did the wages and the consumption. Old industries lost competitive capacity and were closed down. Consequences for the Keynesian state interventionism have been found damaging contextually in this respect, combining impacts of new and old technology.

On the one hand, the closing down of old industries contributed to massive unemployment in most of the Western countries in the relevant years. On the other hand, the expansion and pressure created in the new industries based on ICT required investments, highly skilled and highly paid workers and specialists, which contributed to pressure and high inflation (Cumes 1984). The technological tradeoffs as explanation to the fall of the Keynesian remedies and instruments are demonstrated clearly in Figure 2.

As might be expressed by the supply-side monetarists: policies that restrict the market have never really worked. Well-managed and regulated market growth to stimulate investment, production, productivity and employment, as well as to encourage innovation and a rational use of new technology, is what is needed [Fagerberg, Mowery and Nelson (eds.) 2005]. Furthermore, economy should be approached explicitly in its disaggregated, multi-sector structure, and with steady growth at the micro-economic level; this is a natural interpretation of what Joseph A. Schumpeter argues. In contrast, the international credit and financial crisis of the 2010s has been dominated by no growth at the micro-economic level and recession at the macro-economic level.

THE REGULATORY STATE AND NEO-INTERVENTIONISM

The emergence of the contemporary financial crisis, as already pointed out, had its beginning in the 1970s. The crisis was named a stagflation crisis. Deindustrialization and diminished economic growth in the wake of globalization processes generated unemployment as a threatening impact.

The crisis was met by the national governments with radical change in their monetary policy. Among other things, they started printing money to secure continuous peace in the labor market achieved in the years following the Second World War. The money was invested in work places, in upheaval of nominal salaries, and in the continued building of the welfare state. Despite such actions, the parallel inflation and stagnation problems did not stop. According to Keynesian theory and policy, as we have seen, this should be impossible, and leading economists did not know how to handle the situation and forward advice to the governments.

At last, advices were offered, following an OECD recommendation path (McCracken, OECD 2002). The markets had to be enlarged globally in order to allow businesses to gain access to new markets. It was followed up by unilateral and multilateral agreements and regulations, headed by the European Union (EU) and the World Trade Organization (WTO), to remove trade barriers; free movement of goods, capital, labor and services became the new political spoken slogan. A classic example is the strengthening of the European Commission and the introduction of the Single Market between the years 1988-1992. It also became an important measure to market orientate and commercialize public sector services to make them contribute to the collective national income. Organizational liberation of public institutions and agencies as arm's length bodies, dismissing political instruction authority, meant erecting independent agencies, which became a prevalent political mode of action. The new regulatory state was born and emerged as a form of state organization embedded in the Western democratic capitalism (Veggeland 2009, 2010). The regulatory state was guided by neoliberal ideology, and inspired international agreements and regulations. Those agreements and regulations had opening up new markets globally as a key goal, in order to benefit capitalized industries.

The emergence of the regulatory state supported internationalization and global processes, but the unemployment rates in the Western capitalist countries remained high through the 1990s, see Figure 2. What further happened was that the national states started raising loan abroad guaranteed by government bonds. This was done to develop the welfare state and its services further. However, the unemployment rate continued to be kept high in most Western countries. Again, the high level of unemployment threatened the stability of the labor market, and the government support of welfare arrangements was declining. Public budget deficit started being considered as a practical and functional solution to the problem. Consequently, the state debt arose heavily in countries like the USA and in many EU states in the 1990s and 2000s.

The recession crisis at the time was attempted to be solved by liberalization of the finance sector. This liberalization created an innovative option, namely the option for people to borrow privatized loans from the surplus of financial capital. Low interest rates on privatized loans became a national measure to keep the inflation rate low and stable in accordance with monetary economic theory. The financial institutions traded loan with the guarantee in expected rising prices in the real estate market. Streeck calls this phenomenon "privatized Keynesianism" (2012), i.e., loan-based growth in the private sector instead of the Keynesian principle – public loan to stabilize the effective demand in the economy. There could be, democratically speaking, no question of abolishing allocation of money through privatized loans to social groups and individuals in need, when governments introduced 'deflationary' policies. Real estate bubbles showed up and little by little they cracked; that was the situation in the USA in 2008, and it triggered the financial crisis to arise and to hit economies globally. An international double crisis was a fact, consisting of both dysfunctional public and privatized debt.

The economist Raghuram G. Rajan, writes about the social 'Fault Lines' (2010), indicating here that the society of our time is in trouble. It is not the historical lines that threaten to break into pieces but the society along these lines. He sees political impotence together with missing coherence in the democratic capitalism of today. In particular, he analyzes the many extreme negative consequences of the catastrophic development of economic and social inequality in many Western countries, especially in the USA.

Social justice and democratic government as guarantee for economic equality and good governance is a neglected perception. Rajan points out that for every dollar growth of income between 1976 and 2007, 58% went to the 1% of the richest in the USA. The income of the lower and middle class people stagnated or decreased during the same period, while the richest 10% of the citizens doubled their income manifold.

This created a disorder, which politically was overseen, and the policy lost legitimacy among ordinary people. Rajan put forward this dilemma in his writing, and postulated that politicians, in order to compensate for rising inequality, liberalized the financial capital and facilitated easier access to privatized loans for consumption as a policy turn. It was an innovative way of leveling out economic inequality by offering people seemingly cheap loans. The banks took the opportunity to make profit out of this policy by offering loans with expected rising real estate prices as guarantee, i.e., subprime loan. A large number of people bought real estate to constant rising prices, which were paid by subprime loans. The belief ruled that future prices would continue to rise. When the US Federal Bank raised the interest rate a bit, many families were unable to maintain their loans, i.e., repay interest rate and part payment. This led to financial institutions breaking down and becoming bankrupt. In the context of neo-interventionism and neo-Keynesianism some of the most important great banks were saved by the US government by supply of huge amounts of fresh money. It is now public knowledge: the bank that exposed the federal government to the greatest potential loss during the government bailout was ***Citigroup***, which received a grand total of $476.2 billion in cash and guarantees, according to a new report of the Congressional Oversight Panel which oversees the TARP program.

The contemporary crisis in the USA, EU and other Western states should be named a *double crisis*, because the crisis is intimately bound to both dysfunctional public debt and privatized debt. The footprint of neo-interventionist policies derived from neo-Keynesian theory – see Table 1 – may be observed. On the one hand, governments on both national and EU level intervene in the market economies and put money into saving banks from bankruptcy. Furthermore, supranational authorities claim reduction of public spending, which is followed by interventions to reduce private consumption by forcing forward reduction of salaries together with cuts of pensions. On the other hand, the European governments intervened through the EU and established a stability fund of several €100 billion administrated by the European Central Bank, aiming to be raised to reach €1000 billion in the coming years.

Indirectly but inevitably the governments' new approach and attitude to state intervention became achieved as an innovative mechanism. In 2011 the European Central Bank (ECB) presented an intermediary but long-term solution to heal the actual debt problems of certain states – the Long-Term Refinancing Operation (LTRO). The aim of the operation was, as pointed out before, to support the banks with money by a procedure of money exchange: banks sell expensive old bonds and gilts, which are turned over in the market with 6% - 9% interest rate. These bonds and gilts are sold, according to the new mechanism, to the ECB with fresh money in return. The banks agree on paying the money back in three years' time at the same price. For the money the banks receive they pay an interest of only 1%. The surplus of the capital transaction the banks receive is expected to be reinvested in job creating industries.

This is how neo-interventionism and neo-Keynesianism works out today. The principles of the neo-interventionism in Europe today are mainly administrated through the international organization of the EU. EU's 'The Long-Term Refinancing Operation' (LTRO) and the 'Financial Pact,' are administrated by the ECB and the banks. In contrast to the original Keynesianism principles, they are not administered by national democratic elected governments but by a supranational organization – the unelected EU and its judicial agencies.

As in earlier history of political economy theories, the contemporary international economic and political crisis in the democratic capitalism will find its intermediary solution. Most probably the solution will not go in the favor of liberalized financial capital which will probably come under hard regulatory international control; in Europe control means the EU. It is expected, in line with what Adam Smith and others feared, that industrial monopoly interests will take over because they will be particularly able to create jobs that are needed. In addition, in Europe, central EU power will grow at the expanse of national democratic sovereignty.

Capitalism as an Inherently Unstable System

Economic theory is layered like a cake. Explanations within one layer make sense, but once you move to another layer, they no longer apply. One example is the study, "Can We Avoid Another Financial Crises," by Australian born "neo-Keynesian," Steve Keen. As a compact bomb, it is precisely compactly designed with the aim of creating a theoretical layer as a spearhead that "blows up" neoliberal economic theories, their misconceptions and prejudices; even Keynesianism is impacted throughout the capitalist world. He has stated that "Economics needs reform: both Left and Right are Wrong." He wants his own New Deal, and defines his question within the layer of a corrupt banking system – the system we have now. He explains how it is that banks create money in the form of debt and how this leads to financial instability.

In the study, Steve Keen asks why debt has brought countries such as the United States, the United Kingdom, France and the countries of southern Europe to become "zombie economies." He shows the consequences of debt going ignored, and refers to neo-liberal economic theory where debt is precisely a blind spot in the theory. The message there is "do not worry about debt." Within the EU, it is especially southern European states that are unable to overcome the financial crisis because their market economists in the IMF and the EU Commission deny that debt means anything. Greece is on the edge of collapse. Here, Keen is original, breaking away from the old and famed Keynesian principle of the significance of state economic interventions in times of crisis – usually when taking government loans.

He takes a closer look at the UK and neoliberalism, showing how stable the relationship between UK private loans and GDP had been through a whole century, until Margaret Thatcher's neoliberalism disrupted it all (Keen 2017, p. 17). Debt grew and economists praised the boom that was created. Keen suggests that this wave of neoliberal politics should be called "deform" instead of "reform."

We are still in an economic recession internationally, and market economy models are unable to predict or explain an economic depression. Natural fluctuations in capitalism are viewed as a natural law. *Why is that?*, asks Keen. It is because the depressions are mainly financial. However, market economy cycles in themselves are also a financial cycle, that is, a cycle where loans are built up and later end up in an economic collapse of heavy debt. Hitler had to launch a World War to fight the German debt crisis. This is an example showing that when overloading debt to a political power grouping, the state can start a war in order to take over assets in other countries to compensate for its debt. US economists view President Trump's policy as precisely such a threat.

But nationally and internationally, the growth of debt is overlooked as destructive. Keen calls this "The Barter Illusion," which is the belief in the Barter system, which views all trade in which goods and services are exchanged without money and securities as something that happens as part of exchange transactions. Keen rejects the view of another neo-Keynesian Nobel laureate – Paul Krugman – who believes that banks do not really give credit but only recycle savings as if they were savings banks and not commercial banks. It's the same old lesson, because, Keen says – we own our own debt.

Without complex calculations, we can understand that the years leading to the 2007/8 financial crisis were characterized by increasing wealth for the few and growing banking power, while the vast majority sustained its living standards through loans and a growing welfare state. Yes, says Keen, national economies can be manipulated to flourish by creating "junk economies," i.e., by the state taking up loans and thus increasing demand that prompts growth in terms of value creation measured in GDP. Here Keen is anti-Keynesian. In reality, it's just a postponement, because it simply leads to increasing credit. This is what he criticizes in regard to the aforementioned UK's Margret Thatcher and former American Chairman of the Federal Reserve Alan Greenspan – as well as certain southern European countries. Neoliberal economic ideology brainwashed politicians and other leaders, and many of them actually became bank lobbyists. One reference that Keen – for good reason – does not mention, is a recent survey conducted in the EU, which shows that people have little confidence in politicians, while banks rank much higher in terms of confidence.

The dominant economic models ignored the overload of debt that drives Western capitalism today. How has this become the case? Keen traces back what he calls "endogenous money creation" and notes that the mechanism can easily be remembered as BOMB. This means that bank credit mainly concerns buyers of real estate, companies, etc.

With Steve Keen we can unravel what the current economic policy is about. It's about transforming the future policy to control the curse of debt, i.e., a New Deal of a qualitative new type. Keen's macroeconomic theory should be made known to politicians and key economists internationally. It will be useful in order to create a path forward to avoid a potential upcoming financial crisis.

ACKNOWLEDGMENT

Thanks to Noorit Larsen at Inland Norway University of Applied Social Sciences for important proof reading of the text of my chapter in this book.

REFERENCES

Amdam, Jørgen. & Noralv, Veggeland. (1998). *Teorier om samfunnsplanlegging* [*Theories of social planning*], Oslo: Universitetsforlaget.

Amin, Ash. & Nigel, Thrift. (1995). 'Living in the Global'. Amin, Ash. and Thrift, Nigel (eds): *Globalization, Institutions, and Regional Development in Europe*. Oxford: Oxford University Press.

Arter, David. (1999). *Scandinavian politics today*, Manchester: Manchester University Press.

Bratton, William et al., (eds) (1996*). International Regulatory Competition and Coordination: Perspectives on Economic Regulation in Europe and the United States*, Oxford: Clarendon Press.

Cumes, James W. C. (1984). *The Reconstruction of the Global Economy*, Melbourne: University Press.

Einhorn, Eric S. & John, Logue. (2003). *Modern Welfare States: Scandinavian Politics and Policy in the Global Age*, Westport, CT and London: Praeger.

Egan, Michelle. (2004). 'The Single Market', in Micelle Cini (ed.), *European Union Politics*, Oxford: Oxford University Press.

Fagerberg, Jan., David, C. Mowery. & Richard, R. Nelson. (eds) (2005). *The Oxford Handbook of Innovation*, Oxford: Oxford University Press.

Ferrera, Maurizio. & Martin, Rhodes. (eds) (2000). *Recasting European Welfare States*, London: Frank Cass.

Flora, Peter et al. (eds) (1999). *State formation, nation-building, and mass politics in Europe: the theory of Stein Rokkan, based on his collected works, Comparative European politics*. Oxford: Oxford University Press.

Friedman, John. (1987). *Planning in the Public Domain*, Princeton: Princeton University Press.

Friedman, Milton. (1962). *Capitalism & Freedom*. Chicago and London: The University of Chicago Press.

Friedman, Milton. (1980). *Free to choose*, Harmondsworth, UK and New York: Penguin books.

Giddens, Anthony. (1998). *The Third Way: The Renewal of Social Democracy*, Cambridge: Polity Press.

Hayward, Jack. & Anand, Menon. (eds) (2003). *Governing Europe*, Oxford: Oxford University Press.

Healey, Patsy. (1997). *Collaborative Planning: Shaping Places in Fragmented Societies*.

Jessop, Bob. (1994). 'Post-Fordism and the State', in Ash Amin (ed.), *Post-Fordism: A Reader*, Oxford, UK and Cambridge, US: Blackwell, pp. 249-279.

Keen, Steve. (2017). *Can We Avoid Another Financial Crises*, Amazon.com.

Keynes, John Maynard. (1936). *The General Theory of Employment, Interest and Money* (1964), New York: Hardcourt, Brace and Co.

Knill, Christoph. (2001). *The Europeanization of the National Administrations*, Cambridge: Cambridge University Press.

Krugman, Paul R. (2012). *End this depression now*. New York: W.W. Norton & Company.

Majone, Giandomenico. (1994). 'The Rise of the Regulatory State in Europe', *West European Politics*, Vol. *17*, (3), pp. 77-101.

Majone, Giandomenico. (1997). 'From the Positive to the Regulatory State: Causes and Consequences of Change in the Mode of Government', *Journal of Public Policy*, vol. *17* (3), pp. 139-189.

McCracken, Paul, et al. (1977). *Towards full employment and price stability*, Paris: OECD Publishing.

OECD. (2002). *Distributed Public Governance: Agencies, Authorities and other Government Bodies*, Paris: OECD Publishing.

OECD. (2005). *Modernising Government: The way forward*, Paris: OECD Publishing.

Østerud, Øyvind. (1972). *Samfunnsplanlegging og politisk system* [*Social planning and political system*], Oslo: Gyldendal.

Rajan, R. G. (2010). *Fault Lines: How Hidden Fractures Still Threaten the World Economy*. Princeton: Princeton University Press.

Sachs, Jeffrey D. (2006). 'Welfare States, beyond Ideology'. *Scientific American*, November 2006, p. 20.

Salter, Wilfred E. G. (1969). *Productivity and Technical Change*, Cambridge: Cambridge University Press.

Scharpf, Fritz. (1997). *Games Real Actors play: Actor-Centered Institutionalism in Policy Research*, Boulder: Westview Press.

Scharpf, Fritz. (1999). *Governing in Europe: Effective and democratic*?, Oxford: Oxford University Press.

Schonfield, Andrew. (1969). *Modern Capitalism: The changing balance of public private power*, Oxford: Oxford University Press.

Schumpeter, Joseph A. (1939), *Business cycles: A theoretical, historical, and statistical analysis of the capitalist process*, New York: McGraw-Hill.

Stewart, Michael. (1972). *Keynes and After*, Middlesex, UK and Baltimore, MD, US: Penguin Books.

Storper, Michael. & Allen, J. Scott. (eds) (1992). *Pathways to Industrialization and Regional Development*, London and New York: Routledge.

Streeck, Wolfgang. (1912). *The Burden of the Debt*. Le Monde Diplomatique, January 2012.

Veggeland, Noralv. (1998). *Nye rammer for offentlig planlegging. Internasjonalisering, privatisering* [*New framework for public planning. Internationalization, privatization*], Oslo: Kommuneforlaget.

Veggeland, Noralv. (2007). *Paths of Public Innovation in the Global Age. Lessons from Scandinavia*, Cheltenham, UK and Northampton, MA, US: Edward Elgar.

Veggeland, Noralv. (2009). *Taming the regulatory state: Politics and ethics*, Cheltenham, UK and Northampton, MA, US: Edward Elgar Publishing.

Veggeland, Noralv. (2010). *Den nye reguleringsstaten. Idébrytninger og styringskonflikter* [*The new regulatory state. Ideas and management conflicts*], Oslo; Gyldendal Akademiske.

Veggeland, Noralv. (2016). (ed.), *The Current Nordic Welfare State Model*, New York: Nova Science Publishers.

Veggeland, Noralv. (2017). (ed.), *Administrative Strategies of Our Time*, New York: Nova Science Publishers.

In: Keynesian Policies
Editor: Noralv Veggeland
ISBN: 978-1-53614-026-2

Chapter 5

LOOK AFTER EMPLOYMENT, AND THE BUDGET WILL LOOK AFTER ITSELF

Jesper Jespersen, PhD*
Roskilde University, Roskilde, Denmark

ABSTRACT

According to Keynes's *General Theory of Employment, Interest and Money* the private sector is not self-adjusting and it may get stuck in a position of unemployment equilibrium. The theoretical explanation can be found in his theory of effective demand, which is an equivalent to a theory of structural excess private savings. The mirror picture of the private sector is within a closed economy the public sector. To secure full employment the government has to run a deficit matching the private excess savings. In this case the public sector deficit could be financed automatically by private savings. On the other hand an expansionary monetary policy could facilitate a re-balancing process within the private sector and hereby make a relief to the government budget.

* Professor Dr. Scient. Adm. of Economics at Roskilde University. He has been lecturing in international economy at Copenhagen Business School. He owns a long list of national and international publications. Email: jesperj@ruc.dk

Keywords: effective demand, structural private surplus, structural public deficit, persistent unemployment equilibrium, active fiscal & monetary policy

INTRODUCTION

> "The outstanding faults of the economic society in which we live are its failure to provide for full employment and its arbitrary and inequitable distribution of wealth and income". (Keynes, 1936: 372)

This is the opening sentence of the concluding chapter of *The General Theory of Employment Interest and Money*. This book became a new and path-breaking understanding of the dynamics of a market based macroeconomic system. Keynes was writing on the empirical back ground of high and increasing unemployment in Britain ever since the end of the 1st world war. Keynes was increasingly convinced by these 15 years' record of increasing and persistent high unemployment that the market economy of a private sector was not self-adjusting. The dogma of the (neo)classical economists, that supply creates its own demand was empirically mis-credited. Full employment in any meaningful interpretation of the concept had not been established for much too long to accept this dogma. He was in search for a plausible theoretical explanation.

So, this undeniable empirical evidence of private sector imbalances was his starting point. The new macroeconomic theory did not come easily to Keynes. He was bred up with neoclassical theory learned at the feet of Alfred Marshall back in the early years of the 20th century. The only macro-theory at that time was the quantity theory of money and prices, which relied on the assumption of full employment and based on the axiom of 'supply creating its own demand'. So, unemployment was only considered as provisional and theoretically explained by temporary (labor)market imperfections. The theoretical and empirical contradiction did puzzle Keynes from an early point of his academic carrier, how a theory of scarce resources (i.e., full employment) could be used to explain persistent unemployment? In other word the dominant neoclassical theory was not compatible with real life evidence.

But it took Keynes a life long struggle to get rid of the intellectual chains of the neoclassical paradigm of undertaking macroeconomic analysis. He succeeded in his liberation only step-wise: through *A Tract on Monetary Reform* (CWK IV, 1923) and *A Treatise on Money* (CWK V + VI, 1930), until he in the early 1930s took the final step in this intellectual process, when he realized that the fundamental assumption of the private marked economic system being self-adjusting was an *a priori* analytical straight jacket not substantiated by reality.

General equilibrium models were relatively easy to handle mathematically (Pigou, 1934); but out of touch with '*the economic society in which we actually live, with the result that its teaching is misleading and disastrous if we attempt to apply it to the facts of experience*' (Keynes, 1936: 3).

> "On the one side are those who believe the existing economic system is a self-adjusting system…On the other side of the gulf are those who reject the idea, that the economic system, is in any significant sense, self-adjusting …. Now I range myself with the heretics".
> (Keynes, 1934: 133-36).

It was nothing less than a methodological sea-change when Keynes realized that analyzing reality, it is a fundamental flaw to make the *a priory* assumption that the private sector via price and wage flexibility should be self-adjusting to anything like a full employment (market clearing) equilibrium.

The *Preface* to *The General Theory of Employment, Interest and Money* (Keynes, 1936) tells this intellectual turn around very clearly.

> "The matters at issue are of an importance which cannot be exaggerated". (ibid, p. vi).
>
> "I failed to deal thoroughly with the effects of changes in the level of output…We are thus led to a more general theory, which includes the

> classical[1] theory with which we are familiar, as a special case". (ibid, p. vii)

and at the end of the *Preface*:

> "The difficulty lies, not in the new ideas, but in escaping from the old ones". (ibid, p. viii)

Although it is a preface. The content comes close to being the conclusion of the entire book written as the very final sentences and dated December 13, 1935[2].

The Private Sector Is Not Self-Adjusting

As soon as it is accepted as an empirical fact unveiled by the national statistics that full employment is a rare case lasting unemployment calls for an explanation. The inter war period in Great Britain (and most of Europa) was an obvious case and the US became a case after the Wall Street crash in 1929.

'To escape the old ideas' meant giving up the pre-condition that the macroeconomic development is supply-side determined. Say's Law that 'supply [of labor] creates its own demand' or with Keynes words: Say's Law is equivalent to the proposition that there is no obstacle to full employment' (ibid, p.26). Keynes's new idea is simply to incorporate the demand side into the macroeconomic system. Employment depends on production (Keynes called it 'output') and production depends on (1) Expected demand for goods and services and (2) profitability. It is the combination of (1) and (2), which Keynes called 'the Principle of Effective Demand', see (Jespersen 2012). The entire 1936-book could be read as one long theoretical argument explaining the factors which make an impact on effective demand, and how

---

[1] Keynes called all economists writing before 1936 'classical'.

[2] *The General Theory* was published on February 4th, 1936 – those were the days to get a book quickly through the publishing house.

they are interrelated within a macroeconomic system, what Keynes called 'The economy as a whole.'

That lack of profitability may cause unemployment was a very conventional conclusion. The 'revolutionary' new theory was the importance of 'expected demand'. Accordingly, Keynes focused on 'expectations' and on 'demand.'

a. ***Expectations,*** uncertain knowledge and lack of information are undividable inter-linked. When one recalls that neoclassical market theory securing a Pareto-optimal outcome is relying on a number of restrictive assumption among other full information, it becomes trivial that this theory deviates from reality. When uncertainty prevails, expectations become at least partly subjective. If you know that you do not have all information, what does a rational man do? Looking around, what are other people in the same position doing? They might possess the information you are missing, so herd-effects become rational. People do not act independently of one each other. Waves of optimism and pessimism become a part of decision making into the unpredictable future. As Keynes summaries (Keynes, 1937) about the future we simply do not know and cannot know due to uncertainty.
   When neoclassical macroeconomic theory was re-launched by Lucas & Sargent in the late 1970s (Lucas & Sargent, 1978). They had to face this dilemma of uncertainty causing a fundamental obstacle to the full-employment theory. They cut through this Gordian Knot by assuming the representative individual to possess full and certain knowledge about the full-employment equilibrium. This outrageous unrealistic assumption they phrased *rational expectations*, which with regard to analyzing and understanding reality could be characterized as a rather irrational assumption.
b. ***Demand*** is analytically less elusive than expectations. Keynes made a focus on private consumption and real investment in the *General Theory* and for good reason. In the 1930s these two demand components added up approximately to 80 percent of the GDP (Y).

Public sector demand was small and foreign export highly regulated. I will concentrate on private consumption (C), private savings (S) and real investment (I) in the following paragraphs of this paper. So, it comes close to a closed economy analysis, which subsequently can be applied to an open economy.

c. **Finally,** Keynes asked himself, how can it be that the master of the supply and demand diagram in microeconomics, Alfred Marshall and many other neoclassical economists, only focus on the supply side when it comes to macroeconomics?

PRINCIPLE OF 'EFFECTIVE DEMAND'

In macroeconomic analysis it is important to recall that output (GDP) is equivalent to factor income, and factor income is the main source of purchasing power, which is used to buy output. The causality is somewhat circular: on the one hand output is only produced if firms in aggregate expect demand to be sufficient in the nearer future, on the other hand demand depends mainly (but not solely) on realized factor income (no wage, no private consumption without a welfare state, accumulated savings and/or credit facilities).

Expectations might be wrong. Well, will always be wrong to some extent. We leave this aside for a short while.

If expected demand is equal to realized demand profit maximizing firms are 'happy.' They have no reason to change output (and employment), until expectations do change. Let us focus on this situation with fulfilled expectations:

1. (Output) $Y <= C + I$ (effective demand)
2. (private savings) $S <= Y - C$ (factor income not spend on consumption)

Combining 1. and 2. gives:

3. S <= I (real investment determines savings)

This is the core of *The General Theory*: at the macro level savings are determined by and therefore always equal to real investment, which leaves the level of unemployment indeterminate.

The major part of *GT* is spent on defining *the principle of effective demand* i.e., the theory of employment. It consists of three major sections (or books to use Keynes's own expression) containing the theory of *effective demand:* (1) The propensity to consume (or to save) out of income, (2) The inducement to invest and (3) Money-wages and prices[3].

The analytical conclusion was that output is determined at a level where financial savings (non-consumption) equal real investments, which can happen at any level of employment. Therefore, focus has to be on (1) propensity to consume (save) out of (factor) income and (2) Inducement to invest (which is less dependent on realized factor income, but dependent on the marginal efficiency of capital compared to the long term rate of interest). Keynes's theoretical innovation was to demonstrate that within the macroeconomic system there are no automatic mechanism securing that S = I *at full employment*. Finally in book V on *Money-wages and prices* he explains why a high degree of wage and price flexibility is not a solution to persistent unemployment (or excess employment in war-time).

> The essential character of the argument is precisely the same whether or not money-wage, etc. are liable to change. (ibid, p. 27)

LIQUIDITY PREFERENCE

Within Keynes's macroeconomic system output (and employment) becomes a dependent variable determined by the propensity to save, the

---

[3] If self-called New Keynesian economists ever read *The General Theory* and even come as far as Book V they would be taken by surprise, because the initial chapter has the titles *Changes in Money-Wages*. Here Keynes explains, why flexible wage is no solution to securing full-employment rather the opposite.

inducement to invest *and* the rate of interest. This is the third novelty within *The General Theory* which makes it deviate from neoclassical macroeconomics. The rate of interest is not determined by savings and real investment or the related flow of (financial) funds theory. The rate of interest is determined by financial portfolio adjustments equalizing the stock of money and the stock of other financial assets (government bonds, private debt and shares and foreign exchange (when relevant)).

Keynes was very specific emphasizing that the rate of interest was the relative price balancing demand and supply of financial stocks.

The theoretical implication of the liquidity preference theory was that the rate of interest could not be expected to adjust in such a way that real investment and private financial savings would be identical at full employment. In fact, the only diagram in *The General Theory* is a drawing of the demand and supply schedule of financial flows, where the rate of interest is exogenously determined (by the demand for money relative to (government) bonds). Within this diagram, see below, Keynes demonstrates that given the marginal efficiency of capital a change in the rate of interest will cause the real investment to change and by that output and savings.

Hence, there are two (at least) reasons why the private sector is not self-adjusting: 1. Effective demand might be deficient and 2. The rate of interest is determined by portfolio considerations, i.e., partly by speculation, cf. Chapter 12 in *The General Theory.*

Cause of Persistent Unemployment: Structural Private Sector Savings Surplus

Looking at the private sector in isolation with Keynes's glasses there is no self-adjustment mechanism within a perfect market economy, where uncertainty and lack of information prevail.

If we take Figure 1 as an illustration of a modern economy there are two structural obstacles to full employment:

A structural private savings surplus illustrated by the excess of savings compared to real investment at the level of full employment. If the rate of interest were determined only by 'flow of funds' there would, within this simple illustration, be established a rate of interest making S and I identical; but at an employment level below full employment. Within this analysis a possible solution to unemployment could be to lift the real investment function either by subsidies (or lower taxes) to private business or by increasing public investment, see below.

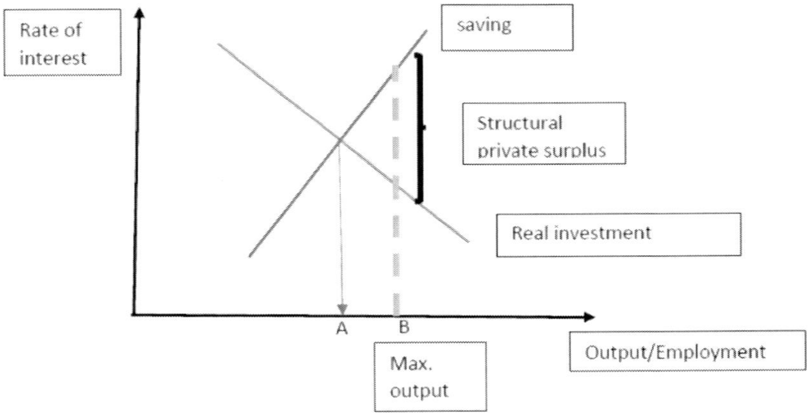

The distance from A to B is structural private sector unemployment caused by the tendency structural sector excess savings.

Note: This figure takes inspiration from Keynes, 1936: p. 180.

Figure 1. Private sector structural excess savings.

Figure 1 illustrates that it is the intersection of private financial saving and real investments, which determine private sector production and employment. These two macro-relations are independent behavioral representations. Real investment depends on MEC (expected rate of return of real capital) and on the rate of interest (of borrowed funds, i.e., determined by liquidity preference). Private Saving depends (mainly) on income, which is determined by output, see equations above.

By looking at Figure 1 it becomes clear that private sector cannot adjust to full employment by itself. The two behavioral relations represent the aggregate decision of millions of households and (at least) thousands of firms. At the macro-level there is no 'adjustment mechanism' which secure that effective demand should converged to a level corresponding to full employment. Private households (and firms) have locked themselves up in a situation with too high propensity to save and/or business with too little incentive to undertake real investments, when MEC is lower than the rate of interest.

This dead-locked employment position illustrated in Figure 1 Keynes called an *unemployment equilibrium.* One can argue about whether it is real investments being too low or the propensity to undertake private saving too high; but the outcome is undeniable: persistent unemployment due to *structural* private sector surplus.

In addition, it is important to understand that this structural private savings surplus will NOT by itself lower the rate of interest. When the economy has settled at an unemployment equilibrium private savings are equal to real investment and there is with unchanged liquidity preference a balance between supply of and demand for financial funds (credit). According to Keynes's (innovative) liquidity preference theory only a change in the expected future rate of interest or monetary policy might have an impact on the composition of money and bonds in private portfolios and hence on the rate of interest.

Private and Public Sectors May Interact to Improve Employment

So, in such cases of persistent unemployment caused by *structural* private sector surplus the obvious question would be, how to increase effective demand for labor? Output and employment could be improved, according to Figure 1, if the private sector could run a savings surplus, which was matched by one (or both) of the external sectors (the foreign and/or the public sector) would run an equivalent savings deficit.

It is trivial to go for an export surplus, which is equivalent to a foreign savings deficit. But all countries cannot have an export surplus (by definition). Say, all Europe suffered from an unemployment equilibrium –

increased export is a no go (a zero-sum game which does not increase effective demand) within Europe (considered as a closed economic system).

Similarly, within a (semi)-closed economy like Great Britain in the inter war period or Europe in the present situation the straight forward policy recommendation would be, instead, to let the public sector run a *structural* budget deficit.

Keynes was very outspoken on what could be done? Although his personal preference was private sector activities. He had to admit that if the private sector were caught in a dead-lock and/or a liquidity trap (of zero-bound rate of interest), it would need a 'helping hand' to reduce unemployment. Adam Smith's 'invisible hand' was not only invisible it was absent at the macro-level. In this situation the government has not only the possibility, but according to Keynes also a moral obligation to increase private employment by public spending on activities, which created more output in the private sector. Looking at the much poorer society of the early 1930s there could easily be set up a long list of needed and necessary wants.[4]

To establish full employment the government, i.e., the public sector, had to run a budget deficit similar to the private sector structural surplus. The ambition of full employment is, of course, very ambitious. Keynes's conclusion is more modest, that high unemployment can be mitigated primarily by increased public spending. (Taxes were in the inter war period quite low and mainly paid by the rich people). Anyhow, the theoretical point was, at least to Keynes, pretty straight forward: increased spending by government on public (domestic) consumption or real investment would have a positive impact on effective demand.

However, at that time it was a theoretical novelty, when Keynes argued within *The General Theory* that the budget deficit could be automatically matched by a private savings surplus of an equal amount! If liquidity

---

[4] Keynes knew that he was up against the so-called Treasury View on public investment, which was thought of to draw on and reduce a given 'pot' of private funds and hereby reduce private incentives to invest. Like today the Treasury had not understood the private savings expand *pari passu* med increased private income. In his despair of this ignorance, he goes on with apocalyptic suggestions like 'Pyramid-building, earthquakes, even wars may serve to increase wealth, if our statesmen on principles of the classical economics stands in the way of anything better, (Keynes, 1936: 129)

preference was unchanged, there would via the expansionary fiscal policy be created an excess of private funds, which had to be 'invested' in government financial liabilities (bonds) or central bank money.

But, as long as this macroeconomic interdependency is not understood, which was the case in the 1930s, the *Treasury View* would prevail, saying that the public sector deficit could be analyzed independently of the private sector imbalances and considered as mainly caused by prodigality of government. Hence, public deficits are a drain on private sector savings available for private investment and had, furthermore, to be paid back by coming generations.

Look After (Private) Employment and the Public Budget Deficit Will Diminish

Keynes's political instinct, being a member of the Liberal Party, was to support and re-balance the private sector and to avoid unemployment. Skidelsky writes,

> 'He [Keynes] brought in the State to redress the failings of society, not because he loved it, but because he saw it as the last resource…
> He was the last of the great English Liberals'. (Skidelsky, 1992: xv)

In addition, Keynes had a somewhat ambivalent relationship to capital formation and private accumulation of wealth. Being a liberal he was concerned that private activity and wealth was not a guaranty of full employment and fair distribution. So, what to do with this excess private savings? To him the answer was to increase private or public real investments in housing, infrastructure and if necessarily in military equipment.

Looking at Figure 1 his political preference was to increase private investment by reducing the rate of interest. According to his newly launched liquidity preference theory Bank of England possessed the political instrument to lower borrowing costs by undertaking Open Market Operations (QE as we call it today).

If the Central bank were successful in lowering the long term rate of interest, employment would improve *and* at the same time the government budget would be structurally relieved for two reasons: 1. A smaller (perhaps disappearing) structural public deficit and 2. Lower interest payments on public debt.

Keynes wrote:

> 'Let us assume that steps are taken to ensure that the rate of interest is consistent with the rate of investment which corresponds to full employment', (Keynes, 1936: 220). In fact, his fear was that within a generation real capital would cease to be scarce and MEC falls to zero. In that case the private sector would suffer from a permanent structural saving surplus. This prospect made him conclude: I conceive, therefore, that a somewhat comprehensive socialization of investment will prove the only means of securing an approximation to full employment, (ibid: 378).

Some years earlier he had made the same projection, but in a more optimistic tune, of society overcoming scarcity to such an extent that accumulated real capital had made it possible to half the average working hour per person within two generations (Keynes, (1931): Economic possibilities of our Grandchildren).

In any case, Keynes's theoretical point is, that the public sector budget (especially when the government runs a deficit) cannot be analyzed in isolation. The economists have to identify the corresponding surplus, which in a closed society has to be in form of private sector excess savings *as long as unemployment prevails*.

In a modern welfare state this link between private sector surplus and public sector deficit is partly exercised via the so-called automatic budget stabilizers. They are activated as soon as the private sector runs into a recession (i.e., excess private savings) causing rising unemployment. In fact, within a modern welfare state the correlation between the rate of unemployment and the public sector budget deficit is quite high. So, the key to public sector budget balance is the private sector. As Keynes said: *look after [private] employment and the budget will look after itself.*

In this macroeconomic perspective it becomes obvious, why a strategy of reducing a public sector deficit, in case of substantial unemployment, by austerity policies is counter-productive, if full employment and prosperity is the aim of the policy.

PUBLIC DEBT, LIQUIDITY PREFERENCE AND MODERN MONETARY THEORY

I continue analyzing a closed society, to make the basic arguments clear. The analysis would also be applicable to an economy with import and export of goods and services, flexible exchange rate and international capital control, like Great Britain in the 1930s and during the Bretton Woods era (where exchange rates were adjustable).

If we take the view of Abba Lerner's *Functional Finance* (1944) re-launched by Randall Wray (2012) under the name of *Modern Monetary Theory* the private and public sector imbalances have to be analyzed simultaneously. In stylized form the public sector budget balance has to be – to secure full employment - a mirror picture of the private sector structural excess savings (positive in most cases, but during the 1960s it could in some countries turn negative).[5]

Hence, the private structural excess savings could therefore equally well be described as an excess demand for external financial asset (at full employment). In a closed economy it means that if the government creates more effective demand, output and employment, the public sector deficit can automatically be financed by private excess savings without making the rate of interest increase.

---

[5] Public debt as a percentage of GDP fell steadily from just after the Second World War until the early 1970erne. Mainly because GDP in current prices (rising inflation) grew faster than the public debt; but in some countries e.g. Scandinavia there was a public sector surplus in many years due to among other thing a private housing boom.

The real challenge is to find the right mix between new issues of government bonds and of central bank money. This mix of bonds and central bank money will, of course, make an impact on the rate of interest dependent on how the private sector liquidity preference develops. If the private sector's liquidity preference is unchanged government can manipulate the rate of interest by changing the proportion of government bond financed debt to the stock of central bank money. This is a policy which central banks in broadly speaking all civilized countries have undertaken during the aftermath of the financial crisis under the name of *Quantitative Easing*. To what extent this policy has been successful it is not up to me to evaluate here. Suffice to say, that the long term rate of interest has never (!) been as low as it had been in the US, UK and euro-zone as long as this monetary policy was in process.

The stock of central bank money has increased speedily without causing wage or consumer price inflation. So, the classical quantity theory of money and prices has obviously been mis-credited. Whereas it is more controversial, if the QE-policy has caused an asset price inflation with implication for future financial stability.

Fortunately, it is less disputed that the QE-policy and the low rate of interest have had a positive effect by reducing the private sector structural excess savings. This positive development has happened via a number of channels. Two shall be mentioned here. The first one is the impact of lower rate of interest on the speed of wealth accumulation in private pension funds, which reduces private passive savings. Secondly, a lower rate of (long term) interest will have an expansionary effect on private real investment. How strong these to effects are depends on circumstances; but will bring the economy closer to full employment and at the same time bring some relief to the public sector budget.

The Misunderstood Macroeconomics Repeats Itself

Franklin D. Roosevelt took office in March 1933 and presented immediately a 'New Deal' to restore the American economy. The government's involvement and regulation were increased in all sectors: banking, labor market, public investment, business support, agriculture, social policy and the gold content of the dollar. All these initiatives were often presented by the President as part of his 'fireside chats' and summed up the following way *'I hope you can see from this elemental recital of what the Government is doing there is nothing complex, or radical, in the process,'* quoted from (Rauchway, 2008: 57).

And Roosevelt was right. He was making this successful policy out of intuition and common sense for two straight forward reasons: 1. The economists of his time assuming a self-adjusting private sector were obviously wrong and the policy recommendations accepted by the previous Hoover administration of aiming at a balanced public budget and dear money had only aggravated and deepened the recession 2. All sectors suffered from lack of purchasing power due to broken banks and a broken market mechanism. On top of these Hoover-failures Roosevelt had had some positive experiences from being Governor of New York State setting up public investment, although in a much smaller scale. What the Americans could see was an economy that started to grow by 8 to 10 percent p.a. each year except for the year 1937/38 and unemployment fell steadily, but not until 1943 unemployment was back where it was in 1929 (ibid: 5). Why did it take such a long time one may ask? An important part of the answer is, because the American economy had got stuck by a total collapse of gross private capital formation from $16 bill. in 1928 to $4 bill. in 1932. The government could only partly fill in this gap by increasing public expenditure by $ 2½ bill. in the mid-1930s (Lewis, 1960: 113). Recovery had to wait for a restauration of business confidence (and the war).

But all way through Roosevelt had difficulties of defending the growing public debt. Here he had to wait for Keynes; but even Keynes had severe difficulties to convince the British politicians of the positive role of public deficit and debt as long as unemployment dominated.

So, it still is – public debt is considered as one of the important macroeconomic imbalances, which has to be addressed separately. Otherwise, the call for austerity policy while unemployment still prevails cannot be understood, unless full employment is no longer at the political agenda.

One may wonder how this misunderstood macroeconomics still can be so widely accepted by economists that it became an undisputed part of the EU policy to aim at a balanced public sector budget independently of unemployment and other imbalances of the private sector. A policy recommendation which has to be followed by all EU-member countries. First step in the implementation of this policy was the Growth and Stability Pact written into the EU Treaty in 1997. No member country should run a current budget deficit above 3 percent of GDP and aim at a balanced budget. If the deficit exceeded this limit, for instance due to a collapse in private investments, the government was asked to make plans how to reduce the deficit by austerity in the middle of a recession!

But, the macroeconomic misunderstanding became is worse in the wake of the great recession, where a number of member-states in the year 2010 undertook an expansionary fiscal policy by expanding the structural budget deficit to match the hugely increased private structural surplus. This expansionary policy had the positive effect of breaking the downward spiral of GDP; but made, on the other hand, the public debt grows. The conventional economists only looking at the governments' budget in isolation saw this development as unsustainable and 'unsound.' On the initiative of the German government it was, therefore, agreed among the EU-member states (except UK and The Czech Republic) to sign the so-called Fiscal Compact, which forbid the member-state at any time to run a structural deficit of more than ½ a percent of GDP. This is equivalent of saying that independently of how severely a private sector is hit by recession (i.e., structural private excess savings) the government is prohibited from undertaking a matching deficit spending (financed by private excess savings).

CONCLUSION

How can it be that this macroeconomic folly repeats itself? One may wonder; but hardly any conventional economist has objected to the 'soundness' of the Stability Pact or the Fiscal Compact. The latter has been implemented into national law by parliament in a number of EU countries among other by the social democratic lead Danish government in 2012 – where the economic recession was at its deepest.

This is a sad story, and I am afraid that one has to wait for another Roosevelt for quite long time. It makes no sense to wait for another Keynes – one is enough; but without impact when the academic economists set another agenda and assume that the private sector is self-adjusting and 'supply creates its own demand'.

I am wondering, like Keynes did, why it is so difficult, when evidence is overwhelming, to get acceptance by the majority of academic economists that

1. The private sector is not self-adjusting;
2. When there is an excess financial saving in the private sector it will cause unemployment;
3. The government may reduce this unemployment by a matching budget deficit (which finances itself);
4. and finally this budget deficit will disappear if the private sector is able to reduce and even to remove the excess savings at full employment.

There are, of course, other remedies to reduce structural excess savings within the private sector: redistributing income and wealth from rich to poorer, investment subsidies, reduced (tax) incentives to private savings (old age pension is heavily subsidized especially for the rich people) or a reduced number of working hours per week.[6]

---

[6] I leave these arguments for another paper, where Figure 1 will be the main analytical model.

References

Jespersen, J. (2009), *Macroeconomic Methodology: a Post-Keynesian Perspective*, Cheltenham: Edward Elgar Publishing.

Jespersen, J. (2012), Keynes's *General Theory* after 75 years: time to re-read and reflect, in Jespersen & Madsen (eds.) (2012), pp. 131-150.

Jespersen, J. and M. O. Madsen (eds) (2012) *Keynes's General Theory for today: Contemporary Perspectives*. Cheltenham: Edward Elgar Publishing.

Keynes, J. M. (1921), *A Treatise on Probability*. London: Macmillan.

Keynes, J. M. (1923), *A Tract on Monetary Reform,* London: Macmillan.

Keynes, J. M. (1930), *Treatise on Money*, vol. 1 & 2, London: Macmillan.

Keynes, J. M. (1931), 'Economic Possibilities of our Grandchildren' in *Essays in Persuasion*, London: Macmillan.

Keynes, J. M. (1934), *Roosevelt's Economic Experiments, The Listener*, 17. January 1934.

Keynes, J. M. (1934), *Is the Economic System Self-adjusting?* The Listener, 21 November 1934.

Keynes, J. M. (1936), *The General Theory of Employment, Interest and Money*. London: Macmillan.

Keynes, J. M. (1937), The General Theory of Employment, *Quarterly Journal of Economics*, 51, 209-23.

Lerner, A. (1944), *The Economics of Control*, New York: Macmillan.

Lewis, W. A. (1960), *Economic Survey, 1919-39*, London: George Allen and Unwin, Ltd.

Lucas, R. E., Jr. & T. J. Sargent (1978), *After Keynesian Macroeconomics,* in *After the Phillips Curve*, Boston, MA: Federal Reserve Bank of Boston.

Pigou, A. C. (1934), *The Theory of Unemployment*, London: Macmillan.

Rauchway, E. (2008), *The Great Depression & The New Deal,* Oxford: Oxford University Press.

Skidelsky, R. (1992), *John Maynard Keynes: The Economist as Saviour, 1920-37*, London: Macmillan.

Wray, L. Randall (2012), *Modern Money Theory: A Primer on Macroeconomics for Sovereign Monetary Systems*, London: Palgrave/Macmillan.

In: Keynesian Policies
Editor: Noralv Veggeland
ISBN: 978-1-53614-026-2

Chapter 6

NEO-KEYNESIAN POLICIES IN INTEGRATED EUROPEAN ECONOMIES: WHAT POLICY CAN BE NATIONAL AND WHAT MUST BE EUROPEAN?

*Ole Gunnar Austvik, PhD**
Inland Norway University of Applied Sciences,
Lillehammer, Norway

ABSTRACT

This chapter discusses the scale and scope of economically integrated countries' room for national political maneuvering in an international economic integration area. The outset is that competition drives prices and expensive national regulations down, thus imposing a ceiling on cost-driving national policies. To limit a following "race-to-the-bottom," EU

* Professor of political economy. By education he holds a doctorate in political science from University of Oslo. He has been working with the Norwegian Institute of International Affairs (NUPI), BI Norwegian Business School and Statistics Norway, and is appointed Senior Fellow at John F. Kennedy School of Government, Harvard University. Email: ole.gunnar.austvik@kaldor.no.

minimum standards set a floor to the extent to which competition can push down such policies. Between this floor and ceiling each country have remaining degrees of freedom for national policy making, including how much taxes can be collected to pay for public expenditures. Hence, to support cost driving policies economically integrated countries need to "pull together" not only to make competition work in non-discriminatory manners, but also to provide revenues to pay for the welfare state, tackle rising inequality issues, and to stimulate economic growth. However, common or coordinated fiscal policies may be difficult to agree on when countries have different needs and views on what is the best policy. Not only long-term and short-term economic interests are confronted, but also domestic winners and losers from free trade, and the visions of the EU as a neo-functional or an intergovernmental regime.

Keywords: Europeanization, European integration, policy formation, regulation, public and private capital, welfare state

INTRODUCTION

International economic integration reduces each nation state's freedom to choose policy independently of others. Unilateral cost-driving regulations and taxes, and macro-economic stimulation, may lead to price increases at home, creating problems for import and export competing industries. Competition drives prices and expensive regulations down, thus imposing a ceiling on cost-driving national policies. To limit a following "race-to-the-bottom," European Union (EU) minimum standards set a floor to the extent to which competition can push down such policies. Between this floor and ceiling each country have remaining degrees of freedom for national policy making, including how much taxes can be collected to pay for public expenditures. For macroeconomic stimulation, there are also significant import leaks to other countries, the more open an economy is, weakening its effect on the national economy. Hence, national autonomy to formulate policy based solely on domestic preferences is balanced against and changed in favor of the benefits expected to accrue from trading in larger markets, to achieve higher economic standards of living. Economically integrated countries need to agree on industrial and economic policies and to "pull together" not only to make competition work in non-discriminatory manners, but also to provide revenues to pay for the welfare state, and to stimulate economic growth. This chapter discusses the scale and scope of economically integrated countries' room for national political maneuvering in an international economic integration area. The first section outlines how international economic integration sets limits to national policy formation. The second section discusses the processes of Europeanization and globalization. The third section focuses on varieties of policy-making for economically integrated countries. Finally, conclusions and policy implications are discussed.

ECONOMIC INTEGRATION AND NATIONAL POLICY FORMATION

The dominating neoliberal international economic system of the past few decades pressures countries to become more similar in a number of economic, social and political affairs, especially within the EU (Austvik 2015:117-121). In microeconomic policy, the Single Market (SM) integrate national markets into a European market, with corresponding harmonization of domestic policies. EU regulations and standards apply equal for all in a non-discriminatory manners. Ideally, the SM is intended to operate as one perfectly competitive market with the same rules and regulations across the Community, similar to a national market. This (theoretically) first-best situation, as defined in economics, exists when markets are unified across borders, and firms adjust production where their respective marginal costs equal a common price, with no national discrimination. With this point of departure, SM policy should be based on competition law and regulation, and (only) correct market distortions (caused by, for example, externalities or monopoly power), so that there will be consistency between companies' desire to maximize profits and the EU desire to maximize European welfare.[1] This is at the core of social efficency in regulatory economics.[2]

However, in the real world, perfect markets are rarely possible. Economics may first of all give insight into the processes around and the purpose of interventions, describing important forces operating towards optimality. Mostly we live in a second-best world where policy measures generally aim for second-best solutions. In a second-best economic integration area, compromises between theoretical first-best solutions and the real market are adopted and recognized, acknowledging that integrated markets are not influenced only by rational economic behavior, efficiency goals and the needs to correct market failures, as defined in economics, but also by diverging institutional, cultural and historical situations and interests. As Lefeber and Vietorisz (2007) note, the economic "efficient pursuit of one particular goal may conflict with the realization of some other, equally or more important social interest. Hence, (economic) efficiency for its own sake cannot be a policy goal." In an economic integration area economic, political, social, and cultural institutions and policies tend to become more similar, but not equal, over time (Bennett 1991), appearing as continuous sequences of negotiations, interpretations, and adaptations (Dolowitz & Marsh 2000:15). While countries converge in policy formation, diverging income distributional and historical situations, levels of economic development, institutional and cultural path-dependencies and identities retain differences and indicate that the same policy is not always desired by, or possible for, all.

---

[1] Under regulation, a "visible hand" is introduced to correct the imperfect market's "invisible hand." By regulating the framework and conditions for how firms may operate, the public authorities seek to achieve what is considered optimal for society. The incentives and disincentives given for pricing and production should create mechanisms that lead to efficient allocation of resources and "acceptable" distribution of income. There are many ways of regulating markets and the behavior of firms, which may result, *inter alia,* in principal–agent problems and gaming between the regulator and the regulated (Train 1991, Austvik 2003).

[2] "Social efficiency" is defined in economics as the optimal distribution of resources in a society, taking into account all external and internal costs and benefits. This occurs when marginal social benefit equals marginal social cost (as opposed to the optimization of private costs and benefits). Social efficiency is closely related to the concept of Pareto optimality, which is a situation where it is impossible to make anyone better off without making someone worse off.

Accordingly, most countries seek an optimal rather than maximal degree of openness and real harmonization of policies with others in their economies. National interests concerning degrees of autonomy and sovereignty, conflicting interests between and within countries, and inertia in markets and politics often contribute to a slowing down of the integration processes. In some areas (for example in agricultural products) complete global free trade may never become a reality. From the outset, the different second-best national situations (as defined in economics), the divergent understanding of rules and regulations (with or without intent), and the gaming around these rules and regulations when it comes to interpretation and implementation hamper a full harmonization of policy practices. Hence, a static economic equilibrium model demonstrates the benefits of free trade in an infinite future. To understand the process of policy harmonization, however, the understanding must become dynamic and more social sciences must be applied.

Within the EU, rules and regulations narrow the room for national political maneuvering through legal harmonization, and emplaces a floor on how far down international competition can push cost-driving regulations and taxes. At the same time, as politics shape markets, markets also shape politics. International markets contribute in determining a ceiling to the national room for political maneuvering. One example is how global free movement of capital gives countries little room for political maneuvering in unilateral national regulations (such as the implementation of a so-called Tobin tax or increased capital requirements for banks), even if international regulations does not forbid neither a unilateral tax or increased equity for banks. To be implemented, policies must be coordinated with more countries as the international capital market restrains national credit and monetary policies. Partly this now takes place for increased bank equities. Hence, international competition as well as supranational harmonization of laws and regulations push governments to solve common problems through common institutions (Drezner 2001:60). Expansionary macroeconomic policies must largely be coordinated with other countries, especially the large ones such as the US and Germany, and gradually also with new economies like China, and discussed in fora like the G-20. The more a country is exposed to international competition, the more probable it is that policy will converge with other countries with the same international exposure, and domestic change must often be done via international cooperation.

While international economic integration represents a win–win situation on aggregated national levels, some countries may win more than other countries. Equally important, it represents a win–lose situation at domestic sectorial levels, causing conflicts, as seen as parts of the reason for various reactions against elites in both the US and Europe. It has also led to a fall in government revenues as a proportion of total value creation in most countries, while private income has increased, cf. Figure 1. World Inequality Report 2018 (WIR2018) demonstrates a number of long-term redistributional effects after the substantial market liberalizations that have taken place since the 1980s. Following the works of Thomas Piketty (2012), it shows how income and wealth in almost all countries in the world has become increasingly more unequally distributed, and is now approaching pre-World War I levels. WIR2018 argue that economic inequality is largely driven by the unequal ownership of capital, and "a very large transfers of public to private wealth occurred in nearly all countries, whether rich or emerging. While national wealth has substantially increased, public wealth is now negative or close to zero in rich countries." Most growth in national income has gone to the private sector, while public revenues and expenses has not increased. The belief in supply side industrial and macroeconomic policies, market liberalization, privatization and competition as drivers for economic growth, has led to a weakening of the possibilities and role for governments to tax and regulate economies with demand side (or Keynesian) policies.

At the same time, most industrialized countries today are welfare states, implying that the most important aspects of people's living standards, education and health should be universally secured. Gøsta Esping-Andersen (1992) distinguishes between three main types of welfare societies; the social democratic (in the Nordic countries), the conservative (in Germany and most of Continental Europe) and the liberal (as in the UK, US and Switzerland). The Nordic welfare models are mainly based on the public paying for the welfare benefits through the tax collection system as a "Single

Payer." Others are financed through various forms of insurance schemes, which then distribute welfare benefits and services. NGOs and individuals can also be part of a welfare system. Independently of the financing of the system, the welfare state is based on the principles of equality, fair distribution of wealth, and public responsibility for those who cannot manage to achieve a minimum level of living by themselves. The extent of the welfare state (what, how and how much it covers) has increased over time, and also the cost of it, and is now an essential part of all welfare states' budgets (mix economies). How much the population pays in the form of taxes, fees or deposits and how much it gets from social security and benefits is central to political debates in all countries. This takes place at the same time as the ability of individual governments to tackle inequality, to maintain and develop welfare states, as well as demand side, or Keynesian, macroeconomic policy, has become more limited. The income side of states that are economically integrated is largely tied to global and European markets and regulations, and the regime for this will contribute in determining the extent and form of their ability to finance their welfare systems.

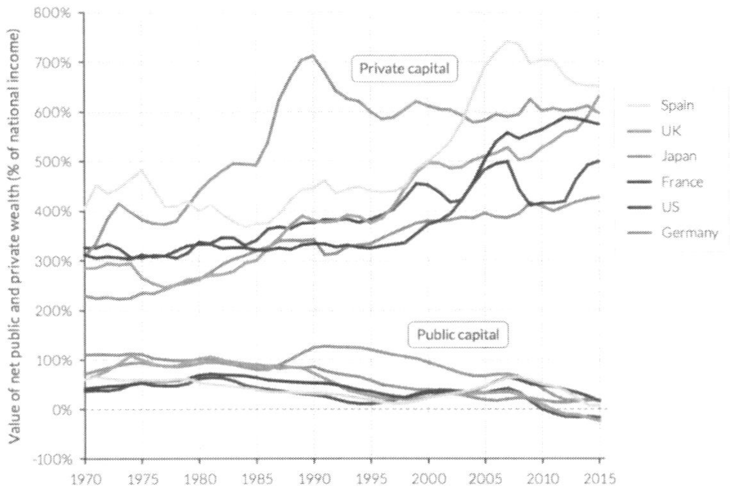

Source: World Inequality Report 2018.

Figure 1. The rise of private capital and the fall of public capital in rich countries, 1970–2016.

Accordingly, economic integration makes the nation state subject to international regulations and market mechanisms, and not just the one that regulates activities of others. What previously most often were national political questions about the rules for economic policy, has become also a commercial, legal and international question of what should and could be policy. At the same time, it is difficult to always make good supranational decisions to the benefit of all. National interests concerning degrees of autonomy and sovereignty, conflicting interests between and within countries, and inertia in markets give limitations to both the global system's and EU's ability to make good common decisions. One example is the scope of the euro-zone, where a single monetary policy appears unfit for those countries that are in rather different economic situations than a core country such as Germany. As countries in the euro area cannot anymore devaluate/depreciate their currency to repair for the loss of competitiveness and overspending, some of them (such as Greece) try internal devaluations (domestic wage and price cuts), strong austerity measures and borrowing money from the surplus euro economies and others. The result is destabilizing unemployment and strong distributional economic effects among persons, regions, governments and countries in Southern Europe and between the North and the South of the EU. While political ambitions made the euro-zone as large as it is, economic theory of an optimal currency area indicate that it should be smaller to work according to its premises.

EUROPEANIZATION AND GLOBALIZATION

Although a frequently used word, Europeanization is not a precise term to describe how countries integrate. Johan P. Olsen (2003:923-924) discusses five uses that should not be competing definitions, but rather understood as simplifying assumptions for a broader meaning. Robert Ladrech (2001:3) has defined it as "a set of processes through which the EU political, social and economic dynamics become part of the logic of domestic discourse, identities, political structures and public policies." The compatibility between EU and domestic policy has increased with structural convergence between institutions and policy (Cowles, Caporaso & Risse, 2001) but also through dynamic processes of adaptation. Globalization has similarly been defined as "norms, institutions, and laws that support global capital accumulation along neo-liberal principles" (Laxer 1995). The processes can lead to a "re-evaluation of interests, re-formulation of conflicting issues and adoption of new perspectives or knowledge" (Claes 2002:300). Hence, Europeanization and globalization have exerted an influence on legal matters, institutions, as well as on norms and ideology as a continuous process. In this context, the EU is a much stronger regime than the WTO, and especially the International Monetary Fund (IMF), giving countries less freedom of action in relation to EU rules and regulations than in the relation to the two global institutions.

At the same time the EU, being a confederation albeit with federal aspects, is weaker to make supranational decisions than a federation like the United States. Although EU policy is more liberal than the mixed economy established by European Keynesian Social Democrats in the post-war II period, it represents a form of mixed economy, rather than a rebirth of the laissez-era policy of the 19th century (no or few public interventions). Unlike in the 19th century, it seeks to reconcile the values of individual freedom and economic growth, with social justice and an even distribution of income. A government should allow markets to work freely if they meet key social goals, and to intervene if they do not. EU's liberal economic approach often allows markets to reach the goals where previously the public was directly involved, for example through state-run businesses and direct interventions. The goals in themselves do not necessarily need to be different, although markets and EU systems of unbundling of businesses, competition and regulations (market liberalization) set a number of boundaries and opportunities for what policy goals and policies can be.

How the EU can or will develop within this liberal paradigm is not obvious. There are more variants of a liberal economic system. Keynes, for example, was also a liberal, but an interventionist liberal, compared with today's dominant perceptions of the state's more neutral role in economic policy. As a variant within the interventionist liberal paradigm is Peter Hall and David Soskice (2001) "Varieties of Capitalism." They argue that there is more than one outcome and choice of policies within a liberal economic regime. John Ravenhill (2014:263) similarly states that «Globalization produces a variety of common pressures to which competing models of capitalism are differently exposed; this exposure tends to promote a dual process of convergence, accentuating the difference between liberal market economies and coordinated economies». Debates about the design of a liberal economic system and types of capitalism, as in Hall and Soskice, and Mjøset and Clausen (2007), shows that liberalism may not necessarily be orthodox. Different variants of economic liberalism must be compatible with the basic ideology of the EU system, albeit contrary to proposals for a change to a non-liberal economic system (such as in Elster and Moene, 1989).[3] Hence, how the EU develops dependsboth on situation, ideological perspective and it's evolution, and will help define the scope of action and political choices for the nation states, as well as for EU's overall economic developments.

Whether the EU will be able to make common decisions to the benefit of all depends on whether it represents a common European identity (common patriotism, desire for cooperation, common values), positions, interests and needs, to give it ability and legitimacy to control and decide over others. Is there such a European identity that enables the EU to represent all the inhabitants from north to south, from east to west? Will the diversity of the EU (language, culture, history and situations) strengthen or weaken its legitimacy and solidarity between member states? To answer, we need to look at its history. While in the 1950s and 1960s, only six countries were relatively similar in the Community, and homogenization of policies across nation states had much rationality. Now there are almost 30 countries that are more geographically dispersed and different. Income and wealth differences, internal migration, external immigration (refugees),

[3] The Norwegian tripartite cooperation is such an example, consisting of employers and workers organizations (called the parties) and the state. The cooperation mainly involves employment and wage issues, but may also affect other parts of the state's economic policy. The tripartite cooperation is often understood as corporatism as a political ideology or practice that gives organized interests systematic influence over social and economic developments. This includes a frontier model based on that wage growth must be adjusted to what international competing industries can afford. In this model, wage growth should not be much higher than by the trading partners, as it would weaken the competitiveness of national industries.

transnational investments and financial crises have contributed to weakening confidence in EU's ability to provide economic and social security and democracy for all. It has contributed to Brexit and other anti-EU turmoil. Currently, not only national economies, but also the EU is under pressure for change. The unrest in many countries, is not only about how the UK and other nation states are to adapt to existing EU law. Equally relevant is how such developments may change the EU. After euro crises, refugee crises and Brexit, it is more open how the EU is moving forward. Here are some alternative (simplified) scenarios:

1. *Muddling through.* The EU continues as now and improves incrementally existing policies in the Single Market and the euro-zone. If higher standards for taxation is established, it could help national governments to tackle inequality and welfare state expenditures. Otherwise, to be robust, this scenario assumes that the problems that have arisen are temporary.
2. *The FTA option.* The EU is gradually repositioning itself in a direction (albeit not fully) of a Free Trade Area (FTA). Migration is restricted within the SM, possibly also the free flow of capital, and the Eurozone is reduced in scope. A disintegration scenario opens up for bilateral agreements within the SM. More integration is postponed on the EU level, but not necessarily abolished for the longer future.
3. *Differentiated integration.* Formally, differentiated integration is accepted in a multi-speed model (forms of á-la-carte or in concentric circles). This complicates and weakens the EU, but issues such as external trade policy (the customs union) could be retained. If countries formally get the option of different forms of membership and not just as exceptions, more options could be developed than what is now simply called membership and non-membership.
4. *More federalism.* More integration, strengthening EU decision-making authority and introduction of a common fiscal policy. A common (or harmonized) fiscal policy can be used as counter-cyclical instrument, and transfers from strong to weak economies

(in practice from northern to southern Europe) could be possible at the European level. More integration requires more supranationality, and transfers of power to EU decision-making bodies, either from the nation states, or as direct taxation of citizens. France's President Emmanuel Macron has suggested ideas based on such ideas, but it does not least require support from German Chancellor Angela Merkel to be realized (and paid for).

Scenario 1 can be the outcome if the EU is unable to make decisions (except for the higher tax elements). It may involuntarily lead to scenario 2. Scenario 2, however, can also be chosen voluntarily. Along with Scenario 3, Scenario 2 represents an intergovernmental approach to EU developments. Both increase the degree of input democracy, but weakens the EU as a decision making body. Scenario 4, in turn, represents a neo-functional approach, where the EU is seeking to integrate itself out of the problems, as with the establishment of the Single Act in the 1980s and the SM in the 1990s. This increases the degree of output democracy.

Most likely, actual outcomes will be some combination of the four scenarios. Partly, what is perceived to be a reasonable, desired and likely development depends on whether one should place an intergovernmental or neo-functional perspective on what the EU is and should be. On this issue, different perspectives may exist among political and economic elites in the population of a country, in the population itself, organizations. A change of ideology may lead to a change in the weighting of preferences and the behavior of institutions, electorate and state structures. In Europe, most political parties, the public and many administrations did, for example, move their basically consensus-oriented social democratic and Keynesian interventionist economic ideology in the 1990s, in a direction that favors more (political "hands off") liberal solutions. This has, inter alia, resulted in a number of New Public Management (NPM) arrangements of unbundling of businesses, competition and regulations of public utilities and services. These include liberalization of markets for telecommunications and energy, privatization of publicly owned companies, in some cases privatization of health care, and more, combined with lower taxes and public spending cuts.

Views from constructivists and institutionalists can be added to this debate. Neo-functionalists and constructivists argue that merging of identities and preferences over time will increasingly lead to more political similarities across countries, and the transfer of power to common institutions to make it work, which is to the benefit of all. Intergovernmentalists and institutionalists explain, however, that resistance to economic integration and the policy converges needed to make such integration a reality remains, citing instances where nation-states and their domestic institutions resist and undermine the gradual transfer of power out of their domains. The bargaining and consensus-building techniques in international organizations are considered by these critics to be refinements of intergovernmental diplomacy where important domestic political autonomy is retained, rather than the ultimate transfer of power to a supranational entity. Nation states may see themselves served by changing the real content of the common policy through delays, innovative interpretation and implementation, and/or find compensatory domestic steps, or put forward new external requirements. Only when economic situations become common a common policy will work adequately, and a full political convergence can take place.

This is reflected in the differentiation of the EU. As the number of member states have increased and the competence of institutions has expanded, the same policy for all has become increasingly difficult to implement. Most Member States participate fully in the Single Market and the Economic and Monetary Union (EMU). However, many MS do not have the euro as its currency (like Sweden, Denmark), some have formal exceptions related to the SM (like the UK before Brexit), and many implement SM rules and regulations in de facto rather different ways. At the same time, among non-MS, some have the euro as its currency without participating in the SM (like Montenegro), and some participate almost fully in the SM (like the European Economic Area, EEA, countries). Turkey participate in EU's customs union, but not in the SM. While attempts to make transatlantic and external services agreements (like TTIP, GATS and TISA) have failed, comprehensive trade agreements are made (like with Canada). At the same time, some non-MS have mainly a WTO membership to regulate their economic relations with the EU (like Russia). With the exception that a few countries are still not members even of the WTO (like Belarus), there is a continuum in European economic integration for countries between being full members of both the SM and the EMU with the same de jure and de facto policy at the one extreme, and (only) a WTO-membership at the other. This continuum is a way of phrasing differentiated European economic integration as a normal state of affairs. For example, Brexit will most likely mean that the UK moves from one differentiated economic integration model with the EU, as a MS, to another differentiated model, as a non-MS. While the political change is significant, the economic difference between before and after may be small (soft Brexit) or quite large (hard Brexit).

Until 2016, much of the debates about global order were about structure and questions whether the United States should actively lead or retire from its hegemonic role in world economy and politics. This is still a theme. However, from 2016, attention has shifted from problems between countries to problems within countries. Populists challenge elites where the truth about the system is expressed as a social construction of the mighty. Many countries do not want the supranational governance that a tighter international regime will imply. The most powerful expression of this is Britain's decision to leave the EU (Brexit), and the election of Donald Trump as American president. The problem is that without a comprehensive international economic regime, countries with open economies will be ruled by international markets and commercial actors. Francis Fukuyama's argument in "The End of History and the Last Man" that Western liberal democracy can be the final form of man-made governance is heavily challenged. In order to create more stability, it is necessary that established political and economic parties and elites do more than to "rebrand" themselves and their ideas. The system must develop a policy that makes Europeanization and globalization more worthy for the interests of the middle and working classes to continue to evolve as a framework for strong welfare states for the majority.

VARIETIES OF POLICY-MAKING

Globalization, Europeanization and the expanding influence of international organizations continue to reshape national public administrations as well as international relations. The pressures for convergence at the supranational scale make the interplay between national and supranational preferences and priorities central. The dynamics of an international economic integration process indicate that lower level of integration pushes for higher levels of integration over time, and trading countries must become more alike in their policies if free trade is to work. Greater integration would speed up growth in a period of recession, but also reinforce the speed of structural change, as reviewed by the Organization for Economic Cooperation and Development (OECD) (2005). From a liberal economic perspective, cooperation is the best response to interdependence and achieving economic win-win solutions. Within single sectors, however, all countries and companies try to reap the benefit of trade in general, and to avoid the problems trade creates for own country/companies, to the disadvantages of other countries/companies. In strategic trade theory, the orthodox liberal understanding of the benefits of trade is replaced by a more interventionist approach, sometimes colored by realist/economic nationalist attitudes (Krugman 1988). Hence, the challenge for an integration process is to prevent unemployment in non-competitive sectors from growing too much when processes are developing rapidly. In such a situation, not only long- and short-term interests are confronted but also winners and losers from trade liberalization. Integration processes should, as a consequence, take time in order to give people, businesses and society time to adjust. The "rich" world has actually given itself half a century after WWII for this adjustment, while new market economies and developing countries are pressured for much faster adjustments.

At the same time, as interdependencies deepen it becomes increasingly more difficult for participants not to reach agreements that further integration. However, the more complex the situation becomes in scale and scope, the more difficult it will be to reach de facto comprehensive supranational arrangements, and as a result, the expansion of maneuvering rooms for national adaptation. International demands about the harmonization of political form and process, but not necessarily about political convergence, makes it possible for countries to have the same policy in terms of rules and regulations, but with rather different political content. In this context, Hirst, Thompson & Bromley (1999) argue that "there are still opportunities for the development of governance mechanisms at the level of international economy that neither undermine national governance nor hinder the creation of national strategies for international control." Europeanization and globalization create political convergence between countries, but different traditions and ideologies also retain divergences. The rules are interpreted, reformulated and implemented within political perspectives, ideology, traditions and path-dependences as continuous processes. Consequently, the effects of the international economy on domestic policy must be understood in the interaction between and relative weight of factors that affect policy. Institutional interests may tip the balance to be more important than economic interests in one situation; other times, institutions need to change due to changed production profile. Ideology can win over industrial policy and economic interests at one time, while exogenous changes in the international political economy may change ideology at another time. Government policies change gradually or abruptly depending on the type of regime (Austvik 2018: 426-430). In general, the principles of political convergence between countries in an economic integration process more clearly define long-term new deals and developments than in the short-term.

Paradoxically, the greater the degree of autonomy a country chooses in an economically integrated world, the less influence it will possess over its own situation. This is because international rules of competition and market mechanisms in many situations de facto may overrule (irrelevant) national decisions, and a country is increasingly "pushed around" and eventually forced to adapt. One extreme example is North Korea, wanting something close to autarky rather than economic integration with the world. The result is substantially lower economic standards, with the following need to close borders to prevent people from trade and/or escape, police control and an authoritarian regime. As a consequence, North Korea must (mostly) act reactively in their policy making to the outside world, albeit the country from time to time makes proactive (even though not always credible) threats. Eventually, the regime will most likely prove unsustainable. Another example is air transportation becoming increasingly cheaper as a form of technical, and not political, initiated trade liberalization. Domestic markets were earlier served by (protected) national airliners. Increasingly these have been subject to international competition. When the difference between domestic and international prices and quality of services have exceeded an acceptable threshold (to be defined), national air traffic policy has eventually converged across countries. A national air policy independent of international regulations is no longer sustainable.

Accordingly, the increased international economic interdependence and complexity of decision-making indicates that more, not less, albeit different, political competence is required for maintaining a maximal degree of national autonomy in comparison with the situation in the 1970s and 1980s, especially for small countries. This is important wherever in the continuum between the WTO and the SM/EMU for European and global economic integration a country positions itself. In this continuum, the choice between maintenance or a change of existing policy and economic and political structure depends on interests, traditions and values, and/or the active creation of visions and ideology. Transnational integration reshapes public administrations as well as international relations. Desires about common regulations are put forward, and administrations receive results they both like and dislike. In a neo-functionalist view, public managers, as in, for example, the EU Commission, are the driving force towards more integration. In an inter-governmental view the counter-parts are more often other nations and governments. Whatever is the reality and each country's desire, the actors relative competencies in economics, policy, politics and law are crucial to which extent national goals can be reached, some times individually, some times together with others.

CONCLUSION AND POLICY IMPLICATIONS

Europeanization and globalization is relatively new in a historical context. The first phase came with the industrial revolution and free markets in the 19th century. After strong setbacks and conflicts in the period 1914-45, the next major phase came with the new international regime after World War II. The third major phase came after the collapse of the Soviet Union in 1991, with the US as a continued global hegemonic superpower in a dominant liberal Western-controlled economic system. Ideologically, the system returned to the time when Adam Smith formulated his arguments about the primacy of the invisible hand of the market and David Ricardo about everyone's benefits from international trade, while Karl Marx and the planned economy is "out." What is special about the third phase is the strong economic growth, its global scope, the speed of change, and thus the strength and speed of the redistribution of income, power and influence that in recent years has created waves of reactions in Western democracies. Some of the political challenge lies in the fact that in democracies integration must be positive for a majority in order for the processes to be supported in elections. If it's not, politicians who want more nationalism get stronger support. In a democracy, voters will vote on other decision makers if they do not regard themselves as well served by the system as the elite manages. Acceptable distribution of income, and respect for the distributional effects that the modernization of societies causes, as for example outlined in Lipset and Rokkan (1967), are prerequisites for national, and thus also international, political stability, with internal and external security policy spillover effects.

Europeanization and globalization take place in parallel. The establishment of the liberal trade regimes (such as the WTO globally and EU regionally) can be seen as schemes similar to and after the French Revolution just over 200 years ago. While the economic integration at that time took place at national level in France, and thereafter between neighboring countries, it now takes place on continents and globally. Neither then nor now, are the benefits of economic integration gained immediately, but mainly after there has been time for readjustments of people and capital. Some manages and/or wants change quickly, some late, and some never. In periods, and to some extent also permanently, there may be strong conflicts of interest between different types of winners and losers in the processes. Experiences about setbacks in economic integration processes that did not manage such changes, have especially been seen in the late 1800s, and between the two world wars. Until 1870, world trade was virtually free, both in terms of products and input factors. Due to the depression following the war between France and Germany (1870-71), the countries chose a more protectionist line. In the interwar period, the same happened. The inter-war period stands out as the worst example of how things can go wrong if the international economic regime does not work.

The EU had also tendencies of disintegration in the 1970s and 1980s. Since non-tariff and hidden trade barriers were not affected by EC-agreement at the time, it was not in fact a complete Single Market, even though it was in the name. Failure to regulate domestic policy that affected competition made Member States introduce hidden barriers to trade as a substitute for the tariffs. However, rather than long-term disintegration, the solution ended up with more integration through the establishment of the internal market and the EMU. Today, the EU has problems again, in particular, the gap between northern and southern Europe is high. Distributional issues and migration are conflictual issues within countries. At the same time, world trade tends towards more bi- and regionalism than multilateralism under the WTO. The question is open again, in the tension between more integration in the form of a common fiscal policy as proposed by President Macron, and degrees of disintegration, as expressed by Brexit and other protests. From an orthodox liberal economic perspective, it can be difficult to understand these challenges. However, this is not only a question of finding the economically most rational first-best solutions in a market-liberal understanding, but also how values, power, influence and distributional issues are balanced. Politicians internationally have after the financial crisis/euro crisis accepted that the current economic system needs to be improved. However, this applies so far mainly to correcting "regulatory errors" more than "structural" challenges of the system. If the societies fail to cope with the distributional and social impacts of a liberal European and global economic order in an acceptable manner, more severe setbacks can take place

Today, international flexible capital make more money than more inflexible labor can from free movement of labor (WIR 2018). The effect of an inadequate international regime for international finance and taxation is that, today, we are seeing trends of strongly increasing income inequalities where capital owners receive an increasing share of economic growth. WIR2018 argues that «tackling global income and wealth inequality requires important shifts in national and global tax policies," including income as well as inheritance taxes. It suggests more transparency, progressive taxation, and that a "global financial register recording the ownership of financial assets would deal severe blows to tax evasion, money laundering, and rising inequality…While land and real-estate registries have existed for centuries, they miss a large fraction of the wealth held by households today, as wealth increasingly takes the form of financial securities." The strong focus on shareholder and stock market values, and a financial sector growing faster than the real economy, spread financial culture throughout society and make decision-making processes increasingly dependent on fast and global financial capital, with consequences for welfare and everyday life ("financialization").

Europe and the world need a functioning European and global trade regime as well as a better financial regime. The situation is different from in the 19th century and the interwar period, as the considerations that modern welfare states today have, given the social and distributional aspects of economic activity, as well as activity itself, were less important for policy, leading to subsequent unacceptable social and economic inequalities, and macroeconomic instability. The role of politics in both national and international economics was moderate and controversial. Today, although there is disagreement about degree and form, there is a consensus that the state has a role in regulating economic activity and the necessity of an international regime that makes predictable rules for the movement of goods, services and capital. This consensus made state interventions possible during the 2008 financial crisis and the euro crisis in 2010, as opposed to after the stock market crackdown in 1929. The Bretton-Woods conference in 1944, establishing the current system, sought to combine realism and liberalism from power relations which existed then. The search for new/revised Bretton-Woods regimes is due to gradually greater imbalances in this system, and because Western economic hegemony is challenged by the strong growth in countries such as China, India, and others. At the same time, any disintegration in Europe would weaken its external competitiveness and combined political influence. That can push higher forms of integration within the EU faster than the internal dynamics would have done without such an "external enemy." The situation can also lead to degrees of protectionism for the EU as a block towards low-cost countries, with the need to strengthen common trade policy. This may result in trade wars, for example between the EU, North America, China and others, for example, if the EU and/or the United States perceive Asian goods so cheap and of high quality that unemployment rises unacceptably.

However, even if one can expect backlashes and stagnation in European and global economic integration processes, it is hard to see that permanent disintegration is attractive to any country after industrial structures and labor markets have been adjusted to international markets and prices. The financial crisis in 2008, the euro crisis in 2010 and other shocks have shown that the system is not good enough today, which has aroused political will to adjust it, but so far not to a more fundamental revision. Crises are often the basis for major changes, as the chaos of the interwar period was a direct precondition for the Bretton-Woods agreement and a new economic order after WWII. As long as major crises are avoided, today's international economic system is likely to continue to a large extent as it is, with adjustments. Whenever possible, parties will seek to influence how the system works, and find creative adjustments to its own benefit, and to avoid disadvantages. A new major crisis could provide a basis for more fundamental reforms that better reflect real economic situations and new global economic powers. A breakdown in the international economy and society, similar to what the Second World War was an expression of, however, seems less likely in the mutually dependent world that has been established. In any case, it will be a test of the assumption that international economic integration, at least within the EU as the most advanced international economic integration area, creates such strong mutual dependence between countries that the system (in some form) as a common interest will survive.

These challenges are concerns both to the European and the global economic regimes, as well as to the nation states. For the EU, sectorial conflicts, and the balancing between short- and long-term interests, can make it difficult to continue integration at the pace neo-functionalists wants. An economic setback with a high unemployment can, to some extent, be helped by protectionist measures, internally as well as externally. The speed of adaptation to new markets and prices for manufacturers and workers indicate that this could be a reasonable strategy in certain situations. Any country wishing to reduce the effects of international markets or policy on the domestic situation can reduce its international exposure, using direct or hidden protectionist measures where possible. At the same time, a common macroeconomic stimulation policy, or one coordinated across EU Member States and/or globally, can also help the situation. Budget increases with higher taxes used to increase government expenditures across Member States would increase activity. Structural changes may take place more strongly and quickly, while protectionism will slow it down. Countries and parties may have different views on what is the best strategy. In a recession not only long-term and short-term economic interests are confronted, but also domestic winners and losers from free trade, and the visions of the EU as a neo-functional or intergovernmental regime.

REFERENCES

Austvik, Ole Gunnar, 2003: *Norwegian Natural Gas; Liberalization of the European Gas Market*. Oslo: Europa-programmet.

Austvik, Ole Gunnar, 2015: "Negotiating and Adapting Optimal Integration. Transnational Economic Integration and the Public Management Challenge." In: Kim, Ashley and Lambright (eds): *Public Administration in the Context of Global Governance*. Cheltenham: Edward Elgar Publishing. pp. 215-233.

Austvik, Ole Gunnar, 2018: *Europeisk integrasjon. Økonomi og politikk* [*European integration. Economy and Politics*]. Oslo: Universitetsforlaget.

Claes, Dag Harald, 2002: "The Process of Europeanization: Norway and the Internal Energy Market." *Journal of Public Policy*, 22, 3. pp: 299–323.

Cowles, Maria Green, Caporaso, James & Risse, Thomas, 2001: *Transforming Europe – Europeanization and Domestic Change*. Ithaca NY: Cornell University Press.

Dolowitz, David P. & Marsh, David, 2000: "Learning from abroad: the role of policy transfer in contemporary policy making." *Governance* 13. pp. 5–24.

Drezner, Daniel W., 2001: "Globalization and Policy Convergence." *The International Studies Review*, Volume 3, Number 1. pp. 53-78.

Esping-Andersen, Gøsta, 1992: *Three Worlds of Welfare Capitalism*. London: Polity Press.

Hall, Peter & Soskice, David, 2001: *Varieties of capitalism: the institutional foundations of comparative advantage*. Oxford: Oxford Uiversity Press.

Hirst, Paul, Thompson, Grahame & Bromley, Simon, 1999: *Globalization in Question* 3rd Edition. Cambride: Polity Press.

Krugman, Paul, 1988: *Strategic trade policy and the new international economics*. Cambridge MA: MIT Press.

Ladrech, Robert, 2001: "Europeanization and Political Parties: Towards a Framework for Analysis." *Queen's Papers on Europeanization*, no. 2. pp. x-x.

Laxer, Gordon, 1995: "Social Solidarity, Democracy, and Global Capitalism," *Canadian Review of Sociology and Anthropology* 32 (3): 287–313.

Lefeber, Louis and Thomas Vietorisz, 2007: "The Meaning of Social Efficiency." *Review of Political Economy* 19 (2): 139–164.

Lipset, Seymour Martin and Stein Rokkan, 1967: *Party systems and voter alignments: cross-national perspectives*. New York NY: The Free Press.

Mjøset, Lars and Clausen, Tommy H., 2007: *Capitalism compared. Comparative social research*, vol. 24. Amsterdam: Elsevier.

OECD, Organization for Economic Cooperation and Development, 2005: *Trade and Structural Change*. Paper. Paris: OECD.

Olsen, Johan P., 2003: “The Many Faces of Europeanization.” *Journal of Common Market Studies*, Vol. 40, pp. 921-952.

Piketty, Thomas, 2014: *Capital in the Twenty-First Century*. Cambridge MA: Harvard University Press.

Ravenhill, John, 2014: *Global Political Economy*. Oxford: Oxford University Press.

Train, Kenneth, 1991: *Optimal Regulation. The Economic Theory of Natural Monopoly.* MIT Press, Cambridge.

WIR2018, 2018: *World Inequality Report*. Paris: http://wir2018.wid.world.

In: Keynesian Policies
Editor: Noralv Veggeland
ISBN: 978-1-53614-026-2

Chapter 7

THE INSTITUTIONAL-ORGANIZATIONAL LEGACIES OF THE NEW DEAL: THE EXAMPLE OF TENNESSEE VALLEY AUTHORITY

Tor Helge Pedersen, PhD*

Inland School of Business and Department of Social Sciences,
Inland Norway University of Applied Sciences, Lillehammer, Norway

ABSTRACT

The Tennessee Valley Authority (TVA) was one of the most important organizations and symbols of the New Deal. The organization solved economic and social problems, and generated both new technological and organizational solutions. This chapter focuses on some of the organizational ideas that can be drawn from it, in other words, what is here called the institutional-organizational legacies. A special focus is devoted

* Associate Professor of Political Science, Inland School of Business and Social Sciences Inland Norway University of Applied Sciences. By education he holds a doctorate of political science from University of Tromsø. tor.helge.pedersen@inn.no.

to the Norwegian context and narrative. Examples of findings are: the idea of grassroots democracy had in TVA two forms; citizen participation and inter-governmental collaboration (e.g., partnerships), whereas the latter is almost a lost organizational legacy. In contrast, it is elements such as planning, regional development and, to some extent, other form of grassroots democracy that had dominated the Norwegian narrative of the TVA. This study also shows that studying these partnerships may teach us about organizational mechanisms for legitimization, as well as about coping with internal and external power realities.

Keywords: regional development, partnership, citizen participation, state intervention, grassroots policy, innovation

INTRODUCTION

The Tennessee Valley Authority (TVA), an enduring symbol of New Deal (Wildavsky 1961), was created in 1933 to provide for flood control, navigation, reforestation and proper use of marginal lands, electricity generation, and agricultural and economic development of the Tennessee River. It was a federal intervention aimed at improving economic and social conditions. As in other countries, in Norway too was it seen as an innovative agency, a democratic ideal, an example for solving economic and social problems with a plan built on democratic values (Brochmann 1945, 11), and as the most important result of Roosevelt's domestic policies (Getz Wold 1947, 5). Knut Getz Wold from the Norwegian Ministry of Social Affairs in 1947, also notes: 'TVA is the most important and lasting result of President Franklin D. Roosevelt's domestic policy. It has transformed the living conditions for the people in a large region. It is in more than one way a beacon for democracy in other countries' (Getz Wold 1947, 5, transl.). In later Norwegian literature, further positive statements can be found: 'TVA is possibly the most discussed project in the New Deal, both in research and as international prototype of regional development' (Kleven 2010, 30, transl.). This is also the case in the American and international literature: 'most extraordinary administrative invention' (Fitzgerald & Neuse 1984, 138); 'an affirmation of positive government intervention where free enterprise feared to tread' (Cole et al. 1984, 166); and 'one of the best-known symbols of American progress, ingenuity, technology, and organizing skills in the entire world' (ibid).

This chapter focuses on some of the institutional-organizational legacies of the New Deal, more precisely, the organizational ideas that the TVA as an example came to symbolize. Some examples can already here be mentioned: Through the organization form of public corporation, the TVA became a pioneer of a new and flexible way of organizing many functions, as well as representing an early case of the rise of unelected bodies (Vibert 2007). As a regional development authority or agency it is seen as the 'granddaddy of all regional development projects' (Scott 1998, 6). There had been suggestions of establishing many TVAs all over USA (Leuchtenburg 1952) as well as several TVA-inspired projects in other countries (Finer 1944; Dahir 1955; Cole et al. 1984; Ekbladh 2002).

As a multi-purpose program, it has been called a Keynesian inspired intervention. One typical interpretation is the following: 'Keynes had provided the model for economic reconstruction, Tennessee Valley Authority had shown how a large region could be lifted out of poverty through planned, state intervention' (Kleven 2011, 51, transl.). As an organization operating with a grassroots policy, TVA came to be connected with ideas such as citizen participation, democratic planning, bottom-up planning, and grassroots democracy. However, the grassroots policy had two aspects: the policy of channeling programs through existing institutions, and the policy of encouraging citizen participation (Selznick 1949). It is especially the former aspect about intergovernmental collaboration (e.g., partnership) that has gotten little attention in Europe, and particularly in Norway. Many of the intergovernmental – and often multilevel – collaborations TVA was engaged in, were called partnerships. This was the case in the different programs and this was the case with the regional development project – it was a regional partnership; 'The purpose is national, but the task is one that calls for a partnership of *every* agency of government, state and local as well as federal, that can further the common purpose' (Lilienthal 1944:118). Selznick (1949, 218) connected 'the concept of regional partnership' to the grassroots policy. He said that the vision of such a working partnership seemed to define the grassroots democracy at work, and 'In the Authority's view, the fundamental rationale of the partnership approach is found in its implications of democracy' (ibid, 37).

The chapter is further organized in the following way: first, we offer an introduction to the TVA as a case. Then I proceed, focusing on some of the organizational ideas that are connected to it. In addition to the technical inventions, TVA had made several contributions to the art of governance as an agency of regional administration. The last part of this chapter is devoted to the partnership idea, the overlooked part of the grassroots policy. In this part, I will explore partnerships in three program areas of the TVA – agriculture, water control and hydroelectric power – as well a regional development.

THE TENNESSEE VALLEY AUTHORITY CASE

The TVA was born in a burst of reforms (Wildavsky 1961). It was authorized by Congress, as part of the New Deal in May 1933, to promote – by its own effort and its example – the control, conservation and wise utilization of natural resources of the Tennessee Valley. The geographical area included all of Tennessee and parts of Alabama, Mississippi, Kentucky, Virginia, North Carolina and Georgia. It was to produce power and supply inexpensive electricity to predominantly rural areas. The TVA was further to manufacture fertilizer, control flooding, increase the utility of waterways (by building ports and widening channels), and build dams. Further, it was to uplift people with cheap electric power, jobs and prosperity.

The background was, as indicated earlier, solving economic and social problems caused by the depression (Finer 1944; Marx et al. 1946). The program was established to modernize a poor region, centered on dams that generated cheap electricity. However, it may be worth noting that it also represented a stage in the 'long fight for public control and operation of the water-power and nitrite-factory projects in the Tennessee River' (Gaus & Wolcott 1940, 76). Established as a public corporation, the TVA represented decentralization within the federal system, 'decentralization of Washington to Knoxville' (Dahir 1955, 15). Further, the TVA Act delegated to the board of directors full discretion to determine organizational structure, staffing, and personnel policies (Hobday 1969). Furthermore, the organization of the TVA was designed as decentralized. Decisions within TVA were to be made at the lowest reasonable level in cooperation with local organizations and citizens. In other words, local actors as agricultural-extension services were brought into the decision-making process. Delegation of authority permits different structures to develop within an organization (Selznick 1949), and one may say that Selznick showed how different types of delegation brought about a series of unanticipated consequences (March & Simon 1958).[1] For example, the position of the Agricultural Relations Department was reinforced 'by the theory of TVA central management which values decentralization within the Authority' (Selznick 1949, 114). TVA also represented decentralization in a world where the trend was centralization (ibid, 22).

TVA was established in an area in which local political agencies already existed – the states, the municipalities, the counties (Finer 1944), as well as representatives from different federal departments. The words Farm Bureau Complex have been used for the strong interests headed by the Land Grant Colleges, the more prosperous farmers represented by the American Farm Bureau Federation, and the Federal Agricultural Extension Service with its county agents (Gamson 1968). TVA could therefore not take its position for granted; 'It had to feel its way. This required the formulation of a policy that would reassure external elements and would so educate its own ranks as to maximize the possibilities of social acceptance' (Selznick 1949, 49). It had to adapt to its environment, an environment with strong conservative and vested interest. The TVA had to define its approach to agencies and institutions that already existed. 'The alternatives seemed to be two: either to take a line which assumed that the TVA itself could and should carry out its programs by direct action; or to accept as legitimate and efficient a method which would seek out and even establish local institutions to mediate

[1] In an earlier article, Selznick expressed his initial assumption: 'The ideals of those who construct the organization are one thing; the "facts of life" operating independently of and often against those ideals are something else again' (Selznick 1943, 48).

between the TVA and the people of the area' (ibid, 37). A decentralized internal organization must be understood in this context.

There were conflicts, both on the board and with external actors. McCraw (1971, 36) points out that when the TVA Act was signed, the 'battle in Congress was over, but the battle in the Valley had hardly begun.' A three-member board of directors was to make the decisions of how to organize and implement the language of the TVA Act (Hargrove 1987a); David E. Lilienthal (power), Harcourt A. Morgan (agriculture) and Arthur Morgan (the general engineering program). There was internal conflict over goals and programs (Selznick 1949; Lepawsky 1948; Colignon 1997), and there were legal attacks from outside, the first six years (Lepawsky 1948). The important achievements of the 1930s and 1940s were the production of electric power, navigation and flood control, and improvement in farming through new fertilizers and technical assistance (Hargrove 1987b). Lilienthal's early priority was the power production. Although not the inventor of it, he later becomes the speaker of the grassroots policy much repeated in the public rhetoric (Lambert 2015). In the 1940s, under Lilienthal's direction, the Authority had shifted its efforts from preserving the rural economy to fostering the growth of manufacturing (Schulman 1991). He now also presented it as a transformative, multipurpose, democratic experiment (Lambert 2015), with a larger mission as a planning agency, by emphasizing democratic planning by the people themselves (Wheeler & McDonald 1986). Lilienthal believed that organizations and publics could be mobilized by ideas – and he gave TVA a stable institutional identity (Hargrove 1987a).

Other New Deal organizations were formed in the period as well: The National Recovery Administration, the Soil Conservation Service, the Resettlement Administration, the National Planning board, and the Rural Electrification Administration. Here, it should be mentioned that the words Agrarian New Deal have been used referring to programs under the U.S. Department of Agriculture. In the 1930s, phrases like democratic planning and grassroots democracy were also employed in other New Deal agencies under USDA (Selznick 1949; Gilbert 2015).

The TVA was also controversial, especially over time. It evoked, for example, claims for being socialistic and unfairly competitive with private enterprises (Perrow 1970; Simon 2011). In the 1960s, it gradually abandoned the grassroots ideal (Schulman 1991). Our focus is mainly early period, when it was a global beacon. In its first years it was primarily a producer and distributor of electric power – a power company (Wildavsky 1961; Hughes 1989). It 'should have been called the Tennessee Valley Power Production and Flood Control Corporation' (Tugwell & Banfield 1950, 50). And when it later expanded its activity into different collaborations, studies of it identified unintended consequences. With vested, conservative interest on the board, the program favored white and wealthy farmers at the expense of poor Afro-American farmers (Selznick 1949; McCraw 1971; Lambert 2015:90). Further, the TVA came in conflict with other New Deal agencies, such as the Farm Security Administration and the Soil Conservation Service, two agencies chiefly concerned with low-income farmers. Furthermore, various policies that had been designed to protect the public interest against special private interests were reversed (Selznick 1949). Too much 'commitment to its agricultural constituency' resulted in that TVA failed to support other agencies created under New Deal (ibid, 263). The organized agricultural establishment held much influence over TVA's agricultural policies.

Selznick (1949) 'examined the design' of the TVA and 'depicted the processes that undermine rational design' (Scott 2014, 138). But Selznick did not deny that the TVA produced profound changes in the Tennessee Valley and contributed to the welfare of its economically deprived people – he just showed that these changes were not as far-reaching as planned. Selznick (1949, 265) concluded that 'the Authority has, on the whole, very effectively achieved some of its major purposes, including the mobilization of a staff of very high quality.' It was because TVA was an example of 'democratic administration that the evidences of weakness in this respect are so important' (ibid, 266). It was a success regarding its major purposes (Wengert 1951, 389; McKinley 1950, 613; Pritchett 1943, 210); 'probably the most impressive physical engineering project since the Panama Canal' (Pritchett 1943, 314). The project management was impressive (Wengert

1951; McCraw 1971). 'TVA's dams practically always ran ahead of schedule, a record unheard of in the private industry. Its labor relations were unbelievably good' (McCraw 1971, 144).

The Organizational Ideas of the TVA

The TVA (or the TVA idea) was comprised of several organizational elements (Selznick 1949; Wengert 1952; Neuse 1983; Ekbladh 2011). Wengert (1952) operates with concepts such as integration, resource development, decentralization, education and planning. Selznick (1949) describes the elements and simplifies them in the following way: 'these minimum essentials may be more clearly understood if they are examined as (1) the concept of managerial autonomy, (2) the partnership of TVA and local government, and (3) the ideal of basing unity of administration upon the natural unity of a region as an area of operation in resource development' (ibid, 29). Neuse (1983) operates with five essential components: regional development, decentralized administration, the active participation of the people of the valley in affairs of the authority, a strong sense of social responsibility, and a commitment to non-political policy-making. In this chapter, we will operate with the following elements: public corporation (federal corporation), unified regional development, a broad mission of regional development (multi-purpose program), democratic method (democratic planning), and a partnership idea.

Public Corporation

In connection with the creation of the TVA, Roosevelt and the Congress went for 'a corporation clothed with the power of government but possessed of the flexibility and initiative of private enterprise' (Roosevelt, quoted in Lilienthal 1944, 53). Lilienthal (1944, 154) also uses the term 'the regional development corporation,' and Selznick (1949, 29) connects it to the concept of managerial autonomy and decentralized administration. Others call it both a regulatory body and a public corporation with economic tasks (Meyer 1957). Although the New Deal is seen as one of the origins of public corporations (Walsh 1978), as well as the first rise of unelected bodies (Vibert 2007), we know that in the 1930s these organizations emerged in other countries as well (Meyer 1957; Hood & Jackson 1991). In fact, as far back as 1904, the Panama Railroad Company had been taken over by United States Government, that had continued to operate it, as remained a private corporation (Finer 1944; Marx et al. 1946; Aharoni 1986). In the UK, the public corporation was connected to so-called Morrison doctrine, first used to justify the way that the London Passenger Transport board was set up in 1933 (Gordon 1938; Hood 1988). We know that Keynes recognized the use of such autonomous bodies within the state (Keynes 1926, 313). The British Broadcasting Corporation (BBC) from 1926 is one such example. And finally, the idea of a corporate form was part of earlier suggestions to use the Tennessee River area, a part of the so-called Muscle Shoals bills dating back to 1919. Those who originally drafted these bills wished to establish an authority that at the same time was a corporation (Finer 1944; Hubbard 1961; Wirtz 1976). In the literature, several reasons for a corporate form can be found. It was to engage in activities typically performed by corporations, such as the production and sale of power and fertilizer (Wirtz 1976). Strategic considerations such as the importance of the waterway system is another reason, and here it is similarities with later cases in other counties where 'national oil companies were created' (Aharoni 1986, 99). A final reason is that a corporation afforded opportunity for regional decentralization and local autonomy in handling the many functions given to it (Pritchett 1937; Selznick 1949). However, Welborn (1984) has later pointed at the problems the corporate form contributed to over the decades. It became the enemy to the other elements.

Unified Regional Development

This element is about TVA as a regional development (and planning) project, and has been seen as the most important contribution to American reforms (Grantham 1983). According to Higgins (1995), Roosevelt regarded it as the first step toward a system of national planning. It was based on the 'ideal of basing unity of administration upon the natural unity of a region as an area of operation in resource development' (Selznick 1949, 29). 'The organization of the Tennessee Valley Authority is an example of this modern idea of regionalism' (Lilienthal 1944, 146). Other words used: unified regional development meaning a holistic approach (Neuse 1983); a regional development agency (Selznick 1949). The regional development element is further called a new model for social and regional planning (Ekbladh 2010), and it was hailed as a model for regional development throughout the world (Cole, Neuse & Sanders 1984). There was no prototype for the TVA as planner around 1938 (Pritchett 1943), but it is claimed that this was a successful element and 'maybe the most lasting contribution' (Lepawsky 1948, 564).

The element described above was a very important inspiration for plans made in the Norwegian Ministry of Social Affairs from 1945-46 (Mydske 1974) and in a public architect organization, BSR that came into operation in 1945 and was engaged in town planning and in reconstruction of burned-down places from World War II. The BSR and its leader Erik Rolfsen wanted to implement TVA-inspired planning in 1948, but it was never realized. However, the plan from the Ministry and Knut Getz Wold around regional (economic) planning arrangements came into operation in 1948, but was only loosely inspired by TVA.[2] In contrast to being highly inspired by it at the start (Mydske 1974; Bugjerde 1981; Thomassen 1997), the actual organizational design in 1948 was much less inspired by the TVA (Thomassen 1997). On the other hand, this was the start of regional policy in Norway. TVA as the most important inspirational source for Norwegian policy came to an end in the fall of 1951 (ibid), right before a new development program – the North Norway Plan – was adopted by the parliament (ibid). Even though this new program had no formal references to TVA, the implemented program had some similarities. One example was

[2] If we read Getz Wold (1947), we can observe that he pays some attention to the department of regional planning in TVA.

that the thematic integration of the North Norway program had similarities with the integrated planning that was conducted by the TVA (ibid, 259).

A Broad Mission of Regional Development

Usually, organizational researchers associate novelty with organizational forms, technology or products. However, the purpose or mission of an organization may also be novel. Lilienthal himself pointed out that there was nothing particularly novel about the individual tasks entrusted to it. 'The new thing about TVA was that one agency was entrusted with them all, and that no one activity could be considered as an end in itself' (Lilienthal 1944, 53). In other words, it is the broad mission that is novel – a multi-purpose program – a broad mandate for regional development, but the statute assigned specific responsibilities to build dams, create and distribute electric power, improve navigations and flood control, and assist agriculture, in part by manufacturing fertilizer (Hargrove 1987b). It was also meant to preserve forest and carry out reforestation, help farmers (especially poor ones) and develop recreation areas. 'The TVA embodied the type of reform that molded economic growth with social change and a flexible style of planning' (Ekbladh 2011, 47), with a 'strong sense of social responsibility' (Neuse 1983, 493), 'an example to solve economic and social problems with a plan built on democratic values' (Brochmann 1945, 11, transl). Its mission made TVA different from other public corporations as well as other organizations.

It took a few years before it became a multi-purpose program and regional planning started in 1938. Before that, it was power production, navigation and flood control that dominated (Wengert 1951). It has been remarked that regional planning became more important when it was necessary for the TVA leadership to promote an 'organizational myth' that kept the Washington politicians and bureaucracies at arm's length (Hargrove 1987b). However, the leaders and the dedicated people in the TVA believed the myth too (ibid). The broad mission of regional development was addressed only through the authorization of planning studies (Hargrove 1987b).

Democratic Method

This element is about democratic planning and citizen participation. The TVA was, according to Neuse (1983, 983), about 'the active participation of the people of the Valley in affairs of the authority.' And Selznick writes the following about the democratic elements in the regional partnership: 'In this way, the farmer or the business man finds a means of participating in the activities of government supplemental to his role on election day' (Selznick 1949, 40). Lilienthal (1944, 78) uses words as 'region-building at the grass-roots.' This component was the first pillar or form of the grassroots approach (ibid; Tugwell & Banfield 1950). Grassroots democracy was at that time not unique to TVA. According to Tugwell and Banfield (1950), other departments and agencies were following the TVA in adopting grassroots planning. Selznick (1949) mentions that other New Deal agencies, under the U.S. Department of Agriculture, were already working in that way. It was Lilienthal that extracted the grassroots idea and developed it into a general philosophy (Hargrove 1987), and he connected to regional planning which started in 1938 (Lepawsky 1948). Lilienthal (1944, 78) claims that they were, already from the outset, aware that regional development 'could become a reality if and only if the people of the region did much of the planning, and participated in most of the decisions' (Lilienthal 1944:78).

Although the TVA model was not selected in the design of the Norwegian regional planning arrangements in 1948, other TVA ideas took hold in Norway. For example, it was much later claimed that despite setbacks in different contexts, 'the idea of bottom-up regional planning was not at all dead' (Kleven 2011, 38, transl.), in other words, one of the forms of grassroots policy that was about participation. Harvold (2002) has pointed out that the debate about communicative planning in the 1990s reflected – or had similarities – with ideas of TVA and Lilienthal. TVA also came to be the common inspirational source of two different (and opposing) planning traditions and planning forms right after the war; the physical planning (i.e., architecture) and regional (economic) planning (and development) represented by regional planning from 1948 (Mydske 1974, 76; Thomassen 1997, 197ff; Kleven 2011, 34). One may say that the two main planning traditions, even today, have a common inspirational source in the TVA (ibid). This element was about how the process should proceed, with participation from citizens.

The Partnership Idea

In much of the American literature on TVA, the term partnership is used for different examples of intergovernmental collaboration, but sometimes also in cases of TVA-private contracts or collaboration (e.g., Neuse 1996, 154; Lambert 2015, 85). There are also those who use other terms such as 'contractual relationship,' 'contract,' 'arrangement,' 'agreement' and 'contractual collaboration' (e.g., Gaus & Wolcott 1940; Finer 1944). Partnership, a form of intergovernmental (and often multilevel) collaboration, was the other pillar or form of the grassroots policy (Selznick 1949; Tugwell & Banfield 1950). In connection with TVA, partnerships were present on two levels: the regional level (Pritchett 1943; Lilienthal 1944; Selznick 1949) and the program level. When it comes to the program level of TVA, Lilienthal (1944) uses the term partnership in several places, and he writes that the device for these partnership relations is the written contract. He also points out that these 'contracts are more than a definition of legal obligations. They constitute, too, expressed agreements on common purposes, often defined in broad terms' (ibid, 119). Lilienthal mentions that there were 'hundreds of such formal contracts between the TVA and every manner of public institution in the Valley, ranging all the way from county library boards to state universities and the highway and conservation commissions' (ibid, 119). He writes that the 'scope of these partnership arrangements is broad and their content as richly varied as the valley's life itself' (ibid, 119). As we will come back to later, there are many examples of partnerships on program level (Lilienthal 1944; Selznick 1949; Clapp

1955). Avery (1954, 10) mentions a partnership in 'the program of malaria control.' Lilienthal describes one organized around industrial research and one in power production. The former partnership agreement on research was a new method of utilizing resources; 'Instead of our setting up entirely new facilities and personnel, this work, wherever possible, has been carried on in partnership with state university engineering or agricultural research department' (Lilienthal 1944, 123). A second partnership example here, focusing on power production and distribution, is described by Lilienthal as 'Now one of the largest power producers in the world, it presents the picture of a joint enterprise of the federal government and hundreds of local communities in six states' (ibid, 125). Selznick reports that in 1943 power was being sold to 83 municipalities and 45 cooperatives, as well as to such large industrial consumers as Alcoa (Selznick 1949). Examples that will be discussed are also partnerships in distribution and sale of electric power (Selznick 1949; Hobday 1969), agriculture (Selznick 1949; Clapp 1955, Sayre 1949; Wirtz 1976), and areas such as navigation, flood control and stream regulation (Roberts 1955).

Organizational Legacies: A Summary

First of all, the components presented above have similarities with what today are studied and sorted under different types of public innovation, to mention a few examples such as organizational innovation (Pope et al. 2006), participatory democratic innovations (Kramer 1969; Geissel & Joes 2013). For example, the broad mission of TVA, is close to what De Vries et al. (2016, 153) call governance innovation, the 'development of new forms and processes to address specific [or several] societal problems.' Next, we have seen that TVA was much referred to in the Norwegian reconstruction debate after World War II (Thomassen 1997). The idea of regional development (and planning) is probably the most important in a Norwegian narrative. It inspired the emergence of a new policy area – regional policy – as well as much planning literature and traditions where the inspiration is mentioned in some of the planning literature (Bugjerde 1981; Thomassen

1997; Kleven 2011). More generally, the American planning ideal's had stronger influence on Norwegian society planning than the British the first 10-15 years after the war (ibid); 'Much of the professional inspiration for reconstruction of Norway after the war came from Keynes' new economics and from Roosevelt's New Deal, especially TVA' (Kleven 2011:29-30, transl., see also Thomassen 1997:76ff). Later studies within Norwegian planning, has seen the idea of democratic planning as a precursor of communicative planning (Harvold 2002).

The idea of public corporations has been little discussed in the Norwegian interpretations of TVA. This idea was about autonomy from Washington, and Getz Wold (1947), found such decentralization, as well as the internal decentralized organization of TVA, to be too radical for Norway (Getz Wold 1947). On the other hand, there may not be large differences between an autonomous agency and a public corporation (Lilienthal & Marquis 1941; Finer 1944), since the 'nature of every public corporation is determined in each particular case by the legislature' (Finer 1944, 113). Selznick used the words authority or agency, but did not pay much attention to this idea in his study; 'The relation of the Authority to federal government – is not directly relevant' (Selznick 1949, 29n). Finally, it should be noted that in the Nordic countries the rule was publicly owned (joint stock) companies and not public corporations (Meyer 1957). For example, when the idea of industrial estates was adopted from UK to Norway, the policy-makers omitted the public corporation element of the original British arrangements.

Even though Eisenhower was an opponent of the TVA and saw it as 'creeping socialism,' ironically, at least the partnership principle became a part of his domestic policy, both as public-private partnerships (Wildavsky 1962; Hargrove 1994; Wheeler & McDonald 1986; Van Dusen 1974; Daynes & Sussman 2010), and public partnerships (Hargrove 1994; Wheeler & McDonald 1986; Clapp 1955a). Eisenhower expressed 'that partnership' was what he favored 'in general for new projects' (Wildavsky 1962:17). But as we know, 'TVA and the states exemplified this method and sought this goal for twenty years' (Clapp 1955, 72). However, the Eisenhower administration had another purpose with the partnerships – 'to shrink the role of Federal government' (Van Dusen 1974, 286); 'Eisenhower's approach was to ensure that federal expenditures were limited and his preference was to see public-private partnerships prevail' (Daynes and Sussman 2010, 123). So we also see that the partnerships principle was used in different ways by the TVA and the Eisenhower administration of the 1950s – and partnerships have in later decades proliferated in American public sector (Kettl (2002). Partnership is an organizational element that is absent in the Norwegian literature on TVA. The word partnership – or a Norwegian translation of the term – is not to be observed in the early Norwegian literature (i.e., Brochmann 1945; Getz Wold 1947; White paper 1952:69) as well as in the later literature (Lorange 1977; Thomassen 1997). A later example is the special edition on partnership in the Norwegian journal Plan (2/2002), has no references at all to TVA. For example, Getz Wold (1947) who is, both in writing and in practice, one of the most important Norwegian 'translators' or mediators of TVA, leaves out partnership in both these regards. He uses other words and descriptions such as contracts about cooperation (ibid, 37), leaving partnership – 'å samvirke' (ibid, 36), 'samarbeide' (ibid, 46) – out. This is also the case with Brochmann (1945), which is more or less a translation of, the book of Lilienthal (ibid, 88, 99).

In the coming sections more focus will be given to partnerships. The most important study here is Selznick, much because he has developed of these elaborated theoretical concepts to analyze these partnerships. Selznick says that he was primarily concerned with 'the TVA's relation to local institutions, as expressed in the implementation of the grass-roots policy' (Selznick 1949, 29n), and he later points out that 'relatively little attention has been paid to the mechanics of its implementation and certainly the experience of other organizations facing the same problems and using voluntary associations has not been seriously studied inside the Authority' (ibid, 219n). His primary focus was on the program of test demonstration farm (distributing fertilizer to farmers) – but he also paid attention to activities such as improving crop-production facilities, organizing rural electrical cooperatives, conservation work, particularly in connection with forestry. In other words, Selznick did not deal directly with functions as generating electrical power, producing fertilizer and flood control.

PARTNERSHIP AS INTERGOVERNMENTAL COLLABORATION

As concluded above, the partnership idea was overlooked in the Norwegian literature about TVA. Before proceeding, we have to mention one important distinction between commercial partnerships and public partnerships: different commercial partnerships are old organizational forms (Weber 1889). The medieval commenda, societas maris and compagnia were historical precursors to later commercial partnerships or firms. For example, the societas maris was a historical precursor to both the modern limited partnership in American venture capital and the Norwegian KS Limited Partnership in shipping.

What one in public administration calls (public) partnership is also old, and older than the collaborative forms in TVA. In fact, the directors of the TVA were aware of that. For example, Lilienthal (1944, 118-9) pointed out that the TVA had not invented the partnership device, and other federal agencies were moving in that direction. Nevertheless, TVA was one early example of intended use of partnerships. Some of the many examples that Lilienthal mentions are: field tests of crop-bearing trees; development of county recreational parks; work toward specific cure for malaria; establishment of woodland wildlife refuges; forest-fire protection; housing; stream pollution and industrial water supply problems; industrial research in flax processing; invention of farming devices – 'hundreds of joint enterprises, great and small' (Lilienthal 1944, 119-20). Selznick (1949, 39) mentions examples such as 'municipal power boards, rural electric cooperatives, schools and library boards; state departments of health, conservation, and parks; state and local planning commissions, agricultural and engineering experiment stations, state extension services and others.' Also, Clapp (1955a) discusses several examples of partnerships: the partnerships land-grant colleges, the state agricultural extension services, and experiment stations as well as those focused on forestry, regional research, and electric-power distribution.

The partnerships had, in many cases, contracts or agreements. Lilienthal (1944, 119) mentions hundreds of 'such formal contracts between TVA and every manner of public institutions in the Valley.' Selznick (1949, 39), in the section about partnership, also writes that 'a list of agencies with which the TVA has maintained some form of cooperative relationship includes nearly all of the governmental institutions in the area' and that the 'form of cooperation with state and local agencies varies, but the pattern of intergovernmental contract has been fully developed.' Lilienthal points out the following about contract, bilateral contract (and partnerships): 'Instead of abstract talk about "co-operation" between local and federal agencies, the device of the contract encourages considerations of specific issues under existing conditions, but within a broad framework of the common purpose of strengthening the region' (Lilienthal 1944:119).

Different partnerships are, in other words, mentioned by Lilienthal, Clapp and Selznick. Referring to earlier studies (Roberts 1955; Hobday 1969), Gordon (1984, 197) points out that 'the incidence of intergovernmental cooperation between TVA and other Valley governments has varied inversely with the degree of centrality of responsibility under the TVA Act.' He also notes 'that in virtually all areas outside the central responsibilities there has been at least some significant intergovernmental cooperation' (ibid, 197). Wirtz (1976, 608) points out that the 'question remains whether these relationships are best characterized as "partnerships" or as something more feudal.' Willbern (1956, 885-6) points out that in the areas such as recreation, forestry, agriculture and city planning, the patterns of partnership were easier and more effective. Hargrove (1994, 107) writes that subsequent 'history would show TVA acting on its own, often in opposition to public opinion in the valley but secure its statutory mandates. This is not to deny the many real partnerships that were formed and continued.' The different partnerships functioned in different ways. In the 1950s TVA was in public-private partnerships, encouraged to do so (Wildavsky 1962; Wheeler & McDonald 1986; Hargrove 1994), but in the power field it was difficult since TVA was an existing institution with powerful political support (Wildavsky 1962). However, it can be debated whether TVA established some sort of public-private partnership with Alcoa already in 1941. Lilienthal (1944, 107-8) does not use the term partnership about this contract and arrangement, but in later literature on Lilienthal we can observe that Lilienthal wrote that 'TVA was virtually into partnership with a huge concern (…) So far as I know, there is nothing like that anywhere in America' (Lilienthal quoted in Neuse 1996, 154; see also Lambert 2015, 85). This assessment is seconded by an Alcoa historian (Neuse 1996, 154). We shall now look at some examples.

The Regional Development Program and the Regional Partnership

As seen earlier, TVA has been called a regional partnership between different institutions and actors (Lilienthal 1944; Selznick 1949; Neuse 1983; Pritchett 1943; Clapp 1955a). Clapp (1955b, 8) mentions federal, state, local governments, cooperatives, other organizations, individuals, and calls it 'The Grand Partnership.' This represented something really novel (Pritchett 1943; Clapp 1955a; Pincus 1945; Selznick 1949) about development of resources. Lilienthal (1944) describes the regional development project as a partnership, and he later claims that they were inspired by Dewey ideas: 'we have taken to heart and sought to put into practice' (ibid, 182).[3] Clapp (1955a) notes the novelty in this federal-state partnership in resource development, and points out regarding the TVA Act that, 'For the first time an administrative agency was created with the

[3] Lilienthal's (1944, 182) claim of inspiration by ideas of Dewey may be supported by studies of the Agrarian New Deal under U.S. Department of Agriculture; 'In fact they drew ideas and inspiration directly from Dewey,' 'instituted key aspects of Dewey's democratic philosophy' (Gilbert 2015,5).

instructions to promote actively a federal-state relationship for regional development along lines more recently spoken of as partnership' (ibid, 73).

Selznick (1949, 37ff) devotes a section to the partnership of TVA and the people's institutions; 'all the agencies concerned with and essential to the development of a region's resources: the local communities, voluntary private organizations, state agencies, and cooperating federal agencies' (ibid, 37). The idea of such a working partnership seemed to define grassroots democracy at work, and the rationale of this 'approach is found in its implications of democracy' (ibid, 37). Finally, the idea of the partnership in regional development was also that 'the farmer or the businessman finds a means of participating in the activities of government supplemental to his role on election day' (Selznick 1949, 40).

Referring to this connection Lilienthal (1944, 118) also talked about 'grass-roots policy of drawing in private organizations and individuals – such as those of farmers, workers, and businessmen.' And he wrote earlier about 'the unique strength of democratic method' for 'stimulating and releasing the individual resourcefulness and inventiveness' (ibid, 77). Selznick, on the other hand, saw in this form of cooptation the rise of calculated bureaucratic strategy.[4] Selznick (1949) connected participation (as one form of the grassroots policy) to formal cooptation, and pointed out that such participation in administration was limited to the sharing of administrative burdens under the label of democracy (ibid, 220). As he pointed out, 'It is easy enough for administrative imperatives which call for decentralization to be given a halo' (ibid, 220), and he continues, saying one cannot 'overlook that pattern which simply transforms an unorganized citizenry into a reliable instrument for the achievement of administrative goals' (ibid, 220). Actually, Selznick formed a hypothesis: 'cooptation oriented toward legitimization or accessibility will tend to be effected

---

[4] Selznick (1949, 13) gives the following definition of cooptation as a mechanism of adjustment: 'coöptation is the process of absorbing new elements into the leadership or policy-determining structure of an organization as a means of averting threats to its stability or existence.' Selznick's notion of co-optation is rooted in the assumption that organizations must either formally or informally adapt to the power realities contained within themselves and their environment.

through formal devices' (Selznick 1949, 260). Participation under the slogan of democracy may be an organizational mechanism for legitimization.

The Agricultural Program

The partnership in this program has also been connected to regional development (Ruttan 1983). We can here talk about partnership as adapting to external power realities: according to Wengert (1952), who also studied the administration of the agricultural program, TVA could have carried it (fertilizer, water control on land) out alone through direct action as Arthur Morgan wanted. Harcourt Morgan wanted a partnership with 'the seven land grant colleges of the TVA states, and the extension services of the U.S. Department of Agriculture' (Dahir 1955, 25). The partnership in the agricultural (farm) program that Selznick studied was about power sharing and can be connected to the theoretical concept of informal cooptation, suggested by Selznick. As mentioned, Harcourt Morgan was in 1933 assigned supervision of all matters relating to agriculture (and the Agricultural Relations Department), including agricultural industries and rural life, as well as of the chemical engineering program (ibid). One of his crucial policy decisions was that TVA should work through the existing land-grant colleges, and county extension agent systems in the Valley – made possible because of his alliance with Lilienthal in conflict over policy with Chairman Arthur Morgan (Colignon 1997). Selznick explains:

> 'Thus the Authority's power to exercise discretion in relation to the broad fertilizer and soil conservation program was concentrated in the hands of the former president of the University of Tennessee' (Selznick 1949:92).
>
> 'As we have seen, the first major act of discretion exercised by the Authority in relation to its agricultural responsibilities was the establishment of cooperative relationships with the land-grand colleges in the Valley. Concomitantly, it was necessary to decide whether the fertilizer program of the Authority would revolve around the production of nitrates' (Selznick 1949:98).

It was especially the partnership with the land-grant college, and colleges and county agent of the U.S. Department of Agriculture, that Selznick (1949) studied and found unanticipated consequences.[5] These existing interests (and the Farm Bureau Federation), especially the land-grant college, took control over the farm program (agricultural program).[6] The cooptation of leaders (e.g., Harcourt A. Morgan) from the Farm Bureau complex into the three-man board was justified under the grassroots policy, which emphasized partnership with local groups in the region. Through cooptation and these partnerships, TVA adapted to powerful agricultural interests to achieve backing for the agricultural program (Selznick 1949) – 'deliberate surrender of TVA's agricultural programs' (Lambert 2015, 90). In addition, these partnerships reduced congressional opposition of TVA in Washington, and in the Valley to other TVA programs, for example, the public power program. However, it is also claimed that Harcourt Morgan's 'agricultural program made considerable contributions to southern agriculture' (Colignon 1997, 157).

Selznick (1949, 262) argues that 'the grass-roots theory became a protective ideology' allowing that one of its major programs has been delegated to an administrative constituency; 'By adopting the grass-roots doctrine the Authority was able to stand as the champion of local institutions and at the same time to device a point of view which could be utilized in general justification of its managerial autonomy within the federal system' (ibid, 262). It was to justify managerial discretion and keep the legitimacy of its program (Lambert 2015). But the 'translation of it into policy commitments, has created serious dissatisfaction between TVA and other branches of federal government' (Selznick 1949, 262).

When the men from the vested, conservative interests were appointed to its board of directors, TVA gradually also adopted the values of these interests; the policies became increasingly conservative and removed from New Deal principles. For example, the TVA created a special relation to the Farm Bureau Federation. Selznick mentions that the 'traditional partnership of the extension service and elements of the American Farm Bureau

---

[5] In contrast to citizen participation, which was about formal cooptation (Selznick 1949).
[6] This organized agricultural establishment is also called the Farm Bureau complex.

Federation raises the question of the extent to which a similar relationship has prevailed between the Farm Bureau and the TVA' (ibid, 141). Later he writes that 'the Farm Bureau used the extension service system as its organizational weapon' (ibid, 158). The bureaucratization set in after this cooptation, and Crozier compares it to Roberto Michels' (1915) findings in his 'Political Parties' study; 'it shows the development of bureaucratic oligarchy behind the veil of democratic procedure' (Crozier 1964, 180). There were unintended consequences involving discrimination, for example, of poor and Afro-American farmers. Further, there were conflicts with other New Deal agencies (Farm Security Administration and Soil Conservation Service) in the late 1930s. 'This resulted in the politically paradoxical situation that the eminently New Deal TVA failed to support agencies with which it shared a political communion, and aligned itself with the enemies of those agencies' (Selznick 1949, 263; see also McCraw 1971, 141-2). Selznick formed a hypothesis that; 'Cooptation which results in an actual sharing of power will tend to operate informally' (Selznick 1949:260). What we learn from Selznick's (1949) study is that cooptation is an organizational mechanism for adapting or adjusting to power realities.

The Water Control Program and the Power Program

The selected cases here are examples of partnerships as symbol and legitimization. The partnerships in the water control program were partnerships (with the states) in the areas of navigation (four cases), power distribution and regulation (four cases), and flood control (two cases). Roberts (1955) studied ten cases of federal-state relations and he started out remarking that Lilienthal and other TVA officials had left key questions regarding partnership unanswered; for example, what 'are the terms of the partnership agreement?' (ibid, 14). Later in his study, he pointed out that the pattern 'which emerges from these events is not one of partnership, nor of continuing interaction between levels of government in working out joint policy, nor of shared responsibility. It is a pattern of firm federal control of basic programs under accountability to the Executive and the Congress'

(Roberts 1955, 90). He further pointed out that the 'TVA has been free to execute its tasks alone' (ibid). There was no good reason why TVA should share these programs with the states (ibid). Roberts also finds that there was no good reason why TVA should share these programs with the states. After all, this was an area with tradition for exclusive federal operation or dominant jurisdiction. Roberts (1955, 93) called the final chapter of his study 'the myth of partnership' and concluded that they were more hierarchical; a 'myth of partnership' had been built around federal-state relationship in the Tennessee Valley. And in questions such as, for example, how to control the river and what to do about navigation facilities, the TVA did not 'partner' with the states.

The second example from the power program, and most emphasized here, is the partnerships around (distribution and) sale of electricity. This or these partnerships, were according to Lilienthal (1944, 125) the most 'far-reaching instance of grass-roots partnership between local agencies and the TVA' (ibid, 125), and 'it presents the picture of a joint enterprise of the federal government and hundreds of local communities in six states, and the reliance for power of more than four million people' (Lilienthal 1944, 125). As one of the later chairmen of the board, also in a positive tone, writes about what he calls a 'Federal-local partnership for Electric Service' (Clapp 1955a, 81), and 'the outstanding example of a true partnership' (ibid, 81); 'The most obvious example of partnership, of course, is the generation and distribution of electricity' (Clapp 1955b, 8). In these partnerships (between TVA, local power boards and municipal governments), TVA owned and operated the generating and transmission facilities, and the local units owned and operated the distribution facilities.

Hobday (1969) also studied these partnerships in the power program both before and after World War II. In contrast to Lilienthal and Clapp, he argued that the rhetoric of partnership was overblown: 'In reality, the contractual relationships between TVA and its municipal distributors fail to meet the partnership test' (ibid, 233); the partnership between the TVA and local governments tended rather toward superior-subordinate relationships rather than a partnership (ibid, 233-4). He could refer to power board members that claimed, 'We are just the lackey of TVA' (ibid, 234). He thus concluded, 'If the status of full partnership is ever to be attained, considerably more give-and-take than has been manifested by TVA in the past will be needed' (ibid, 243). He said that the 'idea of the TVA and the municipalities as partners tends to break down under scrutiny,' because the contract actually left little room for 'discretion by local power systems' (ibid, 233). He even claimed that there existed an 'arm's length' policy (ibid, 38, 158); 'An important part of TVA doctrine holds that municipalities should place their electric system under power boards, thereby removing them from political and other undesirable influences emanating from municipal governments' (Hobday 1969, 236-7). This argument has later been repeated and supported by McCraw (1971), appointing local power boards was 'hardly implying faith in democracy from the bottom up' (ibid, 143), and 'was hardly grass-roots democracy, as Lilienthal suggested' (ibid, 143). In other words, Hobday had a different view than Lilienthal. Lilienthal (1944:123) talked about 'the importance of electricity distribution in the hands of non-political boards made up largely of men with business experience.'

However, Hobday (1969, 33) also finds that 'despite its limitations, the partnership idea was sound because of TVA's need for local support for its program, as seen in the popular support Lilienthal mobilized during the fight with the private utilities; 'the people of the Valley have aided the Authority in its battles with the private lobby in Congress and elsewhere' (ibid). Local distributorship was probably important for political survival and it was Lilienthal that refused the idea of TVA taking care of the distribution function alone 'because he thought the public lacked confidence in the utility industry because of its bigness and remoteness from control' (Hargrove 1994, 55). This must be understood in its historical and policy context. Lilienthal was an anti-monopolist (Colignon 1997), since 1933, he had 'combated threats from both private utility interests and threats from Washington actors to its autonomy' (Lambert 2015, 87), been in bitter fights with private electrical companies, over who should deliver power and at what rates. As Wildavsky writes, 'There is little doubt, however, that continued successful operation of the TVA power system – a living model which might be applied elsewhere – has had a chastening effect on neighboring utilities' (Wildavsky 1962:9). In other words, the partnerships here were about legitimacy, a protective, necessary myth. It is important to note that these partnerships Hobday studied, could have easily been carried out by TVA alone. Also described by Getz Wold without using the word partnership: this is in accordance with the TVA system's attempt to decentralize most of the activity and decisions (Getz Wold 1947). Both these examples above are about TVA ideology and symbols that held Washington politician and bureaucracies (as well as critics) at arm's length. Selznick (1949) uses the word ideology in several places, also as a synonym to doctrine. Later, in 1957 he uses the word myth – and talks about 'that leaders should understand that myths are necessary' and 'create organizational conditions that will sustain' the myth (Selznick 1957, 151). But what we also learn from the TVA case is that ideology is an organizational mechanism for legitimization – a way of adjusting to institutional forces. And as Hargrove (1994, 107) using the word myth, has remarked: 'One must believe that TVA officials were not cynics. They believed the myth, too.' As also pointed out by Selznick in connection with the grassroots policy: 'Whether or not the TVA had developed the grass-roots theory, it would have found it necessary in some way to get along with those forces which might wreck the program if moved to resistance' (Selznick 1949:55). As concluded by Tugwell and Banfield (1950, 49); 'For what was traded for democracy in the valley was support of a sort for the power program.'

CONCLUSION

Although TVA was not directly imitated in Norwegian development programs after World War II, it was a driving force and the origins of ideas that came to take hold in Norway. One example is the idea of bottom-up planning. And the organizations that the TVA inspired the creation of – the regional planning offices (as well as the North Norway Plan) – were integrated in later development funds (Mydske 1974; Bugjerde 1981).

Of all the organizational legacies of the TVA in its formative years, it is the partnership idea we have devoted most attention to here. The idea of partnership, especially the idea of participative (regional) partnership has been a stable idea since 1933 up to the annual reports of the 1980s (Neuse 1983). In the Norwegian literature, partnership is the overlooked idea. The success of these partnerships are, as we have seen, debatable. But, as we also have shown, the partnership idea was central in TVA and its grassroots policy. The emphasis on the partnership idea is therefore the main contribution of this study. In TVA, as an early and comprehensive example, the partnership device was a way to adapt and served as a symbol that reduced opposition in Washington and in the Valley. By studying these partnerships, we may learn about unintended consequences and organizational mechanisms such as ideology, formal cooptation, and informal cooptation. These are organizational mechanisms for legitimization as well as for coping with internal and external power realities.

Acknowledgment

The chapter author would like to thank Noorit Larsen for proofreading.

References

Aharoni, Yair. 1986. *The Evolution and Management of State Owned Enterprises.* Cambridge, Ma: Ballinger Publishing Company.

Avery, Robert S. 1954. *Experiment in Management: Personnel Decentralization in the Tennessee Valley Authority.* Knoxville: University of Tennessee Press.

Brochmann, Georg. 1945. *Eventyret om TVA. Demokrati og plan.* [*The Adventure of TVA: Democracy and plan*] Oslo: Tiden Norsk forlag.

Bugjerde, Audun. 1981. *Norsk distriktsutbygging.* [*Norwegian District Development*] Oslo: Tiden norsk forlag.

Clapp, Gordon Rufus. 1955a. *The TVA: An approach to the development of a region.* Chicago: University of Chicago Press.

Clapp, Gordon R. 1955b. *TVA and its critics*. New York: League of industrial Democracy, Inc.

Cole, William, Neuse, Steven M. & Richard Sanders. 1984. TVA: an international administrative example. *Public Administration Quarterly*, summer, 166-183.

Colignon, Richard A. 1997. *Power Plays: Critical Events in the Institutionalization of the Tennessee Valley Authority*. Albany: State University of New York Press.

Conkin, Paul K. 1983. *Intellectual and Political roots. In TVA: Fifty Years of Grass Roots Bureaucracy*. Edited by Hargrove, Erwin C. & Paul K. Conkin. Urbana: University of Illinois Press.

Crozier, Michel. 1964. *The Bureaucratic Phenomenon*. Chicago: University of Chicago Press.

Dahir, James. 1955 *Regional Building: Community Development Lessons from the Tennessee Valley*. New York: Harper & Brothers.

Daynes, Byron W & Glen Sussman. 2010. *White House Politics and the Environment: Franklin D. Roosevelt to George W. Bush*. College Station, TX: Texas A&M University Press.

De Vries, Hanna, Bekkers, Victor & Lars Tummers. 2016. Innovation in the public sector: A systematic review and future research agenda. *Public Administration* 94 (1):146-166.

Ekbladh, David. 2002. Mr. TVA: Grass-roots Development, David Lilienthal, and the Rise and Fall of the Tennessee Valley Authority as a symbol for U.S. overseas Development, 1933-1973. *Diplomatic History* 26 (3): 335-374.

Ekbladh, David. 2011. *The Great American Mission: Modernization and the Construction of an American Order*. Princeton University Press.

Finer, Herman. 1944. *The TVA: Lessons for International Application.* Montreal: International Labor Institute.

Fitzgerald, Michael R and Steven M. Neuse. 1984. TVA: The Second Fifty Years – a symposium. *Public Administration Quarterly* 8 (Summer), 138-259.

Gamson, William A. 1968. *Power and Discontent*. Homewood, Ill: The Dorsey Press.

Gaus, John M. & Leon O. Wolcott. 1940. *Public Administration and the United States Department of Agriculture*. Chicago: Public Administration Service.

Geissel, Brigitte & Marko Joas. 2013. *Participatory Democratic Innovations in Europe: Improving the Quality of Democracy?* Leverkusen: Barbara Budrich Publishers.

Getz Wold, Knut. 1947. *Plan for velstand: T. V. A. og Norge*. [*Plan for Prosperity: T. V. A. and Norway*] Oslo: N. K. L forlag.

Gilbert, Jess. 2017. *Planning Democracy: Agrarian Intellectuals and the Intended New Deal.* New Haven & London: Yale University Press.

Gladden, Edgar N. 1972. *A History of Public Administration II*. London: Frank Cass.

Gordon, George J. 1984. TVA and intergovernmental relations: variations on a recurring theme. *Public Administration Quarterly (summer):*184-201.

Gordon, Lincoln. 1938. *The Public Corporation in Great Britain*. London: Oxford University Press.

Grantham, Dewey W. 1983. TVA and the Ambiguity of American Reform. In *TVA: Fifty Years of Grass-roots Bureaucracy*. Edited by Hargrove, Erwin C. and Paul K. Conkin, 316-335. Urbana & Chicago: University of Illinois Press.

Hargrove, Erwin C. 1987a. *David Lilienthal and the Tennessee Valley Authority. In Leadership and Innovation*. Edited by Doig, Jameson W. and Erwin C. Hargrove, 25-60. Baltimore & London: The Johns Hopkins University Press.

Hargrove, Erwin C. 1987b. Review; TVA and the Telico Dam 1936-1979. *The American Political Science Review* 81 (2): 645-7.

Hargrove, Erwin C. 1994. *Prisoners of Myth: The Leadership of the Tennessee Valley Authority,* 1933-1990. Princeton, US: Princeton University Press.

Harvold, Kjell-Arve. 2002. Planleggingens "kommunikative vending": Nytt paradigm eller gammel debatt? [The communicative turn in planning: New paradigm or old debate?] *Norsk Statsvitenskapelig Tidsskrift* 18: 356-378.

Higgins, Benjamin (1995) *The American Frontier and the TVA*, Society, march/april: 34-42.

Hobday, Victor. 1969. *Sparks at the Grass Roots: Municipal Distribution of TVA Electricity in Tennessee*. Knoxville: University of Tennessee Press.

Hood, Christopher. 1978. Keeping the Centre Small: Explanation of Agency Type, *Political Studies* 26: 30-46.

Hood, Christopher. 1988. PGOs in the UK. In *Delivering Public Services in Western Europe*. Edited by Hood, Christopher and Gunnar Folke Schuppert, 75-93. London: Sage.

Hood, Christopher & Michael Jackson. 1991. *Administrative Argument.* Aldershot: Ashgate.

Hubbard, Preston J. 1961. *Origins of the TVA: The Muscle Shoals Controversy,* 1920-1932. Nashville: Vanderbilt University Press.

Hughes, Thomas P. 1989. *American Genesis: A Century of Invention and Technological Enthusiasm,* 1870-1970. Chicago & London: The University of Chicago Press.

Huxley, Julian. 1943. *TVA: Adventure in Planning*. London: The Architectural Press.

Johns, Carolyn M., O'Reilly, Patricia L. & Gregory J. Inwood. 2006. Intergovernmental innovation and the administrative state in Canada. *Governance* 19 (4): 627-649.

Kettl, Donald F. 2002. *The Transformation of Governance*. Baltimore and London: The Johns Hopkins University Press.

Keynes, John Maynard. 1926/1963. The End of Laissez-Faire. In *Essays in Persuasion*, edited by Keynes, John Maynard, 312-322. New York: W. W. Norton & Company.

Kleven, Terje (2011) *Fra gjenreisning til samfunnsplanlegging: Norsk kommuneplanlegging 1965-2005* [*From restoration to social planning: Norwegian municipal planning 1965-2005*]. Trondheim: Tapir akademisk forlag.

Kramer, Ralph M. 1969. *Participation of the Poor: Comparative Case Studies in the War on Poverty*. Englewood Cliffs, NJ: Prentice Hall.

Lambert, Jeremiah D. 2015. *The Power Brokers: The Struggle to Shape and Control the Electric Power Industry*. Cambridge, MA: MIT Press.

Leuchtenburg, William E. 1952. Roosevelt, Norris and the "seven little TVAs." *The Journal of Politics* 14 (3): 418-441.

Lepawsky, Albert. 1948. Government planning in the south. *Journal of politics* 10(3): 536-567.

Lilienthal, David E. 1942. *The partnership of federal government and local communities in the Tennessee Valley: A study of 'Grass-roots' democracy in in action.* Address to Decator Chamber of Commerce, July 30, 1942 (pp. 1-14). Knoxville, Tennessee: TVA, mimeo.

Lilienthal, David E. & Robert H. Marquis. 1941. The conduct of business enterprise by federal government. *Harvard Law Review,* 54 (4): 545-601.

Lilienthal, David E. 1944. *Democracy on March*. Harmondsworth & New York: Penguin Books.

March, James G. & Herbert A. Simon. 1958. *Organizations*, 1993 edition. Cambridge, Ma: Blackwell.

Marx, Fritz Morstein et al. 1946. *Elements of Public Administration*. New York: Prentice Hall.

McCraw, Thomas K. 1971. *TVA and the Power Fight*, 1933-1939. Philadelphia: J. B. Lippincott Co.

McKinley, Charles. 1950. The Valley authority and its alternatives. *The American Political Science Review* 44 (3): 607-631.

Meyer, Poul. 1957. *Administrative Organization: A Comparative Study of the Organization of Public Administration*. London: Stevens & Sons Limited.

Michels, Robert. 1915/1962. *Political Parties: A Sociological Study of the Oligarchical Tendencies of Modern Democracy*. New York: The Free Press.

Moulton, Lynne & Helmut K. Anheier. 2002. Public-private partnerships in the United States. In *Public-Private Partnerships: Theory and Practice in International Perspective*, Edited by Stephen Osborne, 105-119. London & New York: Routledge (Taylor & Francis).

Mydske, Per Kristen. 1974. *Den historiske bakgrunnen for fysisk/økonomisk planlegging i Norge* [*The historical background for physical/economic planning in Norway*], Skriftserie om offentlig politikk og adminsitrasjon

[Writing series on public policy and adminsitration], Hefte 2. Bergen: Sosiologisk institutt.

Neuse, Steven M. 1983. TVA at Age Fifty – Reflections and Retrospect. *Public Administration Review* 43 (6): 491-499.

Neuse, Steven M. 1996. *David E. Lilienthal: The Journey of an American Liberal.* Knoxville: University of Tennessee Press.

Perrow, Charles 1970. *Organizational Analysis: A Sociological View.* Belmont, Ca: Wadsworth.

Pfeffer, Jeffrey. 1976. Beyond Management and the Worker: The institutional function of management. *Academy of Management Review*, April: 36-46.

Pincus, William. 1945. Shall we have more TVA's? *Public Administration Review* 5(2):148-152.

Pope, Catherine et al. 2006. Lost in translation: A multi-level case study of the metamorphosis of meaning and action in public sector organization innovation. *Public Administration* 84 (1):59-79.

Pritchett, C. Herman. 1943. *The Tennessee Valley Authority.* Chapel Hill: University of North Carolina Press.

Roberts, Elliott. 1955. *One River – Seven States: TVA-state Relations in the Development of the Tennessee River.* Knoxville: Bureau of Public Administration, University of Tennessee.

Ruttan, Vernon W. 1983. The TVA and Regional Development. In *TVA: Fifty Years of Grass-roots Bureaucracy.* Edited by Hargrove, Erwin C. & Paul K. Conkin, 150-163. Urbana & Chicago: University of Illinois Press.

Sayre, Wallace S. 1949. Review TVA and the Grass Roots. *The American Political Science Review* 43 (5): 1031-1033.

Schulman, Bruce J. 1991. *From Cotton to Sunbelt: Federal Policy, Economic Development, and the Transformation of the South*, 1938-1980. New York & Oxford: Oxford University Press.

Scott, James C. 1998. *Seeing like a State.* New Haven & London: Yale University Press.

Scott, W. Richard. 2014. *Institutions and organizations: Ideas, Interests and Identities.* Los Angeles: Sage.

Selznick, Philip. 1943. An approach to a theory of bureaucracy. *American Sociological Review* 8 (1): 47-54.

Selznick, Philip. 1948. Foundation of the theory of organization. *American Sociological Review* 13 (1):25-35.

Selznick, Philip. 1949. *TVA and the Grass-roots*. Berkeley: University of California Press.

Selznick, Philip. 1950. The Iron law of bureaucracy: Michels' challenge to the left. *Modern Review*, 3 (January): 157-165.

Selznick, Philip. 1957. *Leadership in Administration*. Berkeley: University of California Press.

Simon, Jonathan. 2011. Introduction. In *TVA and the Grass-Roots*. Berkeley: University of California Press.

Thomassen, Øyvind. 1997. *Herlige Tider: norsk fysisk planlegging ca 1930-1965* [*Wonderful Times: Norwegian physical planning c. 1930-1965*]. Doctoral dissertation. Trondheim. NTNU, HF-faktultetet.

Tugwell, Rexford G. & Edward C. Banfield. 1950. Grass Roots Democracy: myth or reality? Review of TVA and the Grass Roots, *Public Administration Review* 10 (1): 47-55.

Van Dusen, George. 1974. *Politics of 'Partnership': The Eisenhower Administration and Conservation*, 1952-60. Dissertation. Loyola eCommons. Chicago: Loyola University.

Vibert, Frank. 2007. *The Rise of the Unelected: Democracy and the New Separation of Powers*. Cambridge: Cambridge University Press.

Walsh, Annemarie Hauch. 1976. *The Public's Business: The Politics and Practices of Government Corporations*. Cambridge: MIT Press.

Weber, Max. 1889/2003. *The History of Commercial Partnerships in the Middle Ages*. Lanham, Ml: Rourman & Littlefield Publishers, Inc.

Welborn, David M. 1984. Persistent Dilemmas: TVA as problem in organizational governance. *Public Administration Quarterly* 8 (2):142-165.

Wengert, Normann. 1951. TVA – symbol and reality. *The Journal of Politics* 13 (3): 369-392.

Wengert, Normann. 1952. *Valley of Tomorrow: The TVA and Agriculture.* Knoxville: The University of Tennessee, bureau of Public Administration.

Wheeler, William Bruce & Michael J. McDonald. 1986. *TVA and the Telico Dam 1936-1979: Crisis in Post-Industrial America*. Knoxville: The University of Tennessee Press.

White Paper no. 69 (1952) *Regional Planning*. Oslo: Ministry of Work and Local Government.

Wildavsky, Aaron. 1961. TVA and power politics. *American Political Science Review* 55 (September): 576-590.

Wildavsky, Aaron. 1962. *Dixon-Yates: A Study in Power Politics*. New Haven & London: Yale University Press.

Willbern, York. 1956. Review: One River – Seven States. *The American Political Science Review* 50 (3): 885-6.

Wirtz, Richard. 1975. The legal framework of the Tennessee Valley Authority. *Tennessee Law Review* 43: 573-612.

In: Keynesian Policies
Editor: Noralv Veggeland
ISBN: 978-1-53614-026-2

Chapter 8

A NEW DEAL FOR NORWEGIAN AGRICULTURE

David Blandford, PhD[1,*], Ivar Gaasland, PhD[2,†] and Erling Vårdal, PhD[3,‡]

[1]The Pennsylvania State University, University Park, PA, US
[2]BI Norwegian Business School, Norway
[3]University of Bergen, Norway

ABSTRACT

As Norway is entering into a post oil age, government money will become scarcer. We argue that the government will put inefficient sectors of the economy under pressure in order to save money. The Norwegian agricultural sector stands out as a god candidate for reform. Sheltered by oil and gas revenues, public expenditure on this disadvantaged sector, which currently only accounts for 0.3% of Norwegian GDP, have been

---

* Professor, PhD of Agricultural Economics. The Pennsylvania State University, University Park, PA, US. Email: dblandford@psu.edu.
† Associate Professor, PhD of Economics, BI Norwegian Business School, Norway. Email: ivar.gaasland@bi.no.
‡ Professor, PhD of Economics, University of Bergen, Norway. Email: erling.vardal@uib.no.

extremely high. If yearly support over the period 1976-2016 is accumulated, adjusted for an interest rate on the same principle as the oil fund, it would give an "agricultural fund" equal to 1/3 of the value of the oil fund (February 2018). We have demonstrated that it is possible to achieve a 1/3 reduction in agricultural support while maintaining Norway's food security objective expressed in terms of current amounts of calories and proteins. A positive side-effect is that greenhouse gas emissions are reduced by almost 40%; i.e., close to the national commitment according to the Paris agreement. Consequently, a policy that is cost efficient with respect to food security is also climate friendly. Under current policy, the lion's share of the budget support is paid out to less efficient and highest polluting production systems, in particular meat from cattle and sheep.

Keywords: farming, restructuring, long-term fiscal sustainability, Norwegian subsidized agriculture, reforms

INTRODUCTION

Since the first discovery of commercially exploitable reserves in 1969, oil and natural gas have dominated the Norwegian economy. The sector has been heavily taxed, and has consequently contributed a substantial amount of money to the Norwegian government. In the first two decades, income was directly included in state accounts. Since 1996 the income has been managed through a sovereign oil fund, with the following rule as a guideline: yearly transfers from the Fund to the government budget shall, over time, follow the expected real return on the Fund. The expected real rate of return of the Government Pension Fund Global is currently set at 3 percent.

A challenge for Norway is that oil and gas reserves are being rapidly depleted. Norway is entering the post-oil age. Wisely, Norway established the oil fund. But even if the fund maintains its real value, it will not follow the growth pattern of the economy. This means that the government must search for money in other places than the oil sector, to finance future public expenditure needs.

Norway has already started the process of ensuring long-term fiscal sustainability. The prime example is the pension reform of 2011. But more reforms are needed. In this respect, there are good reasons to focus on the agricultural sector. Sheltered by oil and gas revenues, public expenditure on the disadvantaged agricultural sector, which currently only accounts for 0.3% of Norwegian GDP, have been extremely high. We will argue that the resource use in Norwegian agriculture, during the oil era, may serve as a good example of the resource curse.

Situated in the northern fringe of Europe, spanning from 58°N to more than 71°N, conditions for farming are difficult in Norway. Due to low temperatures and a short growing season production is restricted to pasture and forage grasses, potatoes and vegetables, grain for feed, and some spring wheat for human consumption. Also, hilly terrain and stony soil makes farming challenging in most parts of Norway. Agricultural area takes up only 3% of the Norwegian land surface.

But, despite the obvious comparative disadvantage of the sector, Norway is more or less self-sufficient in major agricultural products like milk, meat and eggs. This is only made possible through substantial public support. Foreign competition is to a large extent excluded by import tariffs in the range of 200 – 400%, which translate into a market price support of NOK 12 billion. Tax financed subsidies account for roughly an additional NOK 14 billion. Total support in 2016 added up to NOK 26.3 billion, or almost NOK 600 thousand per man-year in agriculture.

The Organisation for Economic Cooperation and Development (OECD) estimates that the total financial support provided to Norwegian agriculture in 2016 was equivalent to 60% of the value of gross farm receipts, which make Norway (along with Iceland) the leader in the amount of support provided to agriculture in the countries monitored by the Organisation (OECD, 2017). The support share in the neighbouring European Union is 21%, while the OECD average is 14%.

The Norwegian government has proposed restructuring the sector on several occasions. Unsurprisingly, proposed policy shifts are extremely controversial and face resistance, particularly from the farmers' unions. Farmers argue that the maintenance of domestic agricultural production is crucial for achieving national food security objectives, in addition to pursuing other aims such as the maintenance of economic activity in rural areas and landscape preservation. Food security, which has been a key policy objective since the end of the Second World War, has been interpreted in Norway as requiring high levels of self-sufficiency in basic agricultural commodities.

So in practice, a key policy objective is to maintain the current self-sufficiency rate. In this chapter we analyse a potential restructuring of agricultural policy that would serve to reduce the toll on public resources while achieving the politically defined food security objective. Constraints imposed by international trade agreements in the World Trade Organisation (Blandford et al., 2010) are taken into consideration. Furthermore, we assume that agriculture should contribute to achieving the commitment to reduce national greenhouse gas (GHG) emissions by 40% by 2030 (compared to 1990 levels), submitted at the UN climate change conference in Paris in November 2015.

In the next section we outline the current situation with respect to long-term fiscal sustainability. In particular, we discuss the potential contribution of the agricultural sector to secure this stability. Then, we present a model analysis of an agricultural policy that is targeted at the politically defined food security objective. This policy favors products that are characterized by a high content of nutrients per unit of resource use; i.e., it motivates an efficient resource use. As we will show, a positive side-effect of a more cost efficient policy is that it also will bring about a substantial reduction in GHG emissions. Finally, in section 4, we provide concluding remarks.

The Need for Redirecting Resources

Since the discovery of oil reserves in 1969, Norway has generally experienced a higher rate of economic growth than other OECD-countries. Because of this, Norway is today one of the richest countries in the world. But the country's oil reserves are in decline. In fact, as Figure 1a) shows, most of the known reserves are depleted. Combined with the collapse in the oil price, as pictured in Figure 1b), the economic outcome from the oil sector is expected to slow down. The petroleum industry will remain important for the Norwegian economy for years to come, but will provide less of a growth impetus than before. So there is a need for major structural adjustments in the economy.

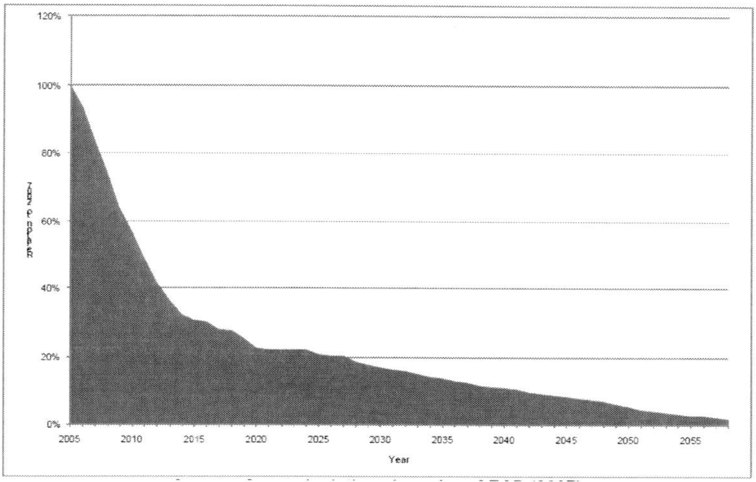

a)

b)

Sources: Royal Ministry of Finance (2017).

Figure 1. The oil sector: prospected reserves and development in world marked price. a) Norwegian petroleum reserves. b) World market price of oil in Brent US dollars.

THE OIL FUND

A major challenge for resource rich countries is to maintain their income level after the resources have been depleted. Norway has prepared for this by building up the oil fund. The fund is based on royalties and tax revenues from oil activity. Figure 2a) shows the development of the fund since its establishment in 1996. We see that since 2006, in particular, the value of the fund has increased substantially.

The fund is used to balance the state budget. In 2001, the parliament voted to adopt a fiscal rule that governs the size of the annual transfer from the fund to the central government budget. According to the fiscal rule the transfer should on average be 4% of the total value of the fund. In early 2017 the percentage was changed to 3%.

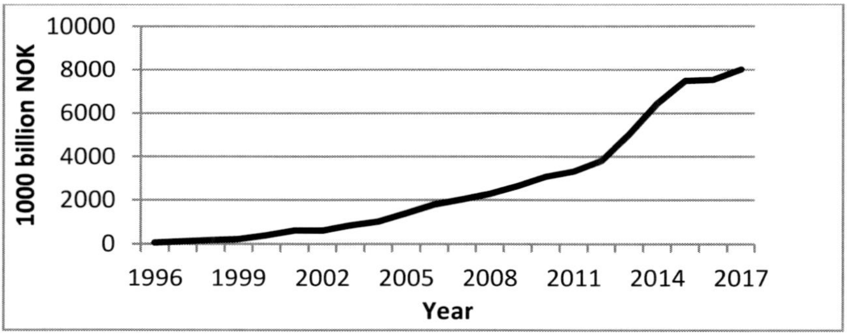

a)

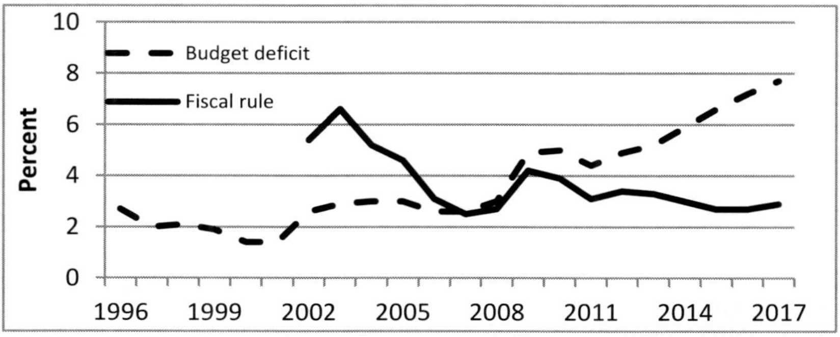

b)

Source: Royal Ministry of Finance (2017).

Figure 2. The oil fund. a) Value of the oil fund (1000 billion NOK) b) Withdrawals from the oil fund (percent).

In Figure 2.b) the solid line shows the transfer from the fund as a percentage of the size of the fund. We see that in the years 2001-2016, transfers have conformed to the fiscal rule, i.e., approximately 4% per year on average. In 2017 the transfer was 2.9%, which is also in accordance with the 3% rule. The dotted line gives the budget deficit as a percentage of GDP.[1] This has been increasing over the years.

PUBLIC REFORMS

As is typical for resource rich countries, part of the income derived from natural resources has been used for welfare benefits. Among the OECD countries, Norway has the most generous arrangement for sickness leave, for example. It is also the OECD country with the highest percentage of the population in receipt of disability benefits.

However, the most important problem is public expenditure related to an aging population. Hagist et al. (2013) pointed out that a continuation of the current policy (as of 2009) will result in a long run gap between government income and expenses. To close the gap, a 17 percentage point increase in total taxes would be needed. Because of this, Norway is expected to face relatively strong pressure on its public finances.

Norway has already taken action through pension reforms enacted in 2011. By this Norway took a significant step towards long-term fiscal sustainability. According to Hagist et al. (2013), the effect of the 2011pensionreform is to reduce the needed 17 percentage point increase in taxes to 12 percentage points. So, the pension reform helps, but clearly a continuous reform process is needed to align public expenditure with income.

[1] Structural non-oil budget deficit measured as a percentage of trend-GDP for mainland Norway.

Oil-Lubricated Farming – The "Agricultural Fund"

As pointed out in the introduction, Norwegian agriculture is heavily subsidized. One reason why the scale of subsidization has been possible is the abundance of means created by the oil sector. Prospects for future oil revenues, in the wake of the 1969 oil discovery in the North Sea, made it politically feasible to reach a historic agreement in the Norwegian Parliament in 1975 to increase support to farmers in order to raise their incomes and increase production. The magnitude of agricultural support since that decision can be illustrated by cumulating yearly support over the period 1976-2016, adjusted for an interest rate on the same principle as the oil fund accumulates. As Figure 3 shows, this would give an "agricultural fund" equal to 3,000 billion NOK (2016-values), which amounts to more than 1/3 of the value of the oil in February 2018.

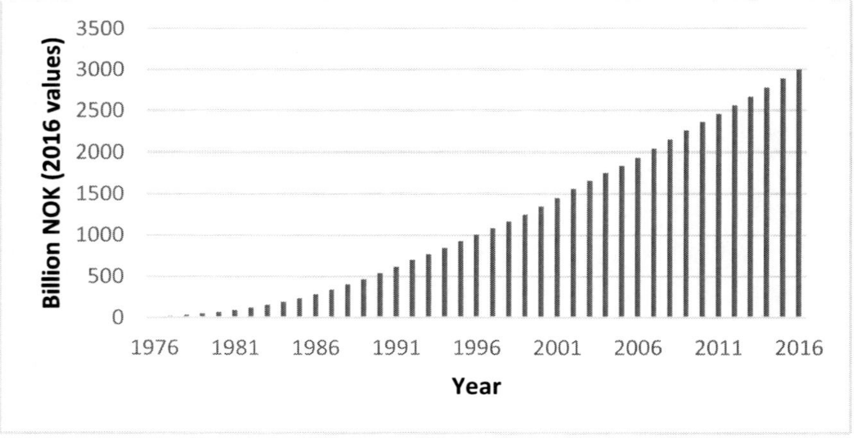

Source: Authors' calculations.

Figure 3. Cumulative agricultural support adjusted for interest rate over the period 1976- 2016.

Consequently, sheltered by oil and gas revenues, public expenditures on the agricultural sector, which currently only accounts for 0.3% of Norwegian GDP, have been extremely high. In spite of the use of significant public resources, the remuneration of farmers is far below the average wage in other industries, and the number of farmers has decreased by 70% during this period. Figure 4 illustrates the low productivity of agriculture; support has more or less exceeded the payments to farmers by a factor of 2 each year. For example, in 2016 the average farmer received NOK 600 thousand in agricultural support. After deducting costs from market income and subsidies received, the farmer is left with only NOK 370 thousand to cover own labour effort and equity.

Obviously, there are more profitable ways to use the public resources that have been channelled into agriculture during the oil era; e.g., investments in infrastructure, research and development, public services, or simply savings for future generations. The resource use in Norwegian agriculture, sheltered by oil and gas money, may serve as a good example of the resource curse.

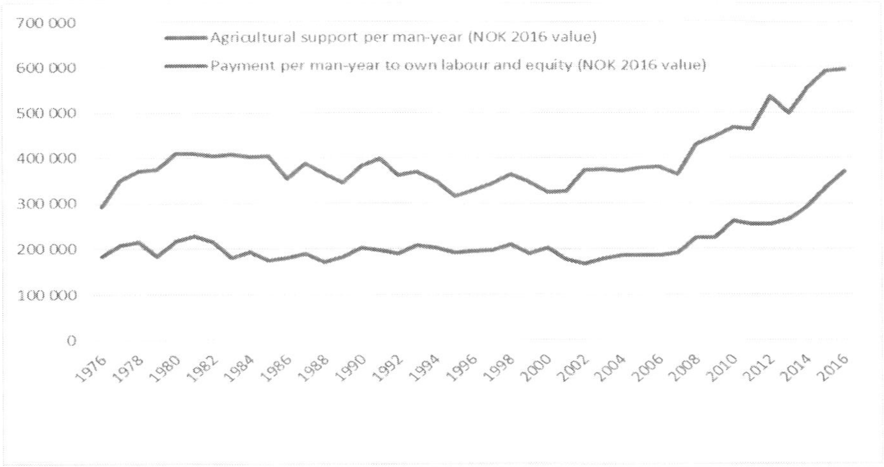

Source: Authors' calculations.

Figure 4. Agricultural support and payment per man-year to own labour and equity (NOK 2016 value).

Despite this, to take away all subsidies for farmers is not practical policy. The approach we will follow is presented in the next section. We first define the public goals for agriculture and thereafter inquire if the government can meet these goals with less subsidization than today.

Reforming Agriculture – A Model Analysis

In this section we illustrate a potential restructuring of agricultural policy that would serve to reduce the toll on public resources while achieving the politically defined food security objective. Constraints imposed by international trade agreements in the World Trade Organisation (Blandford et al., 2010) are taken into consideration. Furthermore, we assume that agriculture should contribute to achieving the commitment to reduce national GHGemissions by 40% by 2030 (compared to 1990 levels), submitted at the UN climate change conference in Paris in November 2015. For analytical purposes we use a partial equilibrium model for Norwegian agriculture that we briefly describe below. A complete presentation of the model is given in Blandford et al. (2018).

The Model and Data

We use a quadratic programming model that maximizes the sum of producers' and consumers' surplus. Domestic demand is represented by linear functions calibrated to price and consumption levels in the base year of 2011, measured at the farm level. Because of the closed-economy characteristics of Norwegian agriculture (high tariffs and restrictive tariff-rate quotas limit the imports of major commodities), the consumption of most products is close to the production levels reported in the first column of Table 2.[2]

Constant returns to scale, i.e., a Leontief-type production function, is assumed with respect to domestic production for each of the main commodities in Norwegian agriculture, based on the coefficients reported in Table 1. Import supply is at given world market prices inclusive of import tariffs, or as determined by tariff-rate quotas.

Restrictions with respect to land that can be used for food grains, land that can be used for either food or feed grains (grain land), and total land are imposed. Total infield land is 1 million hectares (3 percent of total land area). 55 percent of total infield land can be used for grain production, while only 27 percent can provide food grains. The residual is only suitable for growing grass to support ruminants.[3]

The model allows for restrictions with respect to GHG emissions from production (ceilings); domestic consumption of calories and proteins; calories and proteins imported in the form of feed (floors). Shadow prices associated with restrictions can be interpreted as subsidies or taxes necessary to satisfy the restrictions.

Economic welfare is defined as the sum of the producers' and consumers' surplus minus exogenous subsidies and tariff revenues.

---

[2] The main exceptions are consumption of food grain that incorporates about 50 percent ofimports, and some imports of feed grain and protein feed. Imports of other products are low, and within tariff rate quotas, i.e., not subject to most favored nation tariff rates bound through the WTO. Consequently, the first column in Table 2 can be interpreted as the demand for Norwegian products.

[3] The products included in the model occupy 93 percent of available farmland, i.e., we apply 0.93 as a ceiling on total agricultural land in the simulations. Although 27 percent of the total farmland is categorized as food grain quality, only 5 percent is currently used for food grain production. The main explanation is the low quality of Norwegian wheat due to the relatively cold and wet growing season. In the model simulations, the ceiling on food grain land is set to 10 percent of total available farmland. The ceiling on total grain land (inclusive of feed grain) is set to 44 percent of total available farmland (i.e., a 20 percent reduction factor is used to allow for crop rotation).

Table 1. Sectors in the model – production coefficients per kilo of food produced

Product	Land use (10^{-3} ha)	Roughage (feed units)	Feed grain (kg)	Budget support (NOK)	Market price support (NOK)	Costs (NOK)	kcal[2]	Protein[2]	GHG (kg CO_2-e)
Milk (incl.13.8g beef[1])	0.245	0.61	0.24	2.56	1.87	7.77	687	35.6	1.00
Ruminants other									
Beef from fed calves	2.955	8.15	2.06	23.26	21.24	65.26	1,553	190	20.00
Beef, extensive	5.086	13.42	3.70	61.85	21.24	103.85	1,553	190	26.67
Sheepmeat	7.268	23.28	1.96	109.72	2.78	148.89	2,028	172	26.29
Vegetable and grain based products									
Pigmeat	0.840		2.85	1.79	12.83	26.24	2,608	201	4.04
Poultrymeat	0.474		1.61	2.98	25.86	36.09	1,065	156	2.27
Eggs	0.584		1.99	0.69	15.43	22.09	1,250	109	2.00
Food grains	0.256			1.36	0.84	3.79	3,150	114	0.50
Feed grains	0.294			1.56	0.83	3.76	3,150	114	0.50
Potatoes	0.060			0.18	3.36	5.33	590	12	0.50

Notes: [1] Production of beef from culled dairy cattle; [2] Per kg of edible product. NOK denotes Norwegian Krone.

Source: Calculations made by the authors using the database for the sector model of Norwegian agriculture (Jordmod), see Blandford et al. (2015).

ANALYSIS AND RESULTS

The model solution for the current agricultural policy (2011) is given in the first column in Table 2. It more or less replicates current levels of production, land use, GHG emissions, and support levels. As a way to target the agricultural policy at the politically defined food security objective, we replace the current budget support scheme with payments to the farmers that are directly related to a product's content of nutrients (i.e., calories and proteins). This policy would favor products that are characterized by a high content of nutrients per unit of resource use; i.e., motivate an efficient resource use. The current restrictive import barriers that are in compliance with Norway's WTO commitments are maintained in this analysis. While being a major source of inefficiency, the prohibitive import barriers serve to exclude the problem of carbon leakage (i.e., that a reduction in Norwegian GHG emissions is replaced by higher emissions in other countries).

The second column of Table 2 shows that current amounts of nutrients can be supplied with only 2/3 of the current total support level. Note that a positive side-effect is that GHG emissions are reduced by almost 40%; i.e., close to the national commitment according to the Paris agreement. Consequently, a policy that is cost efficient with respect to food security is also climate friendly.

The obvious reason for this convenient result that can be deduced from Table 1 is that products that score relatively well on resource use per unit of nutrient also have a low carbon footprint. In particular, this is plant based food, represented by food grain and potatoes. When it comes to animal products, poultry, pig, eggs, and milk are the most efficient and climate friendly products. Meat from ruminants (cattle and sheep) is not only costly to produce per unit of nutrient, but stands out with extremely high GHG emissions. Also, cattle and sheep receive the lion's share of agricultural subsidies.

Table 2. Model results. Base solution compared to efficient supply of current nutritional levels

Main indicators	Base solution	Efficient nutrient supply	Percent of base solution
Production (mill. kg)			
Cow milk	1,507	1,223	81
Meat	322	247	77
Beef	82	44	54
Culled milk cows	21	17	81
Fed dairy calves	42	27	64
Extensive	19	0	0
Sheepmeat	24	0	0
Pigmeat	130	124	95
Poultrymeat	86	79	92
Eggs	60	59	98
Food grains	179	386	216
Feed grains	927	674	73
Potatoes	250	252	101
Production (nutritional values)			
Million kcal	2,414	2,735	113
Million kg protein	139	139	100
GHG (million kg CO_2 equivalents)	4,544	2,879	63
Farmland in agriculture (mill. ha)	0.93	0.59	63
Grain	0.33	0.31	94
Food grain	0.05	0.10	216
Feed grain	0.28	0.21	74
Grass	0.60	0.28	46
Economic welfare (mill. NOK)	6,572	10,313	157
Producer subsidy estimate (mill. NOK)	19,266	12,780	66
Budget support	11,063	3,286	30
Market price support (mill. NOK)	8,202	9,496	116

The results in Table 2 follow from this reasoning. Ruminant meat production is reduced by 58 percent. Since prohibitive tariffs prevent imports, consumption is reduced accordingly. Smaller impacts are observed for pigs and poultry (5-8 percent reduction). In aggregate, meat production is reduced by about 23 percent, while cow milk supply is reduced by 19 percent. The reduced supply of total nutrients from animals is counterbalanced by increased production of food grains (+116 percent).

Table 3. Market prices: base solution compared to efficient supply of current nutritional levels

Product	Base solution (NOK per kg)	Absolute change (NOK per kg)	Percentage change
Cow milk	4.63	+ 1.75	38
Beef	42.00	+ 21.78	52
Sheepmeat	39.17	+ 43.50	111
Pigmeat	24.25	+ 1.48	5
Poultrymeat	18.15	+ 1.64	9
Eggs	15.53	+ 1.10	7
Food grains	2.43	- 0.84	-35
Potatoes	5.15	- 0.12	-2

Source: Authors' calculations.

The changes in market prices that follow from the policy shift are reported in Table 3. Due to constant returns to scale, the price increase (decrease) for a give product is more or less equal to the reduction (increase) in the subsidy rate. The price increase is particularly high for ruminant meat, reflecting the high resource use associated with the product. It is more moderate for other animal products that more efficiently transform fodder into food nutritional value, while prices of vegetable products fall.

The dietary changes that follow from the policy change in Norway involve a 23 percent reduction in meat consumption and a 20 percent reduction in the consumption of dairy products. In our computation this is counterbalanced by increased consumption of vegetable products, but it could also be combined with higher consumption of fish based on sustainable fisheries. Norway is the world's second largest seafood exporting country (FAO, 2016). Like vegetable products, fish has a low carbon footprint compared to ruminant meat (Winther et al., 2009). It is notable that official dietary advice in Norway and most other rich countries prescribe a shift in consumption from red meat to vegetable and fish products, suggesting that positive health impacts also could be obtained (Helsedirektoratet, 2014; FAO, 2017). Vegetable products are represented in our model by grain and potatoes, but could include legumes, oilseeds, carrots, and other vegetables of high nutritional value that can be grown in Norway.

CONCLUSION

As Norway is entering into a post oil age, government money will become scarcer. The Norwegian government has already introduced reforms, with the pension reform of 2011 as the prime example. But as announced in the last National Budget more is to come; see Royal Ministry of Finance (2017). Pressure will be put on inefficient sectors of the economy in order to save money.

As demonstrated, the Norwegian agricultural sector stands out as a good candidate for reform. Sheltered by oil and gas revenues, public expenditure on the disadvantaged agricultural sector, which currently only accounts for 0.3% of Norwegian GDP, has been extremely high. If yearly support over the period 1976-2016 is accumulated, adjusted for an interest rate on the same principle as the oil fund, it would give an "agricultural fund" equal to 3,000 billion NOK (2016-values), which amounts to more than 1/3 of the value of the oil in February 2018. From this perspective, the resources used on Norwegian agriculture, during the oil era, may serve as a good example of the resource curse.

We have demonstrated that it is possible to achieve a 1/3 reduction in agricultural support while maintaining Norway's food security objective expressed in terms of current amounts of calories and protein. A positive side-effect is that greenhouse gas emissions are reduced by almost 40%; i.e., close to the national commitment according to the Paris agreement. Consequently, a policy that is cost efficient with respect to food security is also climate friendly. Under current policy, the lion's share of the budget support is paid out to the less efficient and highest polluting production systems, in particular meat from cattle and sheep.

The dietary changes that follow from the policy change in Norway involve a 23 percent reduction in meat consumption and a 20 percent reduction in the consumption of dairy products, counterbalanced by increased consumption of vegetable products, but it could also be combined with higher consumption of fish that Norway exports in huge amounts. Official dietary advice in Norway and most other rich countries prescribe a shift in consumption from red meat to vegetable and fish products, suggesting that positive health impacts also could be obtained.

Even if it would be cost effective to pursue a more climate and healthfriendly food security policy in Norway, obtaining political support for such a change would be difficult to achieve. Beef and sheep production are labor-intensive activities, mainly located in rural areas. A reduction in production would likely lead to a decline in agricultural employment. The farm lobby in Norway is politically influential and would probably mobilize to oppose changes in agricultural policy that would lead to a reduction in ruminant meat production.

REFERENCES

Blandford, D., Gaasland, I. and Vårdal, E. (2015). Greenhouse gas abatement in Norwegian agriculture: costs or benefits?' *EuroChoices* 14(2): 34-40.

Blandford, D., Gaasland, I. and Vårdal, E. (2018). Greenhouse gas emissions, land use, and food supply under the Paris Climate Agreement – policy choice in Norway. Forthcoming in *Applied Economic Perspectives and Policy*.

FAO (2016). *The State of World Fisheries and Aquaculture 2016. Contributing to food security and nutrition for all*. Rome.

FAO (2017). *Food-based dietary guidelines*. Rome. http://www.fao.org/nutrient/education/gfood-dietary-guidelines (accessed, November 2017).

Hagist, C., Raffelhüschen, B., Risa, A. E. and Vårdal, E. (2013). Long-Term Fiscal Effects of Public Pension Reform in Norway - A Generational Accounting Analysis. *Nordic Journal of Political Economy*. 38: 1-23.

Helsedirektoratet (2014). *Anbefalinger om kosthold, ernæring og fysisk aktivitet*. [*Recommendations about diet, nutrition and physical activity*]. Rapport IS-2170. Oslo.

Organisation for Economic Cooperation and Development (2016). *Agricultural Policy Monitoring and Evaluation 2016*. Paris. http:// http://www.oecd.org/tad/agricultural-policies/monitoring-and-evaluation.htm (accessed, November 2017).

Ripple, W. J., Smith, P., Haberl, H., Montzka, S. A., McAlpine, C. and Boucher, D. H. (2014). Ruminants, climate change and climate policy. *Nature Climate Change*, 4: 2-5.

Royal Ministry of Finance (2017). *The National Budget 2018.* A Summary. Oslo.

Winther, U., F., Ziegler, E., Skontorp H., Emanuelsson, A., Sund V. and Ellingsen H. (2009). *Carbon footprint and energy use of Norwegian seafood products.* Report SFH80 A096068, SINTEF Fisheries and Aquaculture, Trondheim, Norway.

In: Keynesian Policies
Editor: Noralv Veggeland
ISBN: 978-1-53614-026-2

Chapter 9

NARRATIVES OF SUSTAINABILITY

Arne Johan Vetlesen, PhD*
Institute of Philosophy, University of Oslo, Norway

ABSTRACT

"Sustainable development" has been a key notion in academic as well as political discussion in the last thirty years. This chapter traces the trajectory of the notion since the publication of the so-called Brundtland Report in 1987. Taking the work of Anthony Giddens as my guiding example, I argue that it is no wonder that the idea of "sustainability" has found such favor with the political and business powers that it may be allowing the twin-imperatives of growth and profit to prevail. With no new checks introduced to contain them, let alone question the legitimacy of a globalized economic system that has wrought more devastating ecological harm to the planet for each passing year.

Keywords: sustainable development, capitalism, growth, decoupling, technology optimism

---

* Dr. Philos., Professor of Philosophy at the University of Oslo, studied at the Goethe-University in Frankfurt 1985-1990, author of several books, mainly on ethics, political theory, and environmental philosophy. a.j.vetlesen@filosofi.uio.no.

Introduction

The term «sustainable development» was introduced to the general public in the 1987 report of the "World Commission on Environment and Development", commonly referred to as the "Brundtland Report", since it was chaired by the Norwegian then-Prime Minister Gro Harlem Brundtland. Like the Club of Rome's landmark study of 1972, *Limits to Growth*, authored by Donella H. Meadows et al., the Brundtland Report focused on the possibility that modern industrial society is using up its source materials at an alarming rate, which cannot be maintained for much longer without major change. How to meet this challenge?

UN-Initiated Reports

The Brundtland Report gives a twofold response and represents a new deal regarding sustainability. On the one hand, it recognizes that economic growth is necessary in order to bring greater prosperity to the developing world, i.e., to the countries that historically have not enjoyed the growth in prosperity, measured in GDP, that the leading industrial nations in the world have done, especially since WWII. In this way, continued economic growth of a kind that will benefit the countries hitherto lagging behind as well as those already most affluent is tied to a sense of entitlement and so to a notion of justice: growth would be unjust if it does not correct the historical imbalance between the poor and the rich, taken globally.

On the other hand, the development facilitated by continued economic growth "overall" has to become sustainable. In stating that this constitutes a "must", the Report clearly tries to tackle the problem concerning the "using up" of (limited) source materials (non-renewable natural resources) that the Club of Roma raised with such alarm in 1972, finding considerable public resonance (Meadows et al., 1972). The ecological imbalance caused by taking more from nature than nature is allowed to regenerate and replenish – that is, systemic overshoot – must be contained before it is too late and the consequences become irreversible and beyond human control. What is required is that development be "sustainable": it must be such as to "meet the needs of the present without compromising the ability of future generations to meet their own needs" (Brundtland et al., 1987: 326). Again, a notion of justice is being appealed to, if largely implicitly – namely, the idea that it would be unjust to future (not-yet-born) generations if present ones were to "use up" resources to an extent that leaves less for future humans than has been enjoyed by those now living. The injustice would that of generational egoism, if you like (a moral term not employed by Brundtland). Of course, the preference for the present over the future, giving more weight to a desire that can be fulfilled now than one that can only be fulfilled later, is well known in economics and psychology alike as the problem of discounting, and is viewed as a profound propensity in human nature. What is novel is the context: the ways in which future human beings will likely suffer as a result (however unintended) of the tendency of living humans to put their interests first.

As far as UN-initiated reports go, the Brundtland Report was soon to inspire a number of important declarations about policy changes, nationally as well as globally. Thus, the high-profile 1992 UN Rio Earth summit endorsed a declaration setting out 27 principles of "sustainable development" and recommended that every country produce a national strategy to achieve these results. In the same spirit, a few years later the Treaty of Amsterdam embraced sustainable development as integral to the aims of the EU, and a comprehensive Sustainable Development Strategy was established in 2001.

Academically no less than institutionally, the notion of "sustainable development" has enjoyed almost unprecedented success, being cited by scientists, politicians, and business leaders all around the world. Nevertheless, the notion and the thinking behind it has had a number of detractors ever since it was launched. They argue that its popularity is in large part due to its vagueness, coupled with a have-your-cake-and-eat-it quality. It is difficult to come out against the goals endorsed in the two prime terms, "sustainability" and "development". What is more, it has the ring of good news to all concerned – future as well as present-day humans, the poor as well as the affluent, environmentalists as well as investors – that one can reach both goals at the same time, indeed (to put it more strongly) that the one goal presupposes the other, and vice versa.

Whether that is really so, or simply too good to be true, is a question I will return to below. For now, consider one example showing how the elusive nature of the concept has been sought tackled by avoiding to define it and instead to substitute a set of goals in its place. So, in their book *Implementing Sustainable Development*, William Lafferty and James Meadowcroft argue: "Sustainable development indicates an interdependent concern with: promoting human welfare; satisfying basic needs; protecting the environment; considering the fate of future generations; achieving equity between rich and poor; and participating on a broad basis in decision-making" (2000: 19). It is easy to agree with critics who point out that in amounting to such an all-encompassing list of policy goals acceptable to everyone and offending nobody, the concept is made into a slogan emptied of analytical precision and political bite.

A somewhat more substantial deployment can be witnessed in the "Environmental Sustainability Index" worked out by the Davos-based World Economic Forum, now applied to more than 100 countries. Here, environmental sustainability is defined in terms of five elements (see Esty et al., 2001):

1. The condition of ecological systems such as air, soil and water.
2. The stresses to which those systems are subject, including their levels of pollution.
3. The impact of such stresses upon human society, as measured in terms of factors such as the availability of food and exposed to disease.
4. The social and institutional capacity of a society to cope with environmental hazards.
5. The capacity to create stewardship of global public goods, especially the atmosphere.

Obviously, these are very general statements, abstracting from the highly varied contexts and countries within which the five elements need to be observed.

A striking feature of the policy goals adopted on a worldwide basis since the Brundtland Report is the axiom that development and sustainability are compatible: to succeed, development needs to be sustainable; the requirements for sustainability are such as to facilitate development, not slow it down, let alone forbid it.

To render "development" more concrete, we need to see that it has two different meanings. Development can simply mean economic growth, as measured by GDP, in which case it applies in principle to all countries. But it can also be taken in a more restricted sense, referring to the economic processes that help take people out of poverty. As Anthony Giddens (the prominent British sociologist known for his affiliation with Tony Blair's "Third Way" policies in the 1990s) points out in his 2011 book *The Politics of Climate Change*, this is the sense in which we contrast the "developing" countries with the "developed" ones, adding that in the first sense of the term, considered simply as GDP-measured economic growth, "development" never stops (2011: 62): the more economic growth, the better as far as development is concerned.

The argument of the Brundtland Report is premised on the all-important distinction between so-called "developed" and "developing countries". Giddens remarks that "growth is much less important to the former than the latter", holding that "developed" countries "may continue to expand their economies, but the need for growth is much less pressing" (ibid.). By contrast, Giddens states, "for the poor countries there is a *development imperative*": "It is not only that they have the right to become richer, but that such a process has direct implications for sustainability. Poverty is closely associated with population expansion, one of the root causes of the pressure that is now threatening resources" (ibid.). The poorer countries must be allowed to reach a "certain level of wealth", the more exact definition of which "has to be negotiated politically". What is clear, though, Giddens continues, is that "wherever possible, such as through technology transfer, reductions in emissions – at least relative to past practices in the developed countries – should be sought" (2011: 63). Indeed, the dangers involved in climate change as caused to a large extent by the burning of fossil fuels "will determine in large part how far "development" today can mimic the trajectories followed by the existing industrial countries". Despite the fact that the outcome of those trajectories is today "under immense pressure", Giddens maintains that "a certain "licence to pollute" has to be acknowledged" (ibid.).

THE NOTION OF "SUSTAINABLE DEVELOPMENT"

I have quoted Giddens extensively here because his views are representative of the political and academic consensus: the problems posed by climate change can be, and should be, solved within the framework provided by "sustainable development", politically and economically so as well as analytically. It is not only that "development" and "sustainability" are perfectly compatible, indeed mutually dependent; it is also that the sort of policies that the goal of "sustainable development" recommends will allow us to tackle climate change. This being so, whatever changes the problem of climate change forces upon us, they will not be such as to undermine what the poorer countries are morally entitled to: the "right to become richer" and "a license to pollute".

I see Giddens' highly representative position – though perhaps more so in political circles than in academic ones – as a case of wishful thinking. The compatibility between sustainable development and the need to tackle climate change does not stand up to closer scrutiny; it does not survive a reality check.

To be sure, Giddens himself declares that he will avoid using the notion of "sustainable development" in the remainder of *The Politics of Climate Change*. However, his reasons for doing so have nothing to do with the reality check I have in mind. Rather, Giddens' dissatisfaction is to do with the notion being "more of a slogan than an analytical concept"; indeed, it is "something of an oxymoron" (2011: 71). Nevertheless, "sustainability" is regarded by Giddens as a useful notion, "although itself a little slippery to define, since it concerns an indefinite future. We don't know what technological innovations will occur down the line, and hence assessments of the limits of the earth's resources usually operate under a question-mark" (2001: 61).

I shall come back to the role played by technology in a moment. Before I do so, we should note that Giddens pays some attention to what he calls "over-development", a problem presumably corresponding to that of the "under-development" (my term, not Giddens') seen in poor countries. "Over-development" as understood by Giddens, then, must be acknowledged as a "possibility in the affluent societies". His reasoning is that "the continued expansion of the economy may well bring benefits, but at the same time the problems of affluence tend to pile up". The implication, Giddens goes on to observe, is "not that economic growth has to stop, but that it should not be pursued irrespective of its wider consequences" (2011: 63).

Given this summary of Giddens' view, one thing seems clear: economic growth should continue. It should do so as a matter of moral right in "developing" countries, and it should do so in the "developed" ones with a concern for "the wider consequences", although what exactly these are remains unspecified in Giddens' discussion.

What I find "slippery" and lacking in analytical as well as political bite is not so much the notion of "sustainable development" as such, but Giddens' own position, especially concerning the pivotal issue of the relationship between economic growth and climate change. It all boils down to a very simple question: is economic growth part of the solution to climate change, or is it part of the problem causing it, even reinforcing it?

To see what is at issue here, recall Giddens' statement that "assessments of the limits of the earth's resources usually operate under a question-mark", the reason being that "we don't know what technological innovations will occur down the line". Characteristically, Giddens does not talk about the limits of the earth's resources as something absolute, that is, as constituting a condition whose primacy over all others needs to be recognized. Instead of focusing head-on on the ecological limits as such, Giddens relativizes them in a twofold manner: by connecting them with our assessments of them, and by making the validity of those assessments conditional on future technologies, the when, where and what of whose impacts we in principle cannot know or predict with much certainty. The effect is that a cloud of relativity and uncertainty is made to hang over any mention of the limits of the earth's resources.

Yet there is no denying that "growing the economy" means putting natural resources under more stress, exploiting them to meet the demands of the world's poor and rich alike, enabling the former to adopt the lifestyle and the patterns of consumption enjoyed by the latter, this being their right, one whose lack of realization would amount to injustice and hence be morally unacceptable (to recall Giddens' statement). Now, goes the argument that I take Giddens to implicitly rely on, if the exploitation of the earth's resources may intensify so as to meet the demands of the poor and the rich alike without harming sustainability, this is so because new technologies will be much less environmentally harmful than the ones deployed in the era of fossil-fuels driven industrialism. In other words, technological innovation is the key to the promise of continued, never-ending economic growth on a finite planet; it will allow us to produce, consume, and distribute ever-more goods, for ever-more people, without inducing the unacceptable cost of ruining the planet humans depend upon.

Although Giddens refrains from going into this issue in any detail, his view appears to rely heavily on the idea that technologically driven de-materialization – whereby production and consumption become less resource-intensive per unit of output – is required for the world economy to enjoy constant growth in the foreseeable future. If only technology will help us change *how* we go about using natural resources for human purposes, talk about there being "intrinsic" and absolute limits to that use will prove groundless, proof of misguided techno-pessimism the very moment its opposite is what may save us.

To be sure, the notion of "decoupling" in play here is intriguing: as economic output by way of new, non-fossil-based technologies becomes progressively less dependent on material throughput, the economy can continue to grow without crossing ecological limits or running out of resources. The idea that technological progress will resolve environmental problems is attractive for all sorts of reasons, not least psychological ones: it provides welcome reassurance in rejecting system-related critique and so-called "alarmism" out of hand, since if technological innovations are the solution there is no need to engage in any serious changes in our individual lifestyles and collective practices. Indeed, the constellation "more economic activity – less environmental damage" suggests a win-win situation. It therefore fits nicely with the idea we looked at above: rather than being contradictory and in conflict, development and sustainability are mutually dependent – you cannot have the one without presupposing the other. Crucially, both elements – taken as goals, even matters of entitlement for those concerned – are made possible by continued economic growth (to recall Giddens' argument).

Economist Tim Jackson comments on the promise of "decoupling" in his book *Prosperity without Growth* (published one year prior to Giddens' book yet conspicuously ignored there). Jackson points out that there is as yet no credible, socially just, ecologically sustainable scenario of continually growing incomes for a world of seven, eight or nine billion people. It is entirely fanciful to suppose that "deep" emission and resource cuts can be achieved without confronting the structure of market economies – the very confrontation that the Brundtland Report, followed through the years by scholars such as Giddens, sought to avoid. Nowhere, argues Jackson, is there any evidence that *efficiency can outrun scale* in the way it must do if is to be compatible with sustainability. Far from acting to reduce the throughput of goods, technological progress serves to increase productivity input by reducing factor costs. The phenomenon of "rebound" attests to this: money saved through energy efficiency gets spent on other goods and services (see Jackson 2010: 86, 88, 95).

What prevents "enough is enough" from happening is not lack of knowledge or moral character in the individual consumer. It is the structural reliance of the market system itself on continued growth: on investments continuing to bring profit, on profits continuing to grow. The twin objectives of growth and profit – whereby profit is both growth-dependent and growth-driving – are the system-immanent key characteristics of a capitalist economy; and they happen to be exactly the traits resulting in capitalism's incompatibility with the planetary key characteristics of limits and finiteness. Recent decades have taught us that, as capitalism goes global, all human needs are directed towards the market and all cultures are forced to strive for the very instrument – the market – that relentlessly robs humans of their ability to survive by their own efforts and skills and to live lives that do not in total lead to an overload of the global carrying capacity - the limit that is threatened by the limitlessness of the market and the insatiability of commercialized needs spread by 24/7 advertising. The cycles of creative destruction attest to this, giving the lie to the rhetoric of a win-win alliance between capitalist economy and sustainability, between what is good for the market and what is good for the planet. The harsh reality is that product lifetimes plummet as durability is systematically designed out of consumer goods and obsolescence is designed in. It's not only that everybody has to have a smartphone; you also have to buy a new one ever-more often – what is ideologically sold as consumer choice is instead a matter of sheer technological compulsion, there being no option to keeping up with the newest technology and the newest model. In a word, quality is sacrificed to volume throughput. As Jackson observes, the throw-away society is not so much a consequence of consumer greed as a structural prerequisite for survival – survival of the capitalist system, that is. To an ever greater – not smaller – extent, "the institutions of consumer society are designed to favor a particularly materialistic individualism and to encourage the relentless pursuit of consumer novelty because it is exactly what's needed to keep the economy growing" (Jackson 2010: 163).

The impossibility of infinite exponential growth on a finite planet may appear obvious to most people. But it is has failed to gain traction in neoclassical economic theory, contradicting as it does its very foundation. Herman Daly, perhaps the world's most prominent ecological economist, has noted that economics will remain "autistic" as long as it ignores the fact that "the economy is a subsystem of the ecosystem", and that the containing ecosystem is finite, non-growing and materially closed" (Daly 2007: 2). The fact is that the pattern of scarcity has changed: Manmade capital (labor, technologies) has become relatively plentiful, and remaining natural capital is becoming more and scarcer, subject to over-efficient exploitation to the point of depletion. Manmade and natural capital are complements, not substitutes (as the dominant theoretical paradigm informing and helping justify current practice would have it). As Daly insists, "when factors are complements then the one in short supply is limiting", i.e., natural capital with its flow of natural resources and flux of natural services. To illustrate: the fish catch used to be limited by number of fishing boats and fishermen, now it is limited by remaining stocks of fish and their reproductive capacity; cut timber is no longer limited by saw mills, but by standing forests" (2007: 28, 252). The upshot is as unambiguous as it is anathema to the advocates of business-as-usual coupled with techno-optimism: Any attempt, by way of decoupling or otherwise, to marry economic growth and environmental sustainability will fail because premised on an unrealistically high degree of eco-technological efficiency increase. Regrettably, Daly's well-taken criticisms of neoclassical economic theory's autistic separation from any material content and thus from limits – unchallenged in the Brundtland Report – stop short of a fundamental rejection of capitalism, relying instead on the feeble hope for "a broad moral awakening among capitalists".

As yet, there is no sign of such a thing. To give an example, as the world is receiving the one wake-up call after the other concerning the ecological disaster caused by the ever-increasing global plastic binge, corporations like Exxon-Mobile Chemical and Shell Chemical have just decided to invest more than 180 billion dollars to build new facilities that will help fuel a 40% rise in plastic production in the next decade, exacerbating a plastic pollution crisis that scientists warn already risks "near permanent pollution of the earth", affecting the entire marine food chain. In June 2017, an investigation carried out by *The Guardian* revealed that a million plastic bottles are bought around the world every minute, with the large majority ending up in landfill or the sea; globally, only 10% of plastics are being recycled (see Taylor 2018: 12). Plastic is a telling example of what happens when scientists, based on their most recent findings, sound the alarm bell, with business leaders and politicians responding with statements expressing their "deep concern" with the "serious problems" that have been documented: the problem gets worse. With a few exceptions, this holds for the various problems – designated as so many "challenges" – identified in the Brundtland Report thirty years ago: since then, they have become worse.

A TECHNOLOGICAL SOLUTION IS NEVER COMPLETE AND HENCE IS A QUASI-SOLUTION

Giddens and Brundtland share the kind of routine technology optimism that is characteristic of political and business elites around the world. It is an axiom of faith that humanity will manage the planet – and itself – toward the required transition to sustainability. The mentality in question is captured with great precision in a book written forty years ago by David Ehrenfeld, *The Arrogance of Humanism*. I take it the key assumptions Ehrenfeld listed then ring familiar today as well: that all problems are soluble; that they are so by people; that many problems are soluble by technology, and if not be technology alone, then by politics or economics; that whenever a catastrophe is threatening to happen, knowledge of that fact will motivate people to work together for a solution before it is too late; that while some resources are finite, all finite or limited resources have substitutes such as will be found and developed in time to avert a catastrophic outcome; and that, no matter what sort of danger or risk humanity will be confronted with, human civilization will survive (see Ehrenfeld 1978: 16-17).

Ehrenfeld is especially concerned with the dialectical process whereby a solution to one problem generates a set of problems that eventually preclude solutions. His conclusion, based on a number of case studies in a wide range of fields, is that a technological solution is never complete and hence is a quasi-solution. Each quasi-solution generates a residue of new techno-social problems arising from incompleteness, augmentation, and secondary effects. The new problems will proliferate at a faster rate than solutions can be found to meet them. The resulting increased complexity will in its turn increase costs, decreased resources, require even greater control, and lead to the inertia of social institutions (1978: 107). More than thirty years before the notion of "ecosystem services" gained traction outside the circle of economists, holding that "you cannot manage what you do not measure" and that therefore the way to ensure that endangered ecosystems, habitats, and species be saved is to put a price tag on them, Ehrenfeld observed that "finding a value for some part of nature is no guarantee that it will be *rational* for us to preserve it – the reverse may hold" (1978: 202). Anticipating every argument currently employed in the case for ecosystem services, Ehrenfeld writes:

"It does not occur to us that nothing forces us to confront the process of destruction by using its own uncouth and self-destructive premises and terminology. It does not occur to us that by assigning only instrumental value to diversity we merely legitimize the process that is wiping it out, the process that says, "The first thing that matters in any important decision is the magnitude of the dollar costs and tangible benefits". [...] I am referring not just to the effort to put an actual price on biological diversity but also to the attempt to rephrase the price in terms of a nebulous survival value." (Ehrenfeld 1993: 118)

Allow me to mention here just one of many concrete examples that corroborate Ehrenfeld's argument. In 1973 the applied mathematician Colin Clark wrote a paper about the economics of killing blue whales. The question examined was whether it was economically advisable to halt the Japanese whaling of this species to give blue whale time to recover to the point where they could become a sustained economic resource. The conclusion Clark arrived at was that in fact it was economically preferable to kill every blue whale left in the oceans as fast as possible and reinvest the profits in growth industries rather than to wait for the species to recover to the point where it could sustain an annual catch. To take a more recent example, consider the fate of the rhino is Africa, being one of the "iconic" animals (alongside the polar bear, the tiger, and the orangutan) whose dramatic decline in numbers has received world-wide attention in the last decade. Having reached an all-time-high price in the international market – and be it a black one – poaching of the rhino has tripled in several areas. The market mechanism of supply and demand operates to the effect that as poaching increases, the numbers of rhinos plummet; and the fewer rhinos there are, the more money will be paid for each exemplar being killed, the endpoint being that the very last rhino will command the highest price ever paid for one. In other words, allowing the market to set the price yields the opposite result of that defended by the advocates of putting a price tag on endangered wild animals: the speeding up of the process of extinction. Whether one wants to call this unintended consequence proof of the sometime perversity of the free-market mechanism, or simply the way it works, run-of-the-mill like, yet for the most part inconspicuously so, is a moot question. The fact of the matter is that it's simply how the market works.

World-Wide Impact on New Deal Policies

As Christophe Bonneuil and Jean-Baptiste Fressoz remind us in their recent book *The Shock of the Anthropocene*, the concept of sustainable development derives from the notion of "maximal sustainable yield" conceived by (ecological) fishery science in the 1950s, which in its turn was inspired by the notion of "sustainable (*nachhaltig*) management" developed by German forestry science in the eighteenth century. As Bonneuil and Fressoz point out, all three notions are based on presuppositions that today are proven wrong in that they no longer obtain: "The Anthropocene cancels the peaceful and reassuring project of sustainable development" (2016: 22).

I for one think that the point can be put even more strongly: the success of the notion of sustainable development, measured in terms of its world-wide impact on new deal policies in the field adopted (and those not adopted) during the last three decades, is partly responsible for having led us into the Anthropocene, understood as a danger zone of unprecedented magnitude as far as multi-dimensional ecological catastrophe is concerned. In keeping with Daly's critique, the notion of "sustainable development" has helped maintain belief in the possibility of perpetuating economic growth by means of a bit more "conservation" of the environment, conveniently neglecting the warnings over the impossibility of indefinite growth on a finite planet that not only stemmed from the famous *Limits to Growth* report published by the club of Rome in 1972, but also the work dating back to the 1960s by the economist Nicholas Georgescu-Roegen on entropy and degrowth, captured in what he called "the fallacy of endless substitution", i.e., the fallacy found in the neoclassical school (on which the Brundtland Report tacitly relies) as well as in Marxist economics, failing to recognize the way in which an economy driven by the twin imperatives of growth and profit is bound to undermine resources for which this planet has no substitutes – the fallacy of (mis)treating as mere means, as perfectly replaceable, what is in fact indispensable (see Georgescu-Roegen 1971).

In other words, only by refusing to seriously consider the implications of these insights was it possible go on pretending that the three crucial dimensions could be mutually negotiated within a growth-driven capitalist economy: namely the economic, the social and the environmental. The failure is a two-fold: the economy is not placed within the social, which in itself is framed by a thousand feedback loops within the biosphere and the Earth system. Indeed, the related notions of a "green economy" and of "ecosystem services", in vogue since the 1990s, demonstrate the unwillingness to take on board the bad news: that we have to do with limits, not opportunities; with systemic problems such as require overturning the entire economic framework, not business challenges of a kind wedded to sustaining what has become unsustainable. To the extent that "ecosystem services" – those yielded for humans by, say, bees active in pollination – now are singled out as object of markets, the biosphere, the hydrosphere and the atmosphere are made to appear as mere subsystems of the financial and commodity sphere, thus turning the actual ecological order of primacy on its head: regarding as fixed and unchangeable the current capitalist economic system and the imperatives inseparable from it, and as perfectly elastic and manipulative for human purposes (as expressed in insatiable needs and desires) the material substratum on which all economic activities rely, called "nature". In effect, the social system that desperately needs to change is placed beyond critique, whereas what can only be further changed at the cost of degradation, depletion, and extinction, is subject to ever-intensifying exploitation, rendering the current trajectory self-destructive.

That said, it is easy to see why "green growth" and "ecosystem services" became buzzwords in the wake of the Brundtland Report. Both concepts holds the promise of using the market to solve whatever problems the market has failed to solve thus far – recalling Sir Nicholas Stern's oft-cited statement that climate change is a matter of the biggest "market failure" in history. To be sure, the market economy was for a long time criticized for externalizing its true costs as far as the values provided by nature are concerned, so that a problem like deforestation failed to be accounted for within the given cost/benefit calculus, i.e., the more rapidly and comprehensively deforestation takes place, the better economically speaking, with supply meeting demand, GDP increasing, etc., tacitly presupposing that there will always be "more for the taking". Thus, the thinking behind ecosystem services may be said to change the situation radically in declaring everything affected in/by the economy an "internal" aspect of it and so needing to be accounted for in a manner doing justice to its true importance for the system as a whole. And indeed, this is the logic that allowed the pioneering economist in the field, Robert Costanza, to assess the annual value of the services rendered by the biosphere at about $ 33 billion, or twice the world's GDP. The point about ecosystem services being that they are valuable, the only way to demonstrate the value in question is to measure it qua monetary value, allowing for the perfect commensurability that market transactions crave, in effect subjecting nature *in toto*, in all its qualitative and life-(re)generating dimensions and processes, to quantification. As Bonneuil and Fressoz remark, all values of nature, even those far upstream from production and including the most spiritual (renamed "cultural services"), thus enter into an accounting logic, as illustrated by the adopted policy of International Union for Conservation of Nature to present nature as "the largest company on Earth" (see Bonneuil and Fressoz 2016: 55).

Conclusion

Given my argument that sustainable development is a highly flawed notion, not the solution to the problem but part of the problem and so helping perpetuate and amplify it, what would be the alternative?

There is no simple solution, in large part because the reliance on false ones such as "sustainable development" means that the world has wasted the last three decades seeking for truly efficient ways of tackling the multidimensional ecocrisis. Moreover, what started out as a tacit premise is now becoming visible as a clearly – and invalidly – normative such: talk about "sustainable development" always took for granted that the present economic order is one *worth* sustaining, deserving the contributions, big and small, of each of us to ensure its preservation into the future, thus preventing alternatives involving radical systemic change from being explored. This anti-change bias is built into the concept from its inception.

Thirty years after Brundtland, one thing we do know is that the growth paradigm must be abandoned, in theory and in practice. The fossil fuels driven model of development that has characterized the industrialized Western world for the last three centuries cannot and should not serve as a model to be copied by the currently "emerging" economies of countries like China, India and Brazil. To the contrary, the growth-oriented capitalist model must be recognized for what it is: a warning saying "Don't you do what we have done, lest you cause ecological damage beyond repair, a predicted damage for which no future humans will forgive you." If anything, the current US-led model, now headed by a president who doesn't even acknowledge that climate change exists and is caused by human activity, serves as a case study of what must be avoided at all costs: a recipe for disaster.

The simple fact is that the 7, 4 billion people now living on planet Earth cannot on average enjoy the material standard of living, with the ecological footprint implied, reached by nations like USA or Norway. Justice demands that those who are worst off in today's world must be allowed to rise to a standard of living such as meets their basic needs. For that rise to happen in a truly sustainable manner, however, those who today enjoy so much more than their basic needs require, will need to have their standard of living reduced, considerably and urgently so. In the total picture, the reduction part is just as crucial as the rise one. And for that very reason, the break with an economic system driven by the twin-imperatives of profit and growth that is imperative both as far as distributive justice and ecological limits are concerned. It will be an ugly affair: based on their culturally induced sense of entitlement to have it all, to have more, always more, with no increase in consumption and possessions being regarded as enough, as sufficient, those privileged within the current arrangement will certainly resist systemic change as strongly as their power permits them to (see Kempf 2008). To the extent that that happens, however, such resistance against losing privileges never actually earned will have the one advantage – in the midst of the many downsides and dangers – of bringing the fact of the matter so long kept under the carpet out into the open. That the attainment of a just and ecologically sound economic and political global order, one deserving to be called such, is never going to be easy, provoking brutal, class-based conflicts along the way. In other words, a viable path forward can only be sought by means completely at odds with those advocated by the proponents of "sustainable development". Having deemed it a proof of virtue to evade conflict and sell their model as one allowing for a "win-win" situation, requiring nobody to change their ways in any fundamental manner and to abandon their positions of privilege. As we have learned in the decades since the Brundtland Report was launched and its proposals made the rounds, nothing could be further from the truth.

REFERENCES

Brundtland, Gro Harlem et al., 1987, *Our Common Future*. Oxford: Oxford University Press.

Bonneuil, Christophe and Jean-Baptiste Fressoz, 2016. *The Shock of the Anthropocene*. London: Verso.

Daly, Herman, 2007. *Ecological Economics and Sustainable Development*. Cheltenham: Edward Elgar.

Ehrenfeld, David, 1978. *The Arrogance of Humanism*. Oxford: Oxford University Press.

——— , 1993. *Beginning Again*. Oxford: Oxford University Press.

Esty, Daniel et al., 2001. *Environmental Sustainability Index*. Davos World Economic Forum.

Georgescu-Roegen, Nicholas, 1971. *The Entropy Law and the Economic Process*. Cambridge, MA: Harvard University Press.

Giddens, Anthony, 2011. *The Politics of Climate Change*. Cambridge: Polity Press.

Jackson, Tim, 2010. *Prosperity without Growth*. London: Earthscan.

Kempf, Herve, 2008. *How the Rich are Destroying the Earth*. White River Junction, Vermont: Chelsea Green.

Lafferty, William and James Meadowcroft, eds. 2000. *Implementing Sustainable Development*. Oxford: Oxford University Press.

Meadows, Donella, et al., 1972. *Limits to Growth*. New York: New American Library.

Taylor, Matthew, 2018. "Warnings of "disastrous" plastic binge." *The Guardian Weekly* 5 January: 12.

About the Editor

Noralv Veggeland
Professor of Public Policy
Inland Norway University of Applied Sciences
Lillehammer, Norway
Email: noralv.veggeland@inn.no

The Editor, *Noralv Veggeland*, is a Professor of Public Policy at Inland Norway University of Applied Sciences, Lillehammer, Norway. He is former Director of Nordic Regional Research Institute (NordREFO, Copenhagen. He was twice a visiting professor at Massachusetts State University, Amherst, USA and European University Institute (EUI), Florence, Italy. Earlier Member of the Norwegian Research Council.

Here some few of his latest publications:

Paths of Public Innovation in the Global Age: Lessons from Scandinavia. Cheltenham, UK – Northampton, MA, USA 2007: Edward Elgar Publishing.

Taming the Regulatory State: Politics and Ethics. Cheltenham, UK – Northampton, MA, Cheltenham, UK – Northampton, MA, USA 2009: Edward Elgar Publishing.

Essays on Regulatory Governance. New York 2013. Nova Science Publishers.

Regulatory Governance. Published online as text book/academic book, 2015, Bookboon.com, Copenhagen

Political Economic Realities of Today's Capitalism, Bookboon online October 10, 2017, Copenhagen, http://bookboon.com/en/political-economic-realities-of-todays-capitalism-ebook

The Current Nordic Welfare State Model. (ed.) New York: Nova Science Publishers. 2016.

Administrative Strategies of Our Time. (ed.) New York: Nova Science Publishers. 2017.

INDEX

A

B

C

D

E

F

G

H

I

K

L

M

N

S

T

U

W

Z